Afghanistan

Afghanistan

A Short History of
Its People and Politics

Martin Ewans

HarperCollins books may be purchased for educational, business, or sales promotional use. For information, please write: Special Markets Department, HarperCollins Publishers Inc., 10 East 53rd Street, New York, NY 10022.

First published in the United Kingdom in 2001 by Curzon Press.

First Edition

Printed on acid-free paper

Library of Congress Cataloging-in-Publication Data is available upon request.

ISBN 0–06–050507–9

02 03 04 05 06 RRD 10 9 8 7 6 5 4 3 2 1

Contents

List of Illustrations

ACKNOWLEDGEMENTS

1. British Museum.
2. Musée Guimet.
3, 4, 5. Frances Mortimer Rice.
6, 11. British Library.
8, 36. Anne Holt.
26, 27, 28, 30, 31, 32, 33, 34, 35, 37. Popperfoto.

Although every effort has been made to trace the owners of copyrights, in a few cases this has proved impossible.

List of Maps

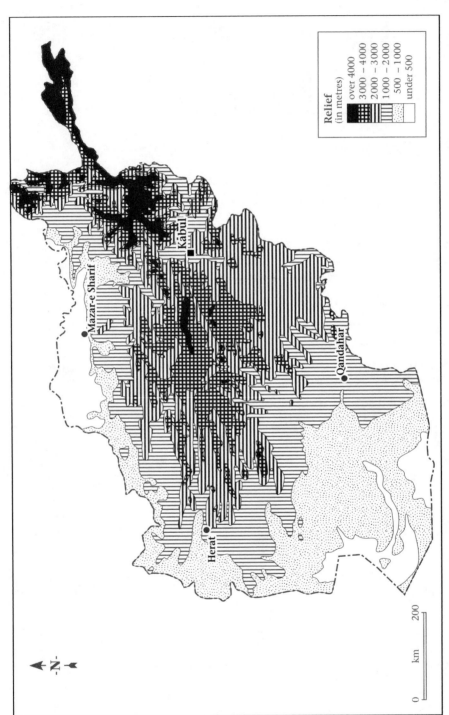

Map 1 Afghanistan: Relief and Main Centres

Relief
(in metres)

over 4000
3000 – 4000
2000 – 3000
1000 – 2000
500 – 1000
under 500

Mazar-e Sharif

Kābul

Herat

Qandahār

N

0   km   200

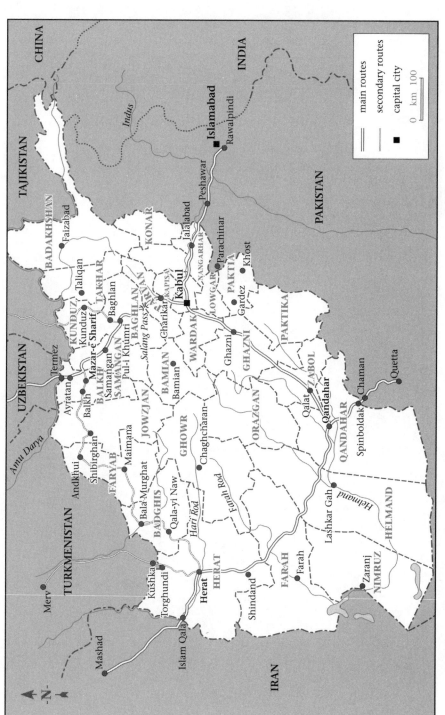

Map 2 Afghanistan: Political and Communications

The Land and the People

A fghanistan is a land of stark and rugged beauty, of snow-covered mountains, barren deserts and rolling steppe. Situated at the eastern end of the Iranian Plateau, it covers some 250,000 square miles, an area about the size of Texas, rather larger than France, rather smaller than Turkey. Some two-thirds of it lie above 5000 feet, and several of its mountains are among the highest in the world. The ranges that bisect the country may be likened to a hand outstretched towards the west, with the wrist lying on the Pamir Knot, the great tangle of mountains at the western extremity of the massive 'arm' of the Himalayas and Karakorams. At the palm of the hand lies the Hindu Kush, the 'killer of Indians', possibly so called in recognition of the Indian slaves who met their deaths as they were taken across its passes to the khanates of Central Asia. Beyond the Hindu Kush is the Koh-i-Baba, a complex of mountains and uplands which gradually tapers towards the west into the 'fingers' of the Band-i-Turkestan, the Safed Koh, the Siah Koh and the Parapomisus Range, each in turn subsiding as it approaches the Iranian frontier. Other 'fingers' run in a more southerly direction, the Suleiman Range close to the eastern frontier with Pakistan, the Kirthar Range which stretches into Baluchistan, and the Paghman Range which provides a scenic backdrop to the country's capital, Kabul. Only to the north and the south-west of the country are lowlands to be found, as the mountains give way in the one direction to the plains of Afghan Turkestan and the banks of the Amu Darya, and in the other to the basin of the Helmand River, enclosing in its semi-circular course the barren expanse of the Dasht-i-Margo, the 'Desert of Death'.

Afghanistan is a land-locked country, with frontiers that were mostly demarcated towards the end of the nineteenth century. To the

1

north, its borders with the Republics of Tajikistan, Usbekistan and Turkmenistan run for some thirteen hundred miles, westwards from the Pamirs along the Amu Darya and then across country to the Hari Rud, the river that marks the northern end of its frontier with Iran. In the far north-east, high in the Pamirs, is a fifty mile border with China, from which runs the so-called Durand Line, the frontier that divides Afghanistan from Pakistan. This winds its way south-westwards for some eight hundred miles and then swings westwards for a further seven hundred, skirting the Helmand valley and meeting the Iranian frontier south of the Hamun, the complex of lakes and marshes into which the Helmand finally drains. The Afghan-Iranian border then runs northwards for nearly six hundred miles, until it meets the Hari Rud.

The Hindu Kush marks the watershed between the Indus and Amu Darya basins, and is part of the mountainous divide that separates Southern from Central Asia. Only on the western side of the country is there an easy route between the two regions, guarded by the ancient city of Herat. The dozen or so passes across the mountains are closed by snow for some six months of the year and only one of them is below 10,000 feet. Despite their difficulty, however, they have been routes of migration and conquest, and have been crossed by successions of merchants and pilgrims, lured from Central Asia and beyond by the material and spiritual riches of the Indian Sub-continent. The even more ancient city of Balkh, now an expanse of jumbled ruins, owed its position on the 'Silk Route' between China and the Mediterranean to its proximity to the most accessible of these passes. Only in recent years has a tunnel been driven below the Salang Pass, creating an all-season road from Afghan Turkestan to the capital and the lands beyond. To the east of the country, the routes to the Indian Sub-continent lie through another line of passes, of which the Khyber Pass is merely the best known.

Afghanistan has a continental climate, cut off from the Arabian Sea monsoon by the mountains lying to its south-east. Its summers are hot and dry and its winters harsh, with great daily and seasonal variations. Rainfall is light, water is scarce and most of the country barren. From the air it resembles a vast moonscape, with only the occasional green of an oasis or a narrow patch of vegetation snaking along a valley floor. All but a fraction of the land area is uncultivable, although there is some rain-fed agriculture in a relatively few fertile areas, and the rivers, nourished by the melting snows, lend themselves to irrigation, at which the Afghans are adept. Many valleys have their *juis*, the artificial watercourses that wind along the hillsides and mark the boundaries between the barren uplands and the fields below, while elsewhere there are *karez*, man-made under-

2

ground channels which run from the edge of the water table to cultivated land, sometimes over considerable distances. The bulk of the population derive their livelihoods from agriculture and pastoralism, or from crafts that are dependent on these activities. Most of the agricultural land is given over to food grains, principally wheat, although cotton, fruit and, latterly, opium, are important cash crops. Although with regional variations, large land holdings have been few and smallholdings the norm, a relative egalitarianism that has meant that the extremes of hunger and malnutrition are not normally as visible in Afghanistan as in some other Asian countries. Such is the marginality of much of the land, however, particularly in the centre and north-east of the country, that severe famines have occurred from time to time. Grazing land is also limited and much of it is only seasonal, so that some two-and-a-half million nomads, the *kuchis*, have from time immemorial moved with their herds and flocks on their annual migrations between the uplands and the plains.

The origins of the peoples who inhabit this high country are as diverse as they are often obscure. Although there has been much intermingling over the centuries, they still have distinct ethnic, physical and linguistic differences. Recent estimates[1] suggest that Afghanistan may have a population of some twenty million, divided into twenty or so main ethnic groups and more than fifty in all. While a majority can speak one at least of the two official languages, Pushtu and Dari, a form of Persian, over thirty different languages are current. The word 'Afghan' has a long history. Mentions of it appear in a Sessanian inscription of the third century AD and in the writings[2] of the Chinese traveller, Hsüan-Tsang, who passed through the country in the seventh century. Later, around the turn of the first millennium, several mentions appear in Muslim records. But there is little doubt that until recently, 'Afghan' was synonymous with 'Pushtoon', the name of the country's largest ethnic group, who have been reckoned to account for about half of the nation. Writing early in the sixteenth century, for example, the emperor Babur names[3] a number of Pushtoon tribes, but always refers to them collectively as 'Afghans', and never as 'Pushtoons'. Even today, the Pushtoons refer to themselves as 'Afghans' and their language as 'Afghani', while the remainder of the country's peoples refer to themselves primarily as Tajiks, Usbeks or whatever, and as Afghans only secondarily, if at all. Variants on the name 'Pushtoon' are 'Pukhtoon' and 'Pathan', the latter being the anglicised term and the two former reflecting the 'soft' and 'hard' dialects of the language, used by the western and the eastern tribes respectively.

At the same time, there are indications that the word 'Pushtoon' may be of even greater antiquity than 'Afghan'. Some[4] see the

3

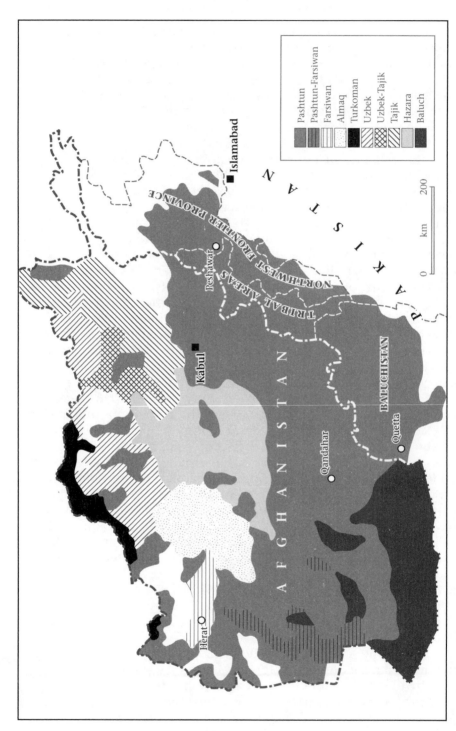

Map 3 Major Ethnic Groups

Pushtoons as the 'Paktua' tribes which are referred to in the Vedas, the sacred texts which originated with the Aryan invaders of the Indian sub-continent some 6000 years ago, particularly since the contexts suggest that the Paktua may have been residents of north-west India. Some also see the Pushtoons as the 'Paktues' whom the historian Herodotus[5], writing in the fifth century BC, includes in several passages among the inhabitants of India. If these interpretations are reliable, the conclusion might be that the Pushtoons can trace their descent from the Indo-Aryans. Others[6], however, see them as having as their ancestors the Ephthalite Hun invaders of the fifth century AD. The one conclusion may not in fact exclude the other, given the degree of racial mingling that exists throughout all the peoples of Afghanistan.

Many of the Pushtoons live in the south and east of the country, while an equal number live across the Durand Line, in the frontier areas of Pakistan. Their language is one of the Indo-Iranian group and is related to Persian. Their tradition is that their descent can be traced from a common ancestor, Qais, a companion of the Prophet Mohammed, whose descendants became in turn the ancestors of the large number of tribes into which they are divided, the two major being the Durranis (formerly the Abdalis), from whom came the Afghan royal house, and the Ghilzai. Both live to the south of the country, the Durranis mostly between Herat and Kandahar, and the Ghilzai between Kandahar and Ghazni. These two tribes have traditionally been antagonistic, and the Ghilzai have tended to be exploited and discriminated against by the Durranis. However the Pushtoon tribes which were better known to the British Army, over many decades of bitter skirmishing on the North-West Frontier, are those of the eastern hills, among them the Wazirs, the Mohmands, the Mahsuds, the Afridis, the Khattaks and the Shinwaris. The main characteristic of the Pushtoons, particularly those of the hills, is a proud and aggressive individualism, practiced in the context of a familial and tribal society with predatory habits, a part feudal and part democratic ethos, an uncompromising Muslim faith and a simple code of conduct. Although the rigidity of this code, the *Pushtoonwali*, has been diminishing over the years, it still establishes obligations of revenge (*badal*), hospitality (*melmastia*) and sanctuary (*nanawati*). Questions of honour (*namus*) and disputes of an economic or political nature have meant that private vendettas and more generalised conflict have been endemic features of Pushtoon life. Vendettas, both individual and collective, have been known to last for generations. Although many Pushtoons have migrated, or have been forcibly moved, to the cities or other areas of the country, Pushtoon society in general remains highly parochial, jealous of its independence and resistant to outside influence. Within the Pushtoon tribes are various sub-tribes and clans (*khels*), sometimes holding land in common. The leaders of the *khels*, the *khans*, often hold their positions by hereditary right, although, in the absence of any firm rules of succession, factionalism has been rife. Also the authority of the *khans* is both dependent on their leadership qualities and is normally tempered, to a greater or lesser degree, by the *jirga*, the assembly in which the elders, and sometimes all the adult men, play a role. As time has passed, however, the *khans* have increasingly acquired economic power and a more feudal system has developed. The underlying ethic, however, has remained one of equality, every adult male having the right to participate in the *jirga* and to contribute to its decisions.

In Afghanistan, Islam is both the national religion and the basis of its overriding culture and values, the majority of Afghans being Sunnis of the Hanafi school. Insofar as there has been a sense of unity in the country, it is Islam, with its concept of community and universality (*umma*), which has superimposed itself on the ethnic diversity and provided the main focus of loyalty. Both in Pushtoon society and more widely throughout the nation, therefore, much influence is exercised by *imams* or mullahs, who may not only have ritual, juridical, medical and educational roles at village and tribal level, but may also exercise an inspirational leadership, particularly when a confrontation with 'infidels', or a cultural threat to the faith, is in question. This influence is all the greater in a society which is largely illiterate, traditional by instinct and mostly ignorant of modern ways of life. Unlike many mullahs elsewhere, those in Afghanistan generally have a secure status, sometimes reinforced by the fact of their being landowners, as well as by their role outside the narrowly religious sphere as mediators, healers and teachers. Higher in the religious hierarchy are the *ulama* or *maulvis,* the scholars who are the repositories of Islamic law and tradition, and the *qazis* and *muftis*, who exercise judicial functions. Further centres of influence are a number of Sufi mystical orders, which have for many centuries inspired a form of spiritualism centred around the veneration of *murshids* or *pirs* (spiritual teachers), or *khwajas* and *sayyids* (presumed descendants of the Prophet). In Afghanistan, two of the most prominent Sufi orders are the Qadiriyya and the Naqshbandiyya, the contemporary leaders of which, Sayyid Ahmad Gailani and Sebghatullah Mujadidi, have also been leaders of Afghan resistance groups. The Qadiriyya order was founded in Baghdad in the 12th century and in the 19th became influential among the Pushtoons, while the Naqshbandiyya order was founded in Bokhara in the 14th century and became particularly strong both in eastern Afghanistan and in Central Asia. It has traditionally been closely involved in politics and opposed to foreign influence. During the late nineteenth and early twentieth centuries, several Sufi *pirs* attracted wide followings and were prominent in uprisings against the British, as the latter tried to establish their ascendancy over the Pushtoon tribes of the North-West Frontier. At local level, the veneration of *pirs* and other holy men is often visible in the form of *ziarats*, shrines which, with their fluttering flags, are a common sight in the Afghan countryside.

Non-Pushtoon peoples have been less influential in the country's history. The next most numerous, at around a fifth of the population, are the Tajiks, communities of whom are to be found in many parts of the country, but who are concentrated in Badakhshan, around Kabul and Herat, and in Kohistan and the Panjshir Valley. Many are traders and artisans, and live in the cities. They appear to be largely of Persian origin and speak Dari, but they also show signs of Mongol antecedents. Because Dari has become the main language of the cities, Tajiks have come to play an active role in the administration and affairs of state, despite their having been mostly excluded from the Pushtoon-dominated officer corps and senior government echelons. To the north of the Hindu Kush are also several peoples of Turko-Mongol origin, who, like the Tajiks, share their ethnic origins with the peoples who live across the border in the former Soviet Union. Prominent among them are a million or so Usbeks, who lived a semi-independent existence under their own *begs* or *amirs* until gradually conquered by the Afghan Amirs, as the latter extended their rule over Afghan Turkestan. The Usbeks are primarily farmers and are noted breeders of horses and karakul sheep. Many migrated into Afghanistan under pressure from Tsarist Russia and the Soviet Union. Like the Tajiks, they have these days mostly lost whatever tribal affiliations they may have had, and, by and large, neither group share the aggressive instincts of their Pushtoon compatriots. The Usbek language is one of the Turkic group, as is that of the other main peoples of northern Afghanistan, the Turkmen and the Khirgiz, both of whom are also partly nomadic but retain some tribal affiliations. The Turkmen, who emigrated from the Soviet Union in the 1920s and 1930s, are also karakul breeders and skilled carpet weavers. The majority of the Khirgiz emigrated to Turkey following the communist coup of 1978.

Another Afghan race who, from their features, clearly have Mongol origins are the Hazaras, a minority group who have traditionally lived an isolated existence in the mountainous centre of the country. The word 'hazar', meaning a thousand, has given rise to the supposition that they may be descendants of Genghis Khan's soldiers or those of some other Mongol invader, the inference being that they arrived 'in their thousands', i.e. as hordes. However some believe that they are, partly at least, the descendants of earlier migrants from Central Asia. Unlike most other Afghans, they are mainly Imami Shias. They speak Hazaragi, a form of Persian, but with Turkic and Mongol accretions. In their relatively barren homeland, they are often sheep breeders, but many of them have migrated to the cities, where they work as porters or undertake other menial occupations. There has in the past been little love lost between them and the other Afghans, who despise them on both religious and racial grounds, while they themselves have a particular hatred of the Pushtoons, whom they see as exploiters and oppressors.

If the Hazaras are to some extent the 'odd men out' in Afghan society, more so are the Nuris or Nuristanis, who live in the north-east of the country and neighbouring Chitral. Until they were converted to Islam at the end of the last century, they were known as *kafirs* (infidels) and practised a polytheistic religion that included a form of ancestor worship, carving strange wooden figures to adorn the graves of their dead. Many of them have light skins and aquiline features, often combined with blue eyes and blond or red hair, so that the romantically inclined have been inspired to suggest that they may have had, among their forebears, Greek settlers or even soldiers of Alexander the Great's army. A more probable theory is that they are one of the aboriginal peoples of Afghanistan, who were pushed into their remote valleys by later migrants. Their several separate languages appear to derive quite closely from a primitive Indo-Aryan tongue. Their strong tribal structure has many similarities with that of the Pushtoons. Scattered around the country are also a variety of other minorities; the Ismailis, another Shia community who live in the north-east of the country; the Baluch and Brahui, who live in the south; the Qizilbash, descendants of the Persian mercenaries who came to Afghanistan in the service of Ahmed Shah in the mid-18th century; the Aimaqs and Farsiwan, with strong Persian connections; and many more.

Both the Tajiks, the Hazaras and the Nuristanis have in the past been the victims of Pushtoon expansionism, and these and other antagonisms persist to the present day. Even within ethnic and tribal boundaries, regional differences are significant. Over most of the country outside the cities and towns, where at least nine-tenths of the population live, the inhabitants have traditionally run their own affairs, with little outside interference. Their villages have been largely self-sufficient communities, dependent on subsistence level agriculture and the rearing of livestock. The state has never been strong enough to establish effective control throughout the countryside and has traditionally done little for it, whether in terms of educational or medical facilities, or of development more generally. Conversely, government revenues have derived largely from foreign subventions or from taxes on commerce and business, rather than from land, agriculture or pastoralism. Despite the bonds of Islam, a sense of national unity has thus always been weak, except when an unusually strong leader has appeared or the nation has come together when threatened by an external enemy. Even then, co-operation has tended to be ephemeral and has lapsed in the face of the country's deep-rooted divisions. In the words of one observer[7]

> Their enmities and bitter struggles spring from the tribal, sub-tribal and regional differences which characterise this most backward of societies – differences which escape definition in terms of modern political theory.

The other side of the coin is that the Afghans share a strong devotion to freedom. They will carry hospitality to embarrassing extremes, but are implacable as enemies. If there has been an overriding feature of their history, it is that it has been a history of conflict – of invasions, battles and sieges, of vendettas, assassinations and massacres, of tribal feuding, dynastic strife and civil war. Rarely have the Afghans allowed themselves, or have allowed others with whom they have come into contact, to lead out their lives in peace.

Perhaps to a greater extent than most countries, therefore, Afghanistan's history cannot be viewed in isolation. As the 'cockpit of Asia', it has, over the millennia, experienced migrations and invasions, and its neighbours have in turn suffered from its attentions. At the same time, Afghans have historically had much in common with their neighbours, in particular in terms of religion, ethnicity and trade. Although never colonised, Afghanistan is part of the colonial history of Tsarist Russia and British India, with a strategic importance that in 1884 brought the two empires to the brink of war. The Soviet Union's disastrous encounter with it in the 1980s was a significant element in the dissolution of the Soviet Union itself. Today, its neighbours are, no less than their predecessors, nervous of its Islamic militancy and concerned to exercise influence in it, or at least to keep it in check. It is a potential participant in regional trade, where its pivotal position could give it a role that it has not possessed since the decline of the Silk Route. More widely, its links with international terrorism and its participation in the drugs trade, as well as what are seen as severe infringements of human rights, are of international concern. The historian of Afghanistan thus has to view its affairs not only in themselves, but also in terms of their regional and global impact. The aim of the narrative which follows is to describe and analyse both the historical and the contemporary interplay of these three perspectives.

CHAPTER ONE

Early History

For a country as closed and remote as Afghanistan, a great deal of archaeological research has been carried out over the years, although relatively little of it has covered the country's prehistory. However enough has been found to show that the region was widely inhabited during the Palaeolithic and Neolithic eras. Evidence also exists of the practice of agriculture and pastoralism some 10,000 years ago. By the sixth millennium BC, lapis lazuli from Badakhshan was being exported to India, while excavations in Sistan and Afghan Turkestan have revealed evidence of a culture allied to that of the Indus civilisation of that time. By the second millennium, lapis lazuli[1] from Afghanistan was in use in the Aegean area, where it has been found in one of the Shaft Graves at Mycenae, while tin, also possibly from Afghanistan, was being carried in a ship which was wrecked at Uluburun, off the Turkish coast, in 1336 BC. From very early times, therefore, the region's commercial links stretched both to the east and to the west.

As is clear from the diversity of the population, as well as from the archaeological and historical evidence, Afghanistan has also over its long history been a 'highway of conquest' between west, central and southern Asia. The country has been incorporated into a series of empires, and successions of migrations and invasions have passed into and through it. One of the main migrations was that of the Indo-Aryan peoples, who spent some time on the Iranian Plateau and in Bactria, before going on to conquer and displace the pre-Aryan peoples of South Asia. It was not until the sixth century BC, however, that the region began to appear in recorded history, as the Achaemenid monarch, Cyrus the Great, extended his empire as far east as the River Indus. His successor, Darius the Great, created various

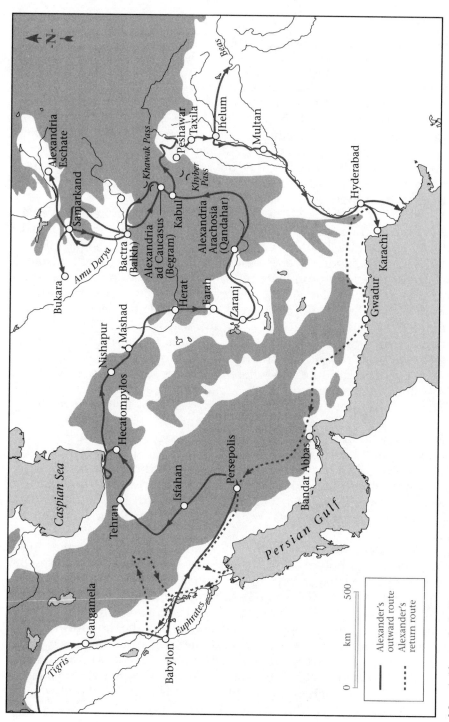

Map 4 Alexander's Route to India

satrapies in the area, among them Aria (Herat), Drangiana (Sistan), Bactria (Afghan Turkestan), Margiana (Merv), Chorasmia (Khiva), Sogdiana (Transoxania), Arachosia (Ghazni and Kandahar) and Gandhara (the Peshawar valley). The Achaemenids appear to have embraced Zoroastrianism, and tradition has it, somewhat uncertainly, that the renowned sage Zoroaster was born and lived in Bactria, and that he died in Bactra (Balkh) around 522 BC. The establishment of the eastern Achaemenid empire involved hard fighting and Persian rule was only maintained with difficulty. Greek colonists were brought in to help consolidate it, but by the fourth century BC, the satrapies to the south and east of the Hindu Kush seem to have regained their independence.

During the latter half of the fourth century, Achaemenid rule gave way to Greek, as Alexander of Macedon, having defeated Darius III in 331 BC at the Battle of Gaugamela, embarked on his epic march to the east. He subdued Persia, and then in 330 entered Afghanistan. As he advanced, he founded cities to protect his conquests, starting with Alexandria Ariana near what is now Herat. He then turned south to the Sistan and eastwards to the Kandahar area, where he founded Alexandria Arachosia. By the spring of 329 BC he had founded yet another city, Alexandria-ad-Caucasum, in the Kohistan valley north of Kabul. He then struck up the Panjshir Valley and north over the Hindu Kush, where his troops suffered severely from frostbite and snow blindness. He seized Bactria and crossed the Amu Darya, where the unfortunate satrap, Bassus, was delivered to him, tortured and executed. He then went on to take Marcanda (Samarkand), and built his remotest city, Alexandria-Eschate, 'Alexandria-at-the-End-of-the-World', on the Sri Darya. Hard fighting followed with the local nomadic tribes until the summer of 327 BC, when, after founding more cities, he retired over the mountains. Before doing so he married a Bactrian princess, Roxane, probably as a dynastic expedient and not, as the romantically inclined would have it, a love match.

Alexander then marched down to India, sending the bulk of his forces and equipment along the Kabul River, while he himself marched with a smaller force up the Kunar Valley and eastwards into Bajaur and Swat. The combined army then crossed the Indus and in 326 BC defeated the local king, Poros, at the battle of Jhelum. By that time, however, his troops had had enough of the unknown and, when he proposed going on beyond the Beas, they mutinied and compelled him to retreat. He built a fleet and sailed down the Indus, and then withdrew partly by sea and partly through the Makran, where his troops suffered severely from shortages of food and water. He died in 323, soon after arriving back in Babylon.

The empire that Alexander established quickly broke up and, in the Punjab, gave way to the Mauryan dynasty under Chandragupta. At the end of the fourth century, Alexander's successor in the East, Seleucus Nikator, suffered a severe defeat at the hands of Chandragupta and was forced to cede to him most of the land to the south of the Hindu Kush. However friendly relations developed between the two kingdoms, a treaty was negotiated and envoys were exchanged. From the middle of the third century BC, under the great Mauryan king, Asoka, Buddhism began to flourish in both India and Afghanistan. Edicts of Asoka, carved on pillars or rocks, have been found in both countries, and bear witness to the strength of his Buddhist convictions. Bactria, however, remained a Seleucid satrapy and was settled by further Greek colonists, and then, also in the middle of the third century, became an independent Graeco-Bactrian kingdom. Over many years, from the 1920s onwards, French archaeologists searched for a Graeco-Bactrian city in northern Afghanistan. In 1963 they eventually found one, at Ai Khanum[2] in Taloqan Province, at the confluence of the Kokcha River and the upper reaches of the Amu Darya. Excavations there revealed the remains of a wealthy and sophisticated Hellenistic city, with a citadel, palace, temples and gymnasium. It appears to have been sacked and burnt at the end of the second century BC, probably by nomad invaders. Around the same time as Bactria broke away from Seleucid rule, the Parthians, originally a Scythian nomad people, supplanted the Seleucids in Persia and established an independent kingdom that was to withstand the Roman Empire and last until 226 AD.

Soon after Asoka's death in 232 BC, the Mauryan Empire declined and in about 184 the Bactrian Greeks, having conquered Aria and Arachosia, captured Gandhara and penetrated as far as the Mauryan capital at Patna. Under Menander, who ruled between 155 and 130, they extended and stabilised their rule in India, with their capital at Shakala (now Sialkot). In India, the Bactrians came under Buddhist influence, although in Bactria itself, Buddhism had not yet penetrated, and the region remained predominantly Persian in culture, although still under Greek rule.

However new actors were now appearing on the scene, with the onset of what has been called 'the great migration of peoples' out of central Asia. Speculation has it that this may have been sparked off by a combination of climatic change, which may have caused the pasture lands of central Asia to dry up, and the construction of the Great Wall of China by the Chinese Emperor Qin Shi Huangdi. Unable to move their flocks eastwards, nomad peoples began to move towards the west. The first of the migrants were the Yüeh-chih, who seem to have been driven from Central Asia by the Hsiung-Nu, later known in the West as the Huns. A majority of the Yüeh-chih began by moving towards Lake Balkhash, in turn driving before them the inhabitants of the region, a Scythian people known as the Sakas. The latter overran Bactria and moved against Parthia, but encountered resistance from the Parthians and detoured southwards to Sistan (Sakastan). From there they moved eastwards into Sind and north-wards to Gandhara and the Indus valley, where they established themselves early in the first century BC. They did not, however, for long remain independent of the Parthians, who in the early first century AD briefly extended their empire as far east as the Punjab. Meanwhile the Yüeh-chih themselves moved westwards and south-wards. Some of them attacked the Parthians, while others crossed the Amu Darya in about 130 BC and conquered Bactria. In around 75 AD they crossed the Hindu Kush under Kujula Kadphises, the leader of one of their five tribal groups, the Gui-shang. They then invaded India, stormed Taxila, the main Parthian city, and defeated the Sakas and their Parthian overlords.

The Gui-shang, or Kushans, as the Yüeh-chih were to be known, proceeded to extend their rule over the whole of the Punjab and the Ganges valley as far as Vatanasi. To the west, they conquered Aria, Sakastan and Arachosia, while to the north, their territories stretched to the Caspian and Aral Seas. Their greatest king, Kanishka, who probably ruled during the second century AD, established a capital at Mathura and a northern capital near Peshawar. A summer capital was also founded at Kapisa in the Kohistan valley. Trading links with the Middle East were revived, as was the Silk Route to China, and the Kushans conducted a thriving trade with Rome and the Han Dynasty. Remarkably, the kingdom that these Central Asian nomads proceeded to establish was notable for both its religious and its artistic achievements. At an earlier stage, they may have been fire worship-pers in the Zoroastrian tradition, and a fire temple dedicated to Kanishka has been unearthed at Surkh Kotal, near Pul-i-Khumri, just north of the Hindu Kush. However Buddhism again flourished and, in its Mahayana form, spread through Afghanistan and along the Silk Route to Central Asia and China. Hellenism seems also to have retained its cultural presence in the area and was reinforced through contacts with Alexandria, so that a combination of Greek and Buddhist influences produced the Indo-Hellenic style of sculpture known as Gandharan, many examples of which, often of great beauty and delicacy, have been found on Afghan sites. Excavations at Kapisa have yielded a magnificent array of some two thousand priceless art treasures, originating from as far afield as China, India, Alexandria and Rome, while what was clearly a complex of flourishing monasteries at Hadda, near Jalalabad, has produced thousands of statues and images in the Gandharan style. Most spectacularly, two huge images of the Buddha have survived at Bamian, carved into the cliff face at the margin of the valley. These probably date from the third and fifth centuries AD, and the number of monastic cells carved into the cliffs around them show that this was a major Buddhist centre. Hsüan Tsang[3], who visited Bamian in the course of his journey in the seventh century, found 'several dozen monasteries and several thousand monks' still in the area.

The Kushans ruled for some five centuries, yielding territory in the mid third century AD to the Persian Sassanid dynasty, which had supplanted the Parthians, but surviving in north-west India until the invasion of the Ephthalites, the White Huns, during the fifth century. The origins of the Ephthalites remain shrouded in mystery. They may have been subjects of the Avars of Mongolia, who broke away and migrated through Turkestan to Bactria, where they drove out the Kushans, crossed the Hindu Kush and occupied north-west India. Unlike earlier invaders, who had accommodated themselves to the pre-existing civilisations, the Ephthalites sacked the cities, slaughtered the inhabitants and dispersed the religious communities. They ruled for about a century, but had to fight off the Sassanids and in 568 succumbed to a joint onslaught by the latter and the Turkish peoples of Central Asia.

A new and more enduring era then started to dawn in Afghanistan, that of Islam. In 637 and 642, the Muslim Arabs defeated the Sassanids, who were exhausted by internal dissension, and in 650 or thereabouts they occupied Herat and Balkh. Beyond that, however, the Arab advance was slow and halting, and was hindered by a succession of conflicts within the Ummayid and Abbasid Caliphates. The Arabs advanced through Sistan and conquered Sind early in the eighth century. Elsewhere, however, their incursions were no more than temporary, and it was not until the rise of the Saffarid dynasty in the ninth century that the frontiers of Islam effectively reached Ghazni and Kabul. Even then, a Hindu dynasty, the Hindushahis, held Gandhara and the eastern borders. From the tenth century onwards, as Persian language and culture continued to spread into Afghanistan, the focus of regional power shifted to Ghazni, where a Turkish dynasty, who started by ruling the town for the Samanid dynasty of Bokhara, proceeded to create an empire in their own right. The greatest of the Ghnaznavids was Mahmud, who ruled between 998 and 1030. He expelled the Hindus from Ghandara, made no fewer than seventeen raids into India and succeeded in conquering territory stretching from the Caspian Sea to beyond Vatanasi. Bokhara and Samarkand also came under his rule. He encouraged mass conversions to Islam, in India as well as Afghanistan, looted Hindu temples and carried off immense booty, earning for himself, depending on the viewpoint of the observer, the titles of 'Image-breaker' or 'Scourge of India'. In Ghazni, he carried out a prestigious building programme and his court became a centre for scholars and poets, including the renowned Persian poet, Firdausi. Ghazni itself was subsequently destroyed several times over, but the remains of three magnificent Ghaznavid palaces are still to be seen at Lashkari Bazar, at the confluence of the Helmand and Argandab Rivers. After Mahmud's death, Ghaznavid power was weakened by a Seljuk invasion from Persia, and was supplanted by that of the Ghorids, who sacked Ghazni in 1150 and established their capital in Herat. Coming from central Afghanistan, the Ghorids, who were also of Turkish stock, then invaded India, where they captured Lahore and Delhi. Their short reign was to go down in history for the construction of the Qutb Minar outside Delhi, the Masjid-i-Juma (Friday Mosque) in Herat and the remote Minaret of Djam in the wilds of the Hezarajat, which was only rediscovered in 1943. In 1215, the Ghorids were in turn conquered by the Khwarizm Shahs, with their capital at Khiva.

There then occurred one of the most cataclysmic events of Afghan history, the invasion of the Mongol hordes under their chieftain Genghis Khan. The latter was a brilliant military commander and administrator, who founded an empire that eventually stretched from Hungary to the China Sea and from northern Siberia to the Persian Gulf and the Indian sub-continent. The origins of his followers are still a matter of dispute, the most likely theory being that they were descendants of the Hsiung-Nu. Genghis Khan's achievement was to weld them into a formidable fighting force, distinguished by its superb cavalry, which was capable of highly disciplined manoeuvre and sustained advance at great speed, even over near-impossible terrain. Genghis Khan himself started life as an abandoned orphan, but managed after many vicissitudes to attract support to the point where, in 1206, he was proclaimed emperor of a Mongol confederation, probably some two million strong. In 1218, out of the blue, he and his followers descended on Turkestan, defeated the Khwarizm Shahs and took Bokhara and Samarkand, which they comprehensively sacked. In 1221 they took Balkh, razed it to the ground and massacred its inhabitants. When the Taoist seer and healer, Ch'ang Ch'un, who had been summoned from China to Genghis' court in Afghanistan, arrived at the city a short while after the massacre, he found[4] that the citizens had been 'removed', but 'we could still hear dogs barking in its streets'. The Mongols treated Herat leniently when it first surrendered to them, but when it rebelled six months later, it was speedily retaken and all its inhabitants were executed, the process

16

taking seven days to complete. Bamian was also razed and its population slaughtered, leaving today only the ruins of two hilltop fortresses, the Shahr-i-Zohak (Red City) and the aptly named Shahr-i-Gholgola (City of Sighs) as evidence of the calamity. Ghazni then suffered the same fate, as did Peshawar, but Genghis Khan did not advance beyond the Punjab, probably nervous of the effect on his army of the heat of the Indian plains. The overall outcome of the Mongol invasion was widespread depopulation, devastation and economic ruin. When the Moroccan traveller, Ibn Batuta, passed through Afghanistan a century later, he found[5] Balkh in ruins and uninhabited, Kabul no more than a village and Ghazni devastated. He reports Genghis Khan as having torn down the mosque at Balkh, 'one of the most beautiful in the world', because he believed that treasure had been hidden beneath one of its columns.

Following Genghis Khan's death in 1227, his sons and grandsons ruled his empire, most of Afghanistan coming under his second son, Jaghatai, whose descendants established themselves in Kabul and Ghazni. Herat alone retained a degree of autonomy under a Tajik dynasty, the Karts. From 1364 onwards, the western part of the khanate came under the control of Tamerlane (a corruption of *Timur-i-Leng* – Timur the Lame), a Turko-Mongol who claimed, apparently falsely, descent from Genghis himself. Tamerlane began by expelling the Mongols from Transoxania and around 1370 proclaimed himself emperor at Balkh. He too went on to create an extensive empire, which included Afghanistan and northern India, and in 1398 he took Delhi and slaughtered its inhabitants. Among his unpleasant habits was that of stacking into pyramids the heads of those he had massacred or incorporating them into walls. In the Sistan, he destroyed the irrigation works that stemmed from the Helmand River, with the result that what had been a prosperous and well-inhabited region was turned into a desert waste. The weathered remains of substantial towns and fortresses even today provide clear evidence of the scale of the destruction, from which Sistan never recovered. However, unlike Genghis Khan, Tamerlane was, despite his barbaric propensities, a man of culture, and he transformed the Timurid capital, Samarkand, into an intellectual and artistic centre. His tomb there is one of the glories of Islamic architecture. His empire began to disintegrate after his death in 1405, but his dynasty, the Timurids, continued to rule in Turkestan and Persia until the early sixteenth century. Under his son, Shah Rukh, Herat became the centre of what has been called the Timurid Renaissance, with a thriving culture notable for its architecture, its literary and musical achievements, and its calligraphy and miniature painting. Shah Rukh's formidable wife, Gohar Shad, was responsible for the building of the Musalla, the complex of mosque, college and mausoleum which, with its several minarets, dominated the Herat skyline over many centuries. The bulk of it was razed at the time of the Panjdeh crisis in 1885, to create a clear field of fire for the defenders of the city, in the event, thought to be imminent, of a Russian attack from the north. Of the minarets which were left, Robert Byron says[6], in his encomium of Timurid architecture,

> Their beauty is more than scenic, depending on light and landscape. On closer view, every tile, every flower, every petal of mosaic contributes its genius to the whole. Even in ruin, such architecture tells of a golden age. ... The few travellers who have visited Samarkhand and Bokhara as well as the shrine of the Imam Riza [in Meshed], say that nothing in these towns can equal the last. If they are right, the Mosque of Gohar Shad must be the greatest surviving monument of the period, while the ruins of Herat show that there was once a greater.

The Timurid Renaissance lasted little more than a century. Following Shah Rukh's death in 1447, ten successive rulers held Herat over a period of a mere twelve years, but it was then taken by another Timurid, Husain-i-Baiqara, who gave it a further forty years of peace and a renewed cultural flowering. The miniature painter Bihzad, the poet Abdurrahman Jami and the historian Mishkwand all embellished his court. Then, during the sixteenth century, two new dynasties began to impinge on Afghanistan. In Persia, the Safavids presided over a national renaissance and survived until well into the eighteenth century, despite conflicts with the Ottoman Turks and the Usbeks, who had moved south into the region around 1500. Also at the turn of the sixteenth century, a descendant of both Tamerlane and Genghis Khan, Mohammed Zahir-ud-din, better known as Babur, assumed power in Kabul and Ghazni. Babur came originally from Ferghana, a small khanate some two hundred miles east of Samarkand. His father having died in a landslip while feeding his pigeons on the wall of his palace, Babur, while still in his teens, conceived the ambition of conquering Samarkand. In 1497, after a seven months' siege, he took the city, but his supporters gradually deserted him and Ferghana was taken from him in his absence. Within a few months he was compelled to retire from Samarkand, and for the next few years he and a small band of followers survived only by living a freebooting existence. Eventually he retook Samarkand, but was again forced out, this time by an Usbek leader, Shaibani Khan, who also took Herat. Once more reduced to destitution, Babur decided in 1504 to trek over the Hindu Kush to Kabul, where the current ruler promptly retreated to Kandahar and left him in undisputed control of the city. Babur became extremely fond of Kabul, and proceeded to settle down and indulge one of his great pleasures, the construction of gardens. In his memoirs, he gives a vivid account of the great ebb and flow of trade which passed through Kabul at that time, but which was later to decline as the sea routes to India were developed. The city, he recorded[7], was

> an excellent and profitable market for commodities … Every year seven, eight or ten thousand horses arrive in Kabul. From Hindustan every year fifteen, twenty thousand pieces of cloth are brought by caravans. The commodities of Hindustan are slaves, white cloths, sugar candy, refined and common sugar, drugs and spices. There are many merchants who are not satisfied with getting three or four hundred per cent.

In 1511, Babur again took Samarkand, but yet again was driven out, so that he finally abandoned his ambitions in that direction and turned towards India. He gradually established his ascendancy over the neighbouring Pushtoon tribes, captured Kandahar and acquired artillery, employing a Turkish gunner to operate it. After several probing raids, he finally launched a full scale invasion of India in 1525 and defeated the Lodi kings, themselves an Afghan dynasty, who had ruled in Delhi since 1451. In 1527 he went on to defeat the Rajputs at Khanua, west of Agra, and established himself at the latter city as the founder of the dynasty of the Great Moguls which was to rule India with glittering magnificence over the following two centuries.

Like Mahmud of Ghazni and Tamerlane, Babur combined military prowess with cultural sophistication. He was an accomplished poet in both Persian and Turkic and was a sensitive observer of nature. Many pages of his memoirs, which he wrote over a period of some forty years, are devoted to the flora and fauna of both Afghanistan and India, and his love of gardening shines through at every turn. His writings also show him to have been a man of great charm, intelligence and humanity. His description of the Timurid court of Husain-i- Baiqara is invaluable as a picture of the age. His judgment of men is sensitive and acute. However, until somewhat late in life, he was also a hard drinker and his health was never good, particularly while he was in India. He died in 1530 and was later buried in Kabul, where his tomb still stands in a garden that he created.

CHAPTER TWO

The Emergence of the Afghan Kingdom

The long period of Mogul and Safavid rule over what is now Afghanistan lasted until the eighteenth century, when it was replaced by that of the Abdali Pushtoons. During the sixteenth and seventeenth centuries, Babur's Mogul descendants exercised a somewhat loose and uncertain rule over Kabul and Peshawar, as well as of the plains between the River Indus and the Suleiman Range, while the Safavids held Herat and the lands to the west. Kandahar was for long a bone of contention between the two powers, and changed hands several times between the middle of the sixteenth century and the middle of the seventeenth. To the north, a number of Usbek khanates maintained their independence in the face of pressures from the south and west. Also during the seventeenth century, various of the Pushtoon tribes combined from time to time to rebel against the Moguls and were at one stage inspired by the warrier-poet, Khushhal Khan Khattak, who has since retained an honoured place in Afghan history. However a judicious mixture of bribery and suppression ensured that the Moguls retained a precarious overall suzerainty.

In 1709, however, a new era dawned, when the Ghilzai tribe, under the able leadership of one of their chieftains, Mir Wais Hotaki, rose in revolt against the Safavids. An astute, wealthy and courageous man, Mir Wais had earlier lived at the Persian court and realised that it was vulnerable. The Ghilzai began by capturing Kandahar, killing in the process the greatly detested Persian governor, who had, in accordance with Safavid policy, tried to force Shi'ism on them, and parties of Ghilzai horsemen were soon riding into Persia in search of plunder. Following Mir Wais' death in 1715 and a contest for the succession, his son Mir Mahmud proceeded to launch a major campaign which in 1722 took him to the Persian capital, Isfahan. On

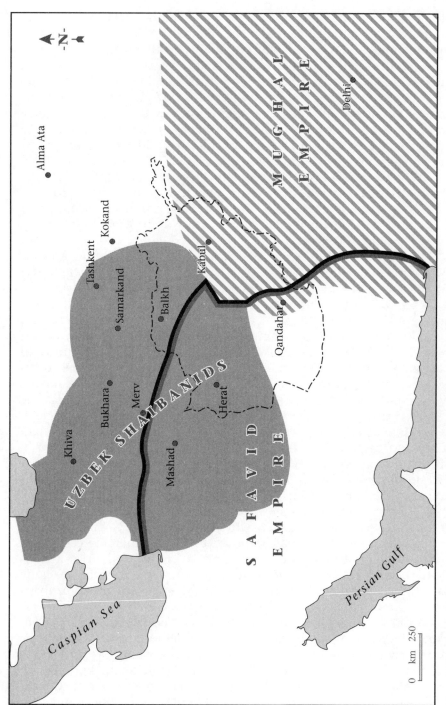

Map 5 The Boundaries of the Safavid and Mogul Empires in the Sixteenth Century

the way to that city, he defeated a considerably larger Persian army supported by 24 cannons under the direction of an itinerant French artilleryman, M. Philippe Colombe, and then, after a long and bloody siege, stormed the city itself. The sack and massacre that ensued were such that Isfahan never recovered its former eminence. Mir Mahmud proceeded to take the Safavid throne, and added to the barbarities he had perpetrated during the siege and capture of the city by inviting a large number of Persian nobles to a banquet, where he had them slaughtered by his troops. His rule over Isfahan did not last long, as he rapidly degenerated into a homicidal maniac, died or was murdered by his own men and was succeeded in 1725 by his cousin Ashraf. The latter defeated an Ottoman army which was also trying to take advantage of Safavid weakness, but in 1729 was in turn defeated near Isfahan by a resurgent Persian army, led by a former camelman and bandit, Nadir Quli Khan.

While the Ghilzai were concentrating on Isfahan, the Abdalis, who had earlier supported the Persian Shah, were also on the move. In 1716 they took Herat and later advanced to Meshed. Nadir was hard put to it to cope both with them and with the Ghilzai, but finally succeeded in driving them back to Herat, which he besieged and captured in 1732. In his moment of victory, he treated the Abdalis, who had three times broken successive truces, with unusual clemency, and he now recruited a number of them to serve in his personal bodyguard. He proceeded to take the Persian throne and, as Nadir Shah, advanced on Kandahar and Kabul, both of which he captured in the course of 1738. From there he marched into India, where his Abdali bodyguard first assisted him in his defeat of a Mogul army and capture of Delhi, and then extricated him from a critical situation as he was trying to force a passage back through the Khyber Pass in the face of strong Afridi resistance. When some of the Abdalis were murdered by a Delhi mob, his vengeance was extreme, with the result that the Indians thereafter described a massacre or reign of terror as a nadershahi. Laden with immense booty, including the Peacock Throne, Nadir Shah returned to Persia, where he continued to campaign against the Ottoman Turks and as far north as Samarkand, Khiva and Bokhara, but in time he too became sadistically paranoid and in 1747 was killed by his own Qizilbash officers.

Nadir's murder created a crisis for his bodyguard, who were at that time commanded by a young Abdali officer, Ahmed Khan. They were outnumbered by the Qizilbash, who greatly resented the privileged position they had held under Nadir Shah, but, having established that the latter was indeed dead, they managed to fight their way out and returned to Kandahar. There, despite his youth,

Ahmed Khan was elected Shah by a *jirga* of the nine Abdali sub-tribes. The traditional story is that after nine days of inconclusive discussion, a noted *darwesh* (holy man), Mohammed Sabir Khan, intervened decisively in Ahmed Khan's favour. When the latter expressed reluctance, the *darwesh* again intervened and ceremonially placed in Ahmed Khan's turban some ears of corn from a nearby field, at the same time proclaiming him Badshah, Durr-i-Dauran (Shah, Pearl of the Age). More mundanely, it is probable that his election resulted partly from his position as the leader of Nadir Khan's formidable bodyguard and partly from the calculation that being both young and a member of the Saddozai clan of the small Popalzai sub-tribe, he would be more likely to be open to manipulation than a leader from one of the more powerful sub-tribes. If so, the Abdalis underestimated him. An astute manager of men, he created an Abdali council, which he was careful to consult as a first among equals, and his attitude towards the other Pushtoon tribes was conciliatory. He was also well aware that the best means of retaining Pushtoon loyalty was to create opportunities for warfare and plunder. Here, he had several advantages. His Ghilzai rivals were enfeebled as a result of their Persian foray and submitted to his rule. Persia was in disarray after the death of Nadir Shah, while the Mogul empire was crumbling. As well as possessing the best fighting force in the region and much of Nadir Shah's treasure, including the Koh-i-Noor diamond, he was also fortunate enough to capture a caravan, which, in total ignorance of Nadir Shah's fate, was returning through Kandahar en route for Persia, loaded with treasure from India. He now had the means to pay his army, conciliate political and tribal rivals, and finance his campaigns. Following his assumption of the title of Durr-i-Dauran, the Abdalis thenceforth called themselves Durranis.

Ahmed Shah Durrani, as he now was, started in 1748 by attacking Ghazni and Kabul, and, when the Qizilbash garrison at Kabul surrendered without a fight, went on to take Peshawar. He then advanced on Delhi and met a Mogul army at Sirhind. Despite great inferiority in numbers, he was gaining the upper hand when his powder train accidentally blew up, killing hundreds of his troops. However he managed to withdraw in good order and, on his return the following spring, met with no resistance from the new Mogul Emperor, another Ahmed Shah. As the price of peace, the latter ceded all the territory earlier held by Nadir Shah, together with the province of Sind. Ahmed Shah then returned to Kandahar and in 1750 marched on Herat. That city having surrendered, he proceeded to Meshed and Nishapur, which, after a wearisome siege in the depths of winter, finally capitulated the following spring. On his way back to Kandahar, he sent an army north of the Hindu Kush, which occupied

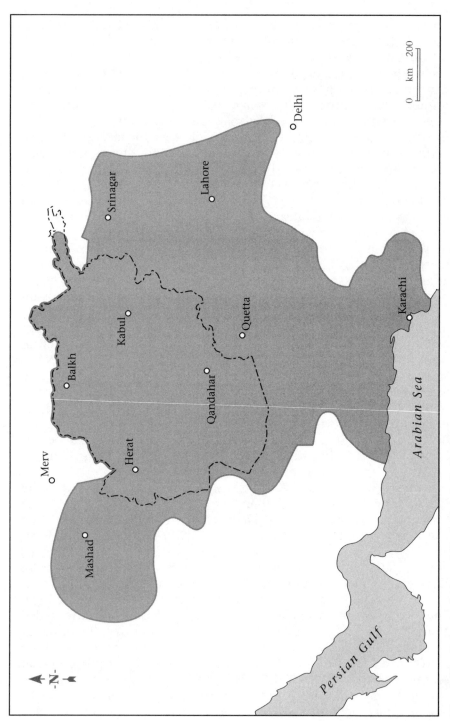

Map 6 The Extent of Ahmed Shah Durrani's Empire

the Usbek and Tajik territories from Maimana through to Badakh-shan, as well as Bamian in the centre of the country. In the winter of 1751 he turned his attention back to India, again captured Lahore after a long siege and once more received the submission of the Mogul Emperor. This gained him the western Punjab, while in the same year he also annexed Kashmir. For the next few years he remained in Kandahar, while he and his fellow tribesmen enjoyed the fruits of their campaigns, but in the winter of 1756 he returned to India, marched on Delhi and sacked it. He contemplated remaining there, but the combination of heat and cholera confirmed his preference for the more equable climate of the hills. He was not, however, to stay away long, for his Indian possessions were soon to be threatened by Maratha armies advancing from the south. In 1761, after two years of inconclusive warfare, the two armies met at Panipat. A massive battle ensued, with possibly some 80,000 men on each side, extended along an eight mile front. At first the Marathas all but breached the Afghan line, but after several hours of fighting, a fierce counterattack led by Ahmad Shah resulted in a sudden Maratha collapse. The subsequent rout and massacre of the Marathas and their large camp following was of epic proportions. This was possibly the most decisive battle to take place on the Indian sub-continent, if only because, had the Marathas won, it is quite possible that they would have remained sufficiently strong to prevent both the emergence of Sikh power and the subsequent British advance to Delhi and the Punjab. As it was, Ahmed Shah and his forces again retired to the hills with their booty, leaving a power vacuum in the Punjab which was soon to be filled by the Sikhs. During the 1760s, Ahmed Shah repeatedly returned to India, defeated the Sikhs and twice sacked and desecrated their holy city, Amritsar. But he was never able to consolidate his victories and each time the Sikhs recovered as he withdrew. Finally he grew tired of campaigning, his health began to fail and he suffered increasingly from what was probably cancer of the face. He died in 1772, aged only fifty and is buried in a still-venerated mausoleum in Kandahar.

At the height of his power, Ahmed Shah's kingdom stretched from the Amu Darya to the Arabian Sea. To the west, it extended beyond Meshed and to the east as far as Delhi, and it also included Kashmir, Sind and most of what is now Baluchistan. An inspired military leader, he was also an astute politician and diplomat who showed an exceptional grasp of the problems of securing and keeping the allegiance of the Pushtoon tribes. While always retaining his dignity and authority, he was a popular ruler who kept himself accessible. He was also a deeply religious and cultivated man who, among other accomplishments, wrote poetry in Pushtu. His weakness was that he and his followers were warriors and freebooters, and in no way were they governors or administrators. Although tempted from time to time, it was never in their nature to undertake the permanent occupation that might have consolidated their conquests in the plains. As a result, Ahmed Shah's empire was never secure while he lived and was to disintegrate after his death, and it is probably for this reason that he has not been accorded the place in history he deserves. But he was the founder of the Saddozai dynasty, which lasted to 1818, as well as, albeit through a different sub-tribe, of the Durrani dynasty which was to rule Afghanistan until 1978. It is understandable, therefore, that the Afghans should have come to regard him as the 'Father of the Nation', although his creation was more of a tribal confederacy than anything approaching a nation state. As a footnote to history, it is perhaps worth recording that he received from the Amir of Bokhara a *kherqa* (part of a cloak reputedly worn by the Prophet Mohammed) which he placed in a mosque in Kandahar especially built to house it. Both the *kherqa* and the mosque have survived to the present day, and the *kherqa* was formally displayed by the Taliban leader, Mohamed Omar, after his men had captured Kandahar in 1994.

Ahmed Shah was succeeded by his second son, Timur Shah, who managed to get the better of a brief struggle with his brother Suleiman Mirza, who had gained support in Kandahar. In 1775, partly to be closer to his Indian possessions and partly to free himself from Durrani pressures, Timur transferred his capital to Kabul, which he used as his summer capital, moving to Peshawar in the winter. He succeeded in keeping the throne – and his large harem – for some two decades, relying less on the support of the tribes than on that of the 12,000 strong personal bodyguard of Qizilbash mercenaries which he had inherited from his father and subsequently enlarged. The Qizilbash also served him as administrators, and were commonly known as the *ghulamshahis,* the 'slaves of the Shah'. Having strong Persian affinities, Timur was, like his father, a cultivated man, with a penchant for architecture and the construction of formal gardens. But he had little stomach for foreign adventure and, compared with much of Afghan history, his was a tolerant and peaceful reign. He had to face a succession of revolts, which his Qizilbash bodyguard managed to suppress, culminating in 1791 in a plot hatched by a combination of Mohmands and Afridis which nearly succeeded. Timur had to conceal himself in the fortress at Peswawar while the Qizilbash dealt with the plotters, and he then proceeded to torture to death two leaders of the conspiracy who had sworn fealty to him on the Koran, a breach of the Pushtoon code of honour for which, if for little else, he was for long remembered. During his reign, a series of revolts broke out across his territories, and Sind and the Amu Darya region became virtually independent. However, nominally at least, at his death in 1793 he still ruled over most of the territory conquered by Ahmed Shah.

A fascinating picture[1] of the Afghans and of Timur's court was provided by an East India Company official, George Forster, who in 1783 undertook a remarkable journey, mostly overland, from Bengal back to England. In the course of it, he passed through Kashmir, Afghanistan and Persia, then took a ship across the Caspian Sea to Baku and Astrakhan, whence he travelled to Moscow and St. Petersburg before finally sailing to England. He was not much impressed by Timur, whom he describes as avaricious, although he does concede that he exhibited 'little injustice or cruelty', and that he allowed foreign merchants 'to enjoy an ample protection and maintain their rights, with a spirit rarely seen in Mahometan countries'. Against the apparent background of apprehension in Bengal that Timur might present a threat to the East India Company's rule, his report was reassuring. He describes Timur as possessing 'little enterprise or vision of mind' and as showing 'little inclination to military action or the aggrandisement of his Empire':

> The facts . . . . do not warrant the opinion that Timur Shah is an object of dread to the bordering states, or that he is justly entitled the comet of the east, who, we have been taught to believe, will, at some unexpected moment, shoot across the Indus and the Ganges, and consume even our remote province of Bengal.

The Afghans themselves he describes as

> a rude unlettered people, and their chiefs have little propensity to the refinements of life, which indeed their country is ill qualified to supply. ... Being generally addicted to a state of predatory warfare, their manners largely partake of a barbarous insolence, and they avow a fierce contempt for the occupations of civil life.

On the relationship between the Pushtoons and their rulers, his comments also had a more than ephemeral validity:

> The government of the Afghans must ever receive a weighty bias from the genius of their ruler, and the degree of authority he may possess. But when not constrained, as in the present reign, by some extraordinary power or capacity of the prince, they disperse into societies, and are guided by the ruder principles of the feudal system. Conformably to this system, the different chieftains usually reside in fortified villages, where they exercise

an acknowledged, though a moderate, sway over their vassals, and yield a careless obedience to the orders of government. Rarely any appeal is made to the head of state, except in cases which may involve a common danger; when I have seen the authority of the Shah interposed with success.

When Timur died in 1793, he left upwards of thirty children by his official wives, of whom over twenty were sons. As he had also failed to nominate a successor, there existed a potent recipe for dynastic strife, or *badshahgardi* (literally 'ruler-turning'), as it was popularly known. The fifth son, Zaman Mirza, who happened to be in the capital, took the throne, with the crucial support of Painda Khan, a Durrani who was the head of the Mohammedzai clan of the powerful Barakzai sub-tribe and had earlier been Ahmad Shah's *wazir*, or deputy. Zaman imprisoned all but two of his brothers and starved them into submission, and then dealt with revolts by the remaining two, Mahmud and Humayun, based on Herat and Kandahar respectively. Mahmud was allowed to stay as governor of Herat after his initial revolt, but Humayun, who, as Timur's eldest son, was a greater threat, was eliminated from contention by being blinded. Zaman conducted several desultory campaigns against the Sikhs and briefly took Lahore in 1797 and again in 1798, but, faced by fresh revolts on the part of Mahmud, ended by withdrawing and leaving the Sikhs in possession of the lands to the east of the Indus. Somewhat improbably, his ineffectual manoeuvrings aroused concern in British India, where there were fears that he might be able to stimulate a general uprising, and the British went so far as to maintain an army in Oudh to counter any invasion that the Afghans might mount. According to Lord Wellesley[2], the Governor-General of India, 'every Mohammedan, even in the remotest region of the Deccan,. . .. waited with anxious expectation the advance of the Champion of Islam'. In reality, the 'Champion of Islam' had only a small, ill-equipped army, which he could barely afford to keep in the field. Whereas Ahmed Shah and Timur had extracted the bulk of their revenues from their Indian provinces and had thus been able to tax the Pushtoon tribes, and in particular the Durranis, relatively lightly, Zaman and his successors found themselves increasingly circumscribed by a lack of funds, a predicament which was worsened by struggles for the succession and a growth in power on the part of the tribal chiefs, who were able to retain appreciable revenues for themselves. Zaman himself is reputed to have been a devout Muslim and something of a scholar. A principled, but mild and malleable character, he played little part in the management of affairs, but left them largely in the hands of his wazir, Wafadar Khan, whose high-handed methods progressively alienated the Durrani chiefs, to the point where, led by Painda Khan, they plotted a revolt. Zaman discovered the plot and executed Painda Khan, an act that prompted an alliance between Fateh Khan, Painda Khan's eldest son, and Mahmud, then in exile in Persia. In 1800, Mahmud and Fateh Khan took Herat and, when Zaman returned hastily from India and marched against them, captured him and had him blinded in his turn. Mahmud seized the throne, but met with immediate opposition from Shah Shuja, Zaman's full brother, who had been holding Peshawar on his behalf. Shah Shuja declared himself Shah and marched on Kabul, but was defeated by an army led by Fateh Khan. Ghilzai revolts over the two following years also failed, as did another attempt by Shah Shuja to take Kandahar, but the latter was eventually successful during 1803. Faced with Shia-Sunni riots in Kabul, Mahmud was unable to control the situation and his opponents gave Shah Shuja the opportunity to take the city. Fateh Khan fled and Mahmud submitted, but this time there was no blinding or execution, a leniency which Shah Shuja was later to regret.

It was during the reign of Shah Shuja that the first official contact was made between the British and the Afghan kingdom, when another East India Company official, Mountstuart Elphinstone, arrived in Peshawar in 1809 on a treaty-making mission to the Afghan court. Elphinstone's lengthy report[3] of his mission has become a classic and, despite the two centuries that have since passed, is still one of the most comprehensive and perceptive accounts of the Afghan kingdom and society that has been written. With the assistance of members of his mission, Elphinstone gives an exhaustive review of the climate, geography, agriculture, commerce and history of Afghanistan, but at the centre of the book are descriptions of its government and society, which he wrote personally. He sees the Afghan kingdom as resembling ancient Scotland, notably in

> the direct power of the King over the towns and the country immediately around; the precarious submission of the nearest clans, and the independence of the remote ones; the inordinate power and faction of the nobility most connected with the court; and the relations borne by all the great lords to the crown. ... There is reason to fear that the societies into which the nation is divided, possess within themselves a principle of repulsion and disunion, too strong to be overcome, except by such a force as, while it united the whole into one solid body, would crush and obliterate the features of every one of the parts.

Elphinstone also argues, however, that for all its anarchy and disorder, the Afghan system avoided much of the corruption and oppression so often found under Asian despotism:

> In Afghanistan. . . . the internal government of the tribes answers
> its end so well, that the utmost disorders of the royal
> government never derange its operations, nor disturb the lives
> of the people. A number of organised and high-spirited republics
> are ready to defend their rugged country against a tyrant; and are
> able to defy the feeble efforts of a party in a civil war.

Summing up a long discussion of the Afghan character, he concludes:

> Their vices are revenge, envy, avarice, rapacity and obstinacy; on
> the other hand, they are fond of liberty, faithful to their friends,
> kind to their dependents, hospitable, brave, hardy, frugal,
> laborious, and prudent; and they are less disposed than the
> nations in their neighbourhood to falsehood, intrigue, and
> deceit . . . . [A visitor] would find it difficult to comprehend how a
> nation could subsist in such disorder; and would pity those, who
> were compelled to pass their days in such a scene, and whose
> minds were trained by their unhappy situation to fraud and
> violence, to rapine, deceit, and revenge. Yet, he would scarce fail
> to admire their martial and lofty spirit, their hospitality, and
> their bold and simple manners, equally removed from the
> suppleness of a citizen, and the awkward rusticity of a clown;
> and he would, probably, before long discover, among so many
> qualities that excited his disgust, the rudiments of many virtues.

Elphinstone was clearly much taken by Peshawar, which he reached
in the spring, and describes in emotive language its gardens, orchards
and fertile and well populated countryside, set against the background of snow covered hills. No less clearly, he much enjoyed the
entertainment laid on for his party, which included dancing girls,
'incomparably superior to those of India in face, figure, and
performance'. He was much impressed by the appearance of Shah
Shuja, 'a handsome man, about thirty years of age, of an olive
complexion, with a thick black beard ... his countenance was
dignified and pleasing, his voice clear, and his address princely'. At
Elphinstone's first audience, the King's attire was so glittering that his
guests at first thought that he was wearing jewelled armour. His tunic
was encrusted with gold, diamonds and gemstones, and he sported
ropes of large pearls, a bracelet bearing the Koh-i-Noor, and a crown
'so complicated, and so dazzling, that it was difficult to understand,
and impossible to describe'. Less impressive, however, was what
Elphinstone could gather of the King's situation. His army had just
been defeated in Kashmir and, more generally, the power and
influence of the crown had, after several years of civil war, greatly
deteriorated in relation to that of the tribes, the army and the nobles

30

of the court. Revenue was short, the tribes rebellious and the army 'more at the disposal of their commanders than at the King's'.

In 1809, only a few weeks after Elphinstone left Peshawar, Mahmud and Fateh Khan took the field, captured Kandahar and Kabul, and met Shah Shuja's forces at Nimla, on the road between Kabul and Peshawar. There Shah Shuja was decisively defeated and, after periods of captivity in Kashmir and Lahore, where the Sikh leader, Ranjit Singh, wrested the Koh-i-Noor from him, he eventually joined Zaman in Ludhiana as a British pensioner. Under the virtually nominal rule of Mahmud, who devoted himself to a dissolute private life, Fateh Khan proceeded to run the kingdom, but in 1818 the two fell out, and Fateh Khan was blinded, and subsequently tortured and brutally killed, by means of progressive dismemberment, by Mahmud and his son Kamran Mirza, a character even more degenerate than his father. This provoked a general rising, led by the Barakzais, who defeated Mahmud and Kamran and drove them to Herat, where Kamran succeeded his father in 1829 and ruled, at least nominally, until 1842. However the Barakzais at that point possessed no strong leader and were unable to agree on a successor. As *badshahgardi* degenerated into anarchy, so the empire created by Ahmed Shah finally disintegrated.

CHAPTER THREE

The Rise of Dost Mohammed

While he was the effective ruler of Afghanistan, Fateh Khan appointed various of his half brothers, who numbered some twenty in all, as governors of provinces. He was careful to move them around in order to prevent their creating over-strong power bases, but two sets of full brothers managed to hold on to their provinces over periods of years, the one in Peshawar and the other in Kandahar. In Peshawar, five brothers, led initially by Ata Mohammed Khan, came to be known, with their descendants, as the 'Peshawar Sirdars', while in Kandahar another five 'Dil' brothers and their descendants, at first led by Purdil Khan, came to be known as the 'Kandahar Sirdars'. Following Fateh Khan's blinding and murder, the remaining brothers began to contend for power, and the ensuing eight years witnessed a kaleidoscope of fratricidal conflict and treachery, with a succession of rivals holding Kabul for shorter or longer periods. Taking advantage of these dissensions, the Sikh ruler Ranjit Singh annexed Kashmir in 1819 and later, after defeating a Durrani army near Attock, extended his authority across the Indus to Peshawar, where he destroyed the buildings and gardens which had so delighted Elphinstone. Until 1834, however, he allowed the 'Peshawar Sirdars' to continue to govern the city and neighbourhood. Ranjit Singh, who had originally been appointed Governor of the Punjab by Zaman Shah, was a ruler of exceptional ability and acumen. In 1809, he had signed a treaty with the British which was to last until his death in 1839, and they came to regard him as a trustworthy leader of a stable buffer state.

Amidst the anarchy that prevailed in Afghanistan, one of the younger of the Barakzai brothers, Dost Mohammed Khan, gradually maneuvered himself into a position of supreme power in Kabul. As the

32

offspring of a Qizilbash mother, he had been looked down on by most of his brothers and had spent much of his youth under the protection of Fateh Khan, for whom he had acted as servant and amanuensis. It was he who was largely responsible for Fateh Khan's downfall, since when, in 1817, the two had marched to Herat to protect it from a threatened Persian invasion, the latter had sent him to seize the city. In the course of the incursion, Dost Mohammed entered the Saddozai harem, where 'amongst other unpardonable deeds, he tore away the jewelled band which secured the *perjamas* of the wife of the prince Malek Kasim. . . . sister of Prince Kamran'[1]. Is was partly in revenge for this insult that Mahmud and Kamran murdered Fateh Khan when, shortly afterwards, he fell into their hands. Dost Mohammed himself fled into exile in Kashmir, where he was held under restraint by Mohammed Azim Khan, Fateh Khan's next senior surviving brother. On Fateh Khan's death, however, he was allowed to depart and moved against Kabul, which at the time was nominally held by Kamran's son Jehangir, but in practice by a Durrani sirdar by the name of Ata Mohammed. Dost Mohammed captured and blinded the later and then attacked the fortress, the Bala Hissar, where Jehangir was taking refuge. 'Young and beautiful', the historian Sir John Kaye records[2], '[Jehangir] was the delight of the women of Caubal, but he had few friends among the chivalry of the empire'. Dost Mohammed blew up part of the Bala Hissar and 'death stared Jehangir in the face'. However, 'the women of Caubal offered up prayers for the safety of the beautiful prince' and he managed to make his escape under cover of darkness and a heavy downpour of rain.

Dost Mohammed was immediately challenged at Kabul by Shah Mahmud and Kamran, but at the last moment, for reasons that are unclear, they lost confidence and retreated to Herat. The country was then again parcelled out among the Barakzai brothers. Mohammed Azim Khan, who had started by bringing Shah Shuja with him but had fallen out with him on the way, retained Kabul for himself, the 'Dil' brothers returned to Kandahar and the Peshawar Sirdars, now led by Sultan Mohammed Khan, again held that city. Dost Mohammed was allotted Ghazni and later also assumed control of Kohistan, which he had earlier held on behalf of Shah Mahmud. With the help of the Qizilbash community, he progressively strengthened his position in Kabul and managed to survive two plots to blind him, one by Mohammed Azim Khan's son, Habibullah Khan, and the other by Sherdil Khan from Kandahar. By 1826, he was strong enough to take full control of the city. In 1834, he had to defend himself from an attack by Shah Shuja, who, encouraged by the British in the form of an advance on his pension, as well as by numbers of Durrani chiefs who resented Barakzai rule, came out of seclusion, concluded a treaty with Ranjit Singh and marched through Sind to Kandahar. There Dost Mohammed and the Kandahar Sirdars defeated him in a close fought battle, which he lost only through lack of money and resolution. No sooner had this threat been dealt with, however, than Dost Mohammed found that Ranjit Singh had taken the opportunity to seize Peshawar. To strengthen his hand in repulsing the Sikhs, Dost Mohammed assumed the title of *Amir ul-Mominin* (Commander of the Faithful) and presented the confrontation as a religious war. However, before he could engage Ranjit Singh in battle, the latter managed to suborn Sultan Mohammed Khan, who deserted and left him with no alternative but to retreat to Kabul. The following year, another attempt, led by Dost Mohammed's son, Mohammed Akbar, resulted in the defeat and death of the Sikh general, Hari Singh, in a battle at Jamrud, but ended with an Afghan withdrawal. In 1836, Dost Mohammed was recognised by his brothers as Amir, although holding little more than the area around Kabul and Ghazni. He continued to smart at the loss of Peshawar; and indeed this loss was to be 'engraved on the heart' of every subsequent Afghan ruler.

A handful of outside observers have left us with a description of Dost Mohammed's character and appearance. One of these was an American doctor, soldier and adventurer, Josiah Harlan, who at one point was a general in Dost Mohammed's army. Harlan describes[3] Dost Mohammed as 'in vigorous health', although slightly stooped, 'which militates against the commanding appearance his person is otherwise formed to impress when animated by conversation or excited by passion'. His dress was 'unaffected and plain', and it seems that he was careful to treat his court in a relaxed manner and as equals, in sharp contrast to Shah Shuja's ornate appearance and habit of standing on his dignity. A view of him later in life, penned by a British officer, Colonel Harry Lumsden[4], was that he was 'tall, of fine physical development, and he truly looked a king ... His manner was courteous, while his keen eyes and vigorous conversation conveyed the idea of great determination combined with astuteness and appreciation of humour ... he called a spade a spade'.

Another observer was Charles Masson, an odd character who knocked around the region for some years and between 1826 and 1838 occupied himself with antiquarian researches in Afghanistan. He was, in fact, as the British discovered, a deserter from the Bengal Artillery by the name of James Lewis, and he eventually received an official pardon for the services he rendered as British agent in Kabul. He was well acquainted with Dost Mohammed, and his observations about him contain much that is of interest. Masson tries to distinguish[5] between what he regards as Dost Mohammed's innate character and the effects on him of an environment 'in which honour could scarcely thrive. ... Had he been born to legitimate power he would have figured very respectably; his talents would have had a fair field for their development and exercise, and he would have been spared the commission of many enormities, then unnecessary'. According to Masson, Dost Mohammed grew up 'untutored and illiterate' and the influence of Fateh Khan, who Masson hints had a propensity to homosexuality, must also have been harmful. 'The example of the dissolute Fati Khan', Masson observes, 'must have had a pernicious effect on the morals of those immediately around him, and Dost Mohammed Khan may claim commiseration when it is considered that he was elevated to manhood amid the disgraceful orgies of his brother'. Dost Mohammed was also, in his youth, addicted to wine and was, apparently, often to be seen in a state of inebriation. As can be inferred from the Herat incident, he was also headstrong, and more than once found himself in trouble as a consequence. Nevertheless, as Masson goes on to say, when he became master of Kabul he 'abjured wine and other unlawful pleasures ...,, overcame the neglect of his youth' and learned to read and write. He apparently studied the Koran daily, as well as history and poetry. In his dealings with his subjects, he was found to be accessible, fair and impartial, and he gained a reputation for justice. Where politics were involved, on the other hand, Masson describes him as 'without principle' and 'as good or as bad as it suited his conceived interests'. Masson cites his rule in Kohistan, where he

> gained his ends by stratagem or by force, but never employing the latter when the former was sufficient. Some of the obnoxious chiefs he inveigled by Korans and false oaths; others by intermarriages – a means not infrequently resorted to by the Durranis, to get their enemies into their power, when other wiles have failed.

Masson notes his slaughter of eight chiefs in Charikar on a single day, and his luring of the most intransigent of his opponents into a neutral fortress and there murdering him, throwing his head down to his retinue outside. When the latter failed in an attack on the fortress, Dost Mohammed 'was left at leisure to rejoice in his victory, and the triumph of his dexterity'. Masson's conclusion is that Dost Mohammed was a 'gallant warrior and shrewd politician', but the ruthlessness and duplicity with which he was forced to act in order to survive meant that while he

> might have an accomplice, he could never have a friend; and his power, erected on the basis of fraud and overreaching, was always liable to be destroyed by the same weapons.

It was Dost Mohammed's misfortune that he ruled in Kabul at a time when two great imperialist powers, Britain and Russia, were extending their conquests, the one to the east and the other to the north, of his domain. Britain had first become concerned about a possible land threat to India in the early 1800s, when the French began to intrigue in Persia and, following the Treaty of Tilsit, the spectre briefly arose of a combined Franco-Russian invasion. By 1814, however, the French threat had receded, and British interest in Afghanistan and its neighbourhood was not to be revived until the late 1820s, when concern began to develop over what was seen as a fresh threat from Russia. In the early 1830s, matters began to come to a head, when the Russians reduced the Shah of Persia to a position of subservience through the Treaty of Turkmanchai and, supremely confident in their ascendancy in the region, turned their eyes to the east. Their first step was to encourage the Shah to take Herat, to which he had maintained a claim, but the death of both the Shah and his heir apparent delayed action until November 1837, when a new Shah, Mohammed Mirza, finally arrived before the city. The general assumption was that after the capture of Herat he intended to aim for Kandahar, from whose Sirdars he had already received overtures. With his army was the Russian envoy at his court, Count Simonich, together with a number of seconded Russian officers and a regiment of Russians deserters under the command of a Polish 'General' Berowski. Together, they should have had little difficulty in taking the city, but, despite the Russian presence, the siege was handled with total incompetence and the defenders were still holding out some eight months later. A contributory factor may have been the chance presence in Herat of an officer of the Bengal Artillery, Eldred Pottinger, who was able to stiffen the defence. Eventually, in June 1838, the British finally bestirred themselves and landed a small force from India on Kharg Island in the Persian Gulf. The Shah was then told by the British envoy, John McNeill, that any occupation of Herat would be considered a 'hostile demonstration against Britain', and that if he wished the force at Kharg to 'suspend the measures in progress for the vindication of its honour', he must at once retire. The Shah had little hesitation in submitting to this combination of bluff and gunboat diplomacy, with the result that the Russians suffered a clear diplomatic and military defeat. Had rational counsels then prevailed in London and Calcutta, that should have been the end of the affair, but events had by then assumed a momentum of their own.

In 1835, shortly after Lord Melbourne's Whig government was formed, with Palmerston as its Foreign Secretary, the decision was taken to appoint George Eden, later Earl of Auckland, to be the Governor-General of India. Auckland had served twenty undistinguished years in Parliament, with a reputation for being conscientious but uninspired, and it was possibly the fact that he was the nephew of a former Governor-General, Lord Minto, that secured him the appointment. It seems that he was a competent administrator, and a reading of his memoranda and despatches (assuming that they were his own work) suggests that he was a careful and intelligent man. However he had no experience of India, nor indeed of foreign affairs more generally, and he was, while well-intentioned, malleable and unassertive[6]. His most senior adviser was William Macnaghten, a brilliant linguist, but one who, until he became Head of the Foreign and Political Department, had spent most of his career as a bureaucrat in Calcutta. In the judgment of many of his contemporaries, he was quite unsuited to foreign affairs and diplomacy, and the general view has been that it was his over-confidence and lack of judgment that, together with Auckland's supineness, were the main causes of the eventual debacle (although he did not live to give his own side of the story). Also influential was Captain Claude Wade, the long-standing Political Agent at Ludhiana, who, from his key vantage point, was a strong proponent of the alliance with the aging Ranjit Singh and the Sikhs, was favourably disposed towards his pensioner, Shah Shuja.

Auckland's instructions[7], sent from London on 25 June 1836, were straightforward, but were couched in such general terms as to give him an almost free hand. He was

> to watch more closely than has hitherto been attempted the progress of events in Afghanistan, and to counteract the progress of Russian influence. ... The mode of dealing with this very important question, whether by despatching a confidential agent to Dost Mohammed of Kabul merely to watch the progress of events, or to enter into relations with this Chief, either of a political or merely in the first instance of a commercial character, we confide to your discretion as well as the adoption of any other measures that may appear to you desirable to counteract Russian influence in that quarter, should you be satisfied. . ..that the time has arrived at which it would be right for you to interfere decidedly in the affairs of Afghanistan. Such an interference would doubtless be requisite, either to prevent the extension of Persian dominion in that quarter or to raise a timely barrier against the impending encroachments of Russian influence'.

Macnaghten and Wade had indeed already taken steps to 'watch more closely' events in Kabul, by appointing as their agent first an Indian by the name of Karamat Ali, and then Charles Masson. Auckland had also, just before receipt of the Secret Committee's Despatch, decided to send an emissary to Dost Mohammed's court, in response to a friendly message[8] received from the latter in the spring of 1836, congratulating him on his appointment and asking for advice over his own relations with Ranjit Singh and 'the settlement of the affairs of this country'. Auckland sent an equally friendly response[9], but excused himself from providing any advice on the lines requested on the grounds that it was 'not the practice of the British Government to interfere with the affairs of other independent states' – a bizarre assertion in the light of what was soon to follow. Auckland's choice for the mission was Alexander Burnes, a bright and ambitious young officer of the Bombay Artillery who had already distinguished himself as a linguist, topographer and traveller. Like Masson, Burnes was no stranger to Afghanistan or to Dost Mohammed. In the early 1830s he had volunteered to travel in Central Asia and succeeded in reaching Bokhara before returning to India via Persia. On proceeding to England in 1833, he published a book[10] on his travels, was lionised by London society and came to be known as 'Bokhara Burnes'. Returning to India, he was employed on a mission to the Emirs of Sind before being chosen in 1836 to go to Kabul.

Burnes and Masson were in substantial agreement about Dost Mohammed. Burnes believed him 'acceptable to the people; and I even think favourable to the prosperity of the country'[11]. He saw him as a 'man of enlightened views ... favourably disposed towards the British Government. ... It would not be difficult to form a connection. ... It would require no great expenditure of the public funds to conciliate this chief, and, it is to be remembered, that he is in possession of the most important position in Asia, as regards the protection of British India'. Masson for his part also saw the Dost as a popular ruler, although he was somewhat less sanguine than Burnes about his reliability. Nevertheless, his considered opinion was that 'if he and his friends ... had been properly treated, they would have done as much as could have been hoped from them'[12]. It is also worth noting that McNeill in Teheran was strongly in favour of reaching an understanding with Dost Mohammed. In a recommendation which foreshadowed later policies, he wrote[13],

> With a little help from us, [he] could be put in possession of Kandahar and Herat. I anxiously hope that aid will not be withheld. A loan of money would possibly enable him to do this and would give us a great hold upon him. He ought to be persuaded to be precluded from receiving any other foreign representation or agent of any kind at his Court, and should agree to transact all business with foreign powers through the British agent. Unless something of this kind should be done, we shall never be secure. ...'.

Despite his instructions and the discretion given to him by Palmerston, Auckland gave Burnes very little in the way of guidance[14]. Masson's comment[15] on the instructions was that they were 'really none at all', and blames Burnes for not contesting them. Initially, Burnes was authorised to do no more than conduct a commercial mission, although, as Masson pointed out[16], trade in and through Afghanistan was in any case almost completely unrestricted and no mission was required to facilitate it. (The instructions incidentally produced the further comment[17] from Masson that '... there was little notion entertained at this time of convulsing Central Asia, of deposing and setting up kings, of carrying on wars, of lavishing treasure, and of the commission of a long train of crimes and follies'.) However, with the inconclusive battle between Ranjit Singh's and Dost Mohammed's armies, the Persian attack on Herat and reports that Dost Mohammed had been making overtures to the Persians and the Russians, it was soon realised that the mission would inevitably have to concern itself with political issues, and Macnaghten sent Burnes supplementary instructions[18]. Nevertheless the latter was given no authority to negotiate, but was told merely to report any 'reasonable propositions' Dost Mohammed might make and await further guidance. More than this, the instructions stipulated that the Government of India's first concern must be for 'the honour and just wishes of our old and firm ally Ranjit Singh'. However, if Dost Mohammed 'looked for terms of peace adapted to a fair measure of his position, such good offices in his favour with the Maharajah [Ranjit Singh] as we can render would be given to him'. Macnaghten went on to authorise Burnes, at his discretion and subject to Wade's approval, to suggest that the good offices might be directed towards the restoration of Peshawar to 'a member of the Barakzye family on the condition of tribute to Ranjit Singh'.

From the outset, therefore, Burnes had very little to offer Dost Mohammed. Despite bringing with him some very inadequate gifts, he was well received, and Dost Mohammed insisted that he was prepared to renounce the overtures he had made to the Persians and the Russians, and that his desire was for friendly relations with the British. But it soon became clear that all would hinge on some acceptable arrangement over Peshawar. Towards the end of 1837, Burnes reported[19] at length on his discussions and recommended strongly that British influence should be exerted to settle the Peshawar issue:

It is surely not asking too much of Ranjit Singh to act with promptitude in the adjustment of a matter which, while it hangs over, brings intrigues to our door, and if not checked may shortly bring enemies instead of messengers. In the settlement of the Peshawar affair we have, it seems to me, an immediate remedy against further intrigue, and a means of showing to the Afghans that the British Government does sympathise with them and at one and the same time satisfying the chiefs, and gaining both our political and commercial ends.

One view is that the enmity between Ranjit Singh and Dost Mohammed was such that there was no scope for reconciliation between the two. However, with a little imagination and diplomacy, it is not beyond the bounds of possibility that an accommodation could have been found, if only because the Sikhs were finding their occupation of Peshawar troublesome and insecure. According to Burnes[20], Dost Mohammed was prepared to 'pay Ranjit Singh allegiance and regular tribute and to send a son to sue for forgiveness'. Alternatives floated were a reversion of Peshawar to Dost Mohammed on Ranjit Singh's death, or to the Barakzai in the person of Sultan Mohammed Khan. Dost Mohammed seems[21] at one stage to have been agreeable to Sultan Mohammed Khan and himself jointly holding Peshawar as tributaries of Ranjit Singh. But Auckland was never willing to open a dialogue with Ranjit Singh and Macnaghten sent Burnes a reprimand[22] for exceeding his instructions. Dost Mohammed, Auckland insisted in a final ultimatum[23], conveyed orally by Burnes, should

> desist from all correspondence with Persia and Russia .... never receive agents from them .... surrender all claims to Peshawar on your own account, as that chiefship belongs to Maharajah Runjeet Singh .... [and] respect the independence of Candahar and of Peshawar. ... In return for this, I promise to recommend to the government that it use its good offices with its ancient ally, Maharajah Runjeet Singh, to remove present and future causes of difference between the Sikhs and Afghans at Peshawar; but as that chiefship belongs to the Maharajah, he may confer it on Sultan Mohammed Khan, or any other Afghan whom he chooses, on his own terms and tribute, it being understood that such arrangement is to preserve the credit and honour of all parties.

Dost Mohammed's immediate reaction was to accept these terms, but he then asked for them to be conveyed in writing, which Burnes was not authorised to do, and jibbed at the need to start by writing a submissive letter to the Sikh leader, in the absence of any willingness on the part of the British to set the ball rolling.

There were several reasons for this somewhat messy, but conclusive, end to Burnes' mission. One was that Macnaghton and

Wade trusted Ranjit Singh and the Sikhs (with whom, after Ranjit Singh's death, British India would be at war in less than a decade), and 'were not ready to desert a profitable Sikh alliance for a doubtful Afghan one'[24]. They knew little, and trusted less, of Dost Mohammed, and even appeared to believe that Kamran in Herat was a stronger and more reliable power. Another was that while Burnes was in the midst of his mission, the whole issue was complicated by the appearance in Kabul of a Russian agent, a Lieutenant Vitkievitch, bearing, ostensibly, letters from the Tsar and the Shah of Persia. Purely by chance, he had been spotted while crossing Persia by one of McNeill's staff, and British suspicions were aroused even before he arrived in Kabul. Quite what his status was, and what the Russian motives were in sending to Kabul this solitary, junior officer, remain obscure. There was a suggestion that, like Burnes originally, his main purpose was commercial, but there is little doubt that his mission also had political objectives. In the light of their instructions from London and the prevailing climate of Russophobia, it was entirely predictable that Auckland and his advisors should have put the worst interpretation on it. The irony of the situation was that that, as with his earlier overtures to the Russians and Persians, Dost Mohammed, in dealing with Vitkievitch, was probably only trying to put pressure on the British, and did not realise how counterproductive his action was. Burnes lingered some further weeks in Kabul following Dost Mohammed's rejection of Auckland's terms, but, seeing Dost Mohammed in talks with Vitkievitch and realising that the situation was hopeless, packed his bags and left Kabul in April 1838. On arriving in India, he restated[25] his views on the desirability of reaching an accommodation with Dost Mohammed, but, seeing that the tide was flowing strongly the other way, and no doubt fearing that his own career might suffer if he continued to swim against it, he also went along with the view that was gaining ground there, that the now elderly Shah Shuja should once again be brought out of exile and restored to the Afghan throne. As Burnes put it, 'as for Shah Shooja-ool-Moolk, the British Government have only to send him to Peshawar with an agent and two of its own regiments as an honorary escort, and an avowal to the Afghans, that we have taken up his cause, to ensure his being fixed for ever on the Throne'. This was a significant and, for Burnes, a fatal piece of advice. Vitkievitch's fate was also tragic. Accounts differ as to whether or not his activities were repudiated in St. Petersburg, but, for whatever reason, shortly after his return there he committed suicide.

CHAPTER FOUR

The First Anglo-Afghan War

During the early months of 1838, and in the face of the continuing siege of Herat and evidence of Russian intervention in both Persia and Afghanistan, where there were also reports of an agreement, guaranteed by the Russians, between Persia and the Kandahar Sirdars (which Burnes had tried to prevent and had again been reprimanded for his pains), so Auckland became convinced that he would have to switch from a passive to an active policy and exercise the discretion given him to 'interfere decidedly in the affairs of Afghanistan'. Dost Mohammed having, in his view, rejected his offers of good offices with the Sikhs and sold out to the Russians and Persians, he now adopted the proposal, which had been advanced by Macnaghten and Wade, to restore Shah Shuja. To effect this, his initial strategy was to revive and extend the 1833 treaty between Shah Shuja and Ranjit Singh, and to persuade the two to invade Afghanistan. British support would be given in the form of money and British officers, but no British troops would participate. In May 1838 Macnaghten was sent to put this proposition to Ranjit Singh and, after a long negotiation, secured a treaty[1] which provided, in return for Sikh support, undertakings that Shah Shuja would abandon all claim to Peshawar and would pay Ranjit Singh the equivalent of £20,000 annually. This sum, to be guaranteed by the British Government, was in effect tribute, although thinly disguised as payment for the maintenance of 5,000 troops in the Peshawar area, to be sent to Shah Shuja's aid whenever needed. Shah Shuja had little choice but to accept this treaty, and indeed, such was his ambition for the Afghan throne, he made little difficulty over it. It was duly signed by all three parties in the course of July.

Auckland's advisers were unanimous that Shah Shuja should easily recover his throne. How they came to believe that the Afghans would accept an invasion by their Sikh enemies, or the rule of a Saddozai 'superannuated puppet'[2] who had on more than one occasion been ejected from the country, remains unexplained. But a worse error of judgement was to follow: almost insensibly, a decision was reached in the late summer of 1838 to commit British troops to the venture. One likelihood is that the Commander-in-Chief in India, General Sir Henry Fane, was highly dubious of the trustworthiness of Ranjit Singh and the ability of Shah Shuja's raw levies to prevail in Afghanistan, and was insistent that, if the venture was to be undertaken at all, there must be no half measures. Another is that there was a concern that if the Sikhs, whose army, on the parade ground at least, seemed hardly less impressive than the Company's, were to gain control of Afghanistan on their own, they might become sufficiently strong to pose a threat to the British position in northern India. Also it was cheaper to use British troops than to pay for large new levies for Shah Shuja.

However, there seems to have been more to it than this. The overall policy, which had started by being one of gradual commercial penetration and dependence on the Sikh alliance, had, by November 1838, been transformed into one of extending British influence into Afghanistan and establishing it as a fully fledged buffer state. As Auckland put it in an informal letter[3], the purpose was, 'to raise up an insurmountable and, I hope, lasting barrier to all encroachments from the Westward, and to establish a basis for the extension and maintenance of British influence throughout Central Asia'. The adoption of this expansionist strategy makes much more intelligible the decision not only to commit British troops, but to persist with the venture even after the Persian withdrawal from Herat and the Russian disavowal of Simonich and (possibly) Vitkievitch. This led Kaye to the judgement[4] that a project that was in any case one of 'doubtful honesty and doubtful expediency' had been converted to one which was 'at once a folly and a crime'. To try to justify the invasion, Auckland issued in October 1838 what was to be known as the Simla Manifesto[5], a patently dishonest piece of propaganda, designed to blacken Dost Mohammed and whitewash Shah Shuja and Ranjit Singh. Dost Mohammed, it alleged, 'avowed schemes of aggrandisement and ambition injurious to the security and peace of the frontiers of India; and ... openly threatened ... to call in every foreign aid he could command [so that] ... we could never hope that the tranquillity of our neighbourhood could be secured, or that the interests of our Indian Empire would be preserved inviolate'. In a no less blatant untruth, the Manifesto alleged that 'It had been clearly ascertained from the various officers who have visited Afghanistan, that the Barakzye chiefs, from their divisions and unpopularity, were ill fitted under any circumstances to be useful allies to the British Government'. The popularity of Shah Shuja, on the other hand, 'had been proved ... throughout Afghanistan by the strong and unanimous testimony of the best authorities' (unspecified). The Manifesto added (in words that are uncannily similar to those used by the Russians at the time of their 1979 invasion), 'the Governor-General confidently hopes that the Shah will be speedily replaced on his throne by his own subjects and adherents; and when once he shall be secured in power, and the independence and integrity of Afghanistan established, the British army will be withdrawn'.

When, towards the end of 1838, news of the Manifesto and of the intention to invade reached London, there was considerable public and parliamentary concern. Several of its critics saw[6] the key issue, that the problems were likely to begin when the military successes had ended and means had to be found to keep Shah Shuja on his throne. In response to parliamentary pressure, the government published[7] the correspondence that had preceded the decision to invade, but, without admitting the fact, made extensive cuts before publication. A reading of the passages omitted reveals a number of concerns; to distance the government, and Palmerston in particular, from Auckland's policy, to vindicate Auckland himself, to blacken Dost Mohammed, to depict Burnes as having been in favour of Auckland's policies, and to play down the Russian angle, in the interests of good relations with that country. However, Palmerston and the British Cabinet were not deflected. They had already endorsed Auckland's plans, although, such was the slowness of communication, up to three months in either direction, that it was only after he had sent his army on its way that he received the relevant despatch[8]. This specifically approved the choice of Shah Shuja, the assembly of 'a considerable force composed partly of British troops', and its invasion of Afghanistan, subject, at Auckland's discretion, to 'one more attempt to conciliate and secure the alliance of the Chiefs of Cabool and Candahar' (which Auckland chose not to do). 'The Shah's retreat from Herat ...', the despatch continued, 'may make these measures unnecessary: but even in that case you would do well to lose no time in attempting to recover your influence in Afghanistan; and to establish your relations with the Chiefs of that country upon a more satisfactory basis than you have hitherto been able to obtain'. The draft of the despatch carries a note by Hobhouse, the President of the Board of Control, that it had been approved by the Cabinet. While it still gave Auckland some discretion, it provides conclusive evidence of the British government's role. The policy may have been Auckland's (or Macnaghten's), but the government had, from its original instructions to its final word, full responsibility for what was to follow.

Towards the end of 1838, therefore, the requisite force was assembled and its leadership appointed. Now knighted for his services in Kabul, Burnes had confidently expected to be chosen as political adviser to the force, but Auckland thought it advisable to give this appointment to Macnaghten, with the proviso that once Shah Shuja had been reinstated, Macnaghten would leave and Burnes remain as permanent envoy to the Shah's court. At this point, the Sikhs, whose fulfilment of the Tripartite Treaty had been doubtful from the outset and who appreciated rather better than Auckland what the risks were, did no more than send in a force through Peshawar, the size of which Kaye describes[9] as 'absolutely contemptible', with Claude Wade attached as its political and military adviser. Ranjit Singh also objected to the main force marching through Peshawar, and so it was ordered to advance via Kandahar, with an immense train of 38,000 camp followers, 30,000 camels and a large herd of cattle. If there was one thing on which its British officers were clear, it was that they were going to have a comfortable campaign. One regiment took with it its pack of foxhounds, another employed two camels merely to carry its stock of cigars, junior officers were accompanied by as many as forty servants and one senior officer needed as many as sixty camels to carry his personal effects. In December 1838, thus encumbered, the 20,000 strong 'Army of the Indus' set out on its invasion. 'Poor dear peaceful George has gone to war' wrote[10] Auckland's sister, Emily Eden, 'rather an inconsistency in his character'.

The route taken by the 'Army of the Indus', lay in a south-west direction from Ferozepur, across the Indus at Bukkur and thence north-westwards to the Bolan Pass. As it proceeded, its fringes were harassed and plundered by Baluch tribesmen, and it was almost immediately confronted with acute problems of supply. Provisions were supposed to have been collected at the entrance to the Pass, but with a poor harvest in the area the previous year, little had been found. Towards the end of March the column reached Quetta, where it came close to starvation. At this point, however, Burnes, whose task it had been to secure a safe passage from the Khan of Kalat, managed to procure some 10,000 sheep, and so saved the day. The force then continued to Kandahar, which the Sirdars had abandoned and which it entered on 25 April.

Initially, the townsfolk gave the army an enthusiastic welcome, and Macnaghten reported[11] to Auckland that Shah Shuja had been received 'with feelings nearly amounting to adulation'. However, two weeks later, when all the troops had arrived and a ceremonial review took place, few local Afghans bothered to turn up. Also, when Macnaghten tried to conciliate the Durrani chiefs with lavish gifts of money, he was only partially successful in the face of widespread resentment at the presence of foreign troops. The army stayed in Kandahar for some two months, waiting for the arrival of fresh supplies, and then resumed its march. On 21 July it reached Ghazni, where it found itself before a heavily defended fortress under the command of one of Dost Mohammed's sons, Ghulam Haider Khan. For some inexplicable reason, it had not brought its siege artillery beyond Kandahar, but a solution was provided by a deserter from the Ghazni garrison, who revealed that, alone of the gates of the city, the great Kabul Gate had not been bricked up. The gate was therefore blown and an assault party succeeded in storming the fortress. There was some hard fighting within the walls, but the attackers had little difficulty in overwhelming those inside and capturing Haider Khan. Dost Mohammed's plan had been to make a stand at Argandeh, a few miles outside Kabul, while forces led by his sons took the invading army in the rear. There were now, however, numerous desertions among his troops and a rebellion in Kohistan, his overtures for peace were rejected and he had no option but to flee. Although pursued by a party of cavalry which was sent out in pursuit, he managed to make his escape across the Hindu Kush.

Meanwhile, on 7 August, Shah Shuja entered Kabul in state, but the absence of popular enthusiasm was immediately apparent, and it soon became clear that, as the critics had predicted, the British army could not be withdrawn without serious risk to the Shah's position. Apart from his evident unpopularity, it emerged that such revenues as he could raise would be quite insufficient to maintain him, and that his own force was too small and unreliable to keep him in power. Auckland needed the army back to guard against unrest in India, and was concerned to reduce the expense of maintaining it in Afghanistan, but 'these objects would be ill attained at the price of leaving unaccomplished the great purposes with which the expedition to Caubul was undertaken'[12]. Eventually it was decided to withdraw all but one division, which garrisoned Kandahar, and two brigades, which remained at Kabul.

The immediate problem, with the winter coming on, was where to station the troops left in Kabul. The obvious place was the Bala Hissar, but Shah Shuja objected strongly that the fortress overlooked his palace and the city, and that its occupation would create the impression that the British were in charge and that their presence would be permanent. Macnaghten conceded the point and the army moved to a newly constructed cantonment a mile away. From a military point of view, this cantonment was highly vulnerable. It was overlooked from the nearby hills, and the trees and buildings around it obstructed fields of fire. It was surrounded by a low wall and ditch, which the Afghans could 'run over with the facility of a cat'[13], and was so extensive that the available troops could not easily both defend it and make sorties into the surrounding countryside. Even worse, its commissary was housed in a building outside its perimeter. This was the first of the succession of military miscalculations that were to contribute to the ultimate disaster.

Late in 1839, news began to come in of a Russian advance towards Khiva, the motive of which was undoubtedly to counter the British 'forward policy' in Afghanistan. The Russians were nervous of the possibility of British encroachments into their commerce in Central Asia, as well as of the influence that a Muslim power with British support might exercise on the khanates of the region. Macnaghten panicked, and proposed to respond by sending a force across the Hindu Kush. As it turned out, however, the Russian venture was a miserable failure. It encountered exceptionally severe wintry conditions and, by the spring of 1840, the British were relieved to hear that it had withdrawn to Orenburg. Of an original force of some 5,000 men, some 1,000 died. The mere fact that it had taken place, however, had the effect of strengthening the British determination to persist with their Afghan policy.

During the winter of 1839–40, discontent started to spread in Kabul, although for many months it barely broke the surface. A main complaint was over the growing cost of food and other necessities, for which the occupying army was competing in the market. In the manner of many occupying armies, the members of this one also started to play fast and loose with the ladies of the city, both married and unmarried, and this caused great resentment. The troops also drank in public, and their attitude towards the locals was careless and overbearing, as was that of the 'politicals'. There was meanwhile a growing need to hand out subventions in order to persuade the tribal leaders, particularly among the Ghilzai who commanded the Kabul-Peshawar road, to acquiesce in the occupation. These leaders were additionally antagonised because the British took it upon themselves to raise a cavalry force for Shah Shuja, so that they lost the payments they traditionally received for providing 'feudal' cavalry for the Shah.

As if all this were not enough, Dost Mohammed then escaped from Bokhara, where he had been held virtually as a prisoner, raised a force of Usbeks north of the Hindu Kush and in September 1840 advanced on the small garrison at Bamian. Macnaghten was distraught[14] – 'the Afghans are gunpowder, and the Dost is a lighted match' – but the garrison had been strongly reinforced during the summer and, when the combined force met Dost Mohammed's army a few miles out of the town, they achieved a decisive victory. However Dost Mohammed was not finished. He soon reappeared in Kohistan, now with Tajik support, and a further engagement took place. Dost

Mohammed had the better of this, but seems at that point to have lost heart. One evening in November, while Macnaghten was taking his daily ride outside Kabul, he was approached by another rider, who turned out to be Dost Mohammed offering his surrender. He was duly sent under guard to Ludhiana, where he was given a pension and was held in the very house formerly occupied by Shah Shuja.

As the winter of 1840–41 approached, therefore, it seemed that all was going reasonably well. In the course of the winter, a Durrani rising near Kandahar was suppressed by the forces there, and in the summer of 1841, both the Durrani tribes on the Helmand and the Ghilzais in western Afghanistan rose, but were defeated in a series of engagements. British optimism was reinforced, even though there still seemed no reasonable prospect that the whole British force could be withdrawn. The country, Macnaghten reported[15] in August, was 'perfectly quiet from Dan to Beersheba'. The following month, he learned that he was to be appointed Governor of Bombay and was looking forward to leaving Afghanistan for good. On the military side, a new commander, General Elphinstone, had been appointed earlier in the year. A cousin of Mountstuart Elphinstone, he had fought with distinction at Waterloo and, after many years on half pay, had been recalled to active duty and appointed military commander of Oudh. He was now suffering from severe gout and was not far short of a state of senility. Under Elphinstone was another new appointee, Brigadier Shelton, who despised Elphinstone to the point of insubordination. The army, meanwhile, stayed in its cantonment. It had been joined by wives and families, and, to the bemusement of the Afghans, whiled away the time by indulging in cricket, horse racing, amateur theatricals, skating, shooting and fishing (and disporting itself with the ladies of the town). A number of officers, including Burnes, had taken up residence in the city, where the army's treasury was also located.

As the winter of 1841 approached, and unperceived by the ever-optimistic Macnaghten, Afghan resentment continued to grow. The immediate cause of the crisis that broke out in October of that year was a decision by the new Tory government in London to reduce expenditure, and Macnaghten consequently received instructions to reduce further the size of the occupying army and to cut back his subventions to the Ghilzai tribes, who promptly retaliated by closing the road to Peshawar. In Kabul itself, friendly Afghans had for some time been telling the British that a rising was being planned, but their warnings had gone unheeded. On 2 November, a mob attacked Burnes' house and, after several hours' fighting, the small number of defenders were overwhelmed, and Burnes and his brother were killed. Shah Shuja sent a force to rescue him, but it was unable to make headway in the narrow streets of the city. From the cantonment, where a message calling for assistance was received and the noise of the affray was clearly audible, no help at all was provided. After much order and counter-order, a force under Shelton was sent to the Bala Hissar, but went no further.

The success of this initial venture sparked risings across the country. A small force leaving Ghazni for the capital was annihilated, while only two officers and a sepoy survived a desperate retreat from the outpost at Charikar. In Kabul, the failure of the army to rescue Burnes, or even to take effective retribution for his death, encouraged those who were opposed to the British occupation, or who were looking for easy loot. The area around the cantonment was soon swarming with hostile Afghans, who laid siege to the commissariat fort. As Elphinstone and his colleagues dithered, this was abandoned, as also, after a spirited defence, was the garrison's grain store in the city. An attempt was made on 13 November to dislodge the Afghans from the hills surrounding the cantonment and for a short while achieved its objective. But the Afghans returned and, when a further sortie was made on the 22nd, the British force broke under heavy fire and retreated in disorder. The British command was now wholly paralysed and the troops, who were too few in number to defend themselves effectively, thoroughly demoralised.

On 25 November, therefore, a truce was called and Macnaghten began negotiating. The Afghans' initial objective seems to have been simply to get the British out of the country, realising that to attempt anything more extreme would be to invite retribution. But their attitude hardened with the arrival of Dost Mohammed's son, Mohammed Akbar, who had been living in Turkestan and who now assumed the leadership of the insurgents. Macnaghten tried, unwisely, to effect some double dealing and, at a meeting which took place on 23 December, he was killed, possibly by Mohammed Akbar himself. His mutilated and headless body was then displayed at the entrance to the Kabul bazaar.

Negotiations continued after Macnaghten's death, under the increasing constraints of shortage of supplies and the onset of winter. Early in January, after a treaty had been concluded with the Ghilzai chiefs promising a safe passage out of Afghanistan, some 4,500 troops and 12,000 camp followers left the cantonment and headed through the passes to Jalalabad. By the time they had reached the first of the passes, the Khurd Kabul, many were dead from exposure in the freezing conditions and Shah Shuja's contingent had defected en masse. Some 3,000 more died the next day when, despite the treaty, they came under heavy fire as they crowded through the Pass. Defections, exposure and Ghilzai attacks continued to take their toll, until by the end of the fourth day only 120 European soldiers and some 4,000 camp followers were still trying to fight their way through. Two days later a mere eighty survivors made a final dash for safety, but their numbers dwindled to the point where no more than twenty were left, most of whom perished in a last stand at Gandamak. Six officers on horseback succeeded in escaping, but of these five were later caught and killed. Only a single man, Dr Brydon, wounded and on a dying horse, managed to beat off his pursuers and reach Jalalabad. For several days and nights, the Jalalabad garrison burnt lamps and sounded bugles every quarter of an hour, but nobody else appeared.

The impression has persisted that Dr Brydon was the only survivor of the retreat from Kabul. In fact, over a hundred British captives were rescued the following year by the 'Army of Retribution', as were some 2,000 Sepoys and camp followers. Others also survived, some to reappear over time, others never to return to India. In the 1920s, members of the British Legation in Kabul were invited[16] to meet two very elderly ladies, who turned out to be survivors of the retreat who, as babies, had been rescued and brought up by local families. They had lived all their lives as Afghans, but, in their old age, they had wished to meet some of their original compatriots.

So perished the Army of the Indus, a victim of political misjudgement and military incompetence. Auckland, who had already asked to be relieved of the Governor-Generalship, left India a few weeks later. The last word perhaps lay with Dost Mohammed. 'I have been struck with the magnitude of your resources, your ships, your arsenals', he is reported to have said, 'but what I cannot understand is why the rulers of so vast and flourishing an empire should have gone across the Indus to deprive me of my poor and barren country'.

CHAPTER FIVE

Dost Mohammed and Sher Ali

Following their 'signal catastrophe' in Afghanistan, the British had three objectives. The first was to relieve the garrisons which were still there and rescue the captives. The second was to 're-establish our military reputation by the infliction of some signal and decisive blow on the Afghans'. The third was then to withdraw altogether from Afghanistan 'not from any deficiency of means to maintain our position, but because we are satisfied that the king we have set up has not, as we were erroneously led to imagine, the support of the nation over which he has been placed'[1]. Two columns were sent, one to Jalalabad and the other to Kandahar, where British garrisons were holding out. In Kandahar, the British force repulsed a strong attack by Durrani tribesmen, while in Jalalabad, the garrison sallied out against Mohammed Akbar's forces, which were massing in preparation for an attack on the town. What started as a desperate last throw was soon overwhelmingly successful and Mohammed Akbar fled to the hills, taking the British captives with him. The question now was whether these victories could be considered sufficiently decisive to re-establish Britain's military reputation. Ellenborough, the new Governor-General, thought that they were, but his generals were most reluctant to leave and clear hints[2] were coming from London that something more decisive was expected.

In July, therefore, the generals were given discretion to 'retreat' via Kabul. A large Afghan force was defeated between Kandahar and Ghazni, while an army commanded by Mohammed Akbar, who had been weakened by desertions, was also put to flight in the course of the British advance from Jalalabad. In September the British reentered Kabul and soon afterwards found and recovered the captives. As acts of retribution, they destroyed the great Kabul bazaar, one of the sights of Central Asia, and sent a force to the Kohistan village of Istalif, where it killed all the adult males, raped and killed many of the women, looted everything movable, and destroyed buildings and trees. Istalif, which had had little to do with the opposition to the British, was one of the most ancient and attractive of Afghan villages, and is popularly believed to have been given its name by Alexander the Great after the Greek word for 'grape'. The force then went on to Charikar, parts of which it also destroyed. Having completed these tasks, the combined army withdrew by way of the Khyber, harried by Afridi tribesmen as it went.

It then only remained to count the cost of the war – principally the loss of between 15,000 and 20,000 soldiers, together with an unknown number of camp followers, and an expenditure that has been estimated at some £17–20 million[3]. More than 50,000 camels were also lost, with damaging consequences for the economy of the region. There were also severe knock-on effects for the Indian economy as a whole, while, in non-material terms, the British lost considerable respect among their Indian subjects. In Afghanistan itself, more serious for the longer term was the loss of any sense of trust and friendship between Afghan and Briton. In British minds, Afghans acquired a reputation for barbarity, treachery and fanaticism. This is all the more sad, as before the First Afghan War, Masson was only one of many visitors who found the Afghans exceptionally friendly and tolerant. According to Masson[4],

> It is a matter of agreeable surprise to any one acquainted with Mahommedans in India, Persia, and Turkey, and with their religious prejudices and antipathies, to find that the people of Kabul are entirely [devoid of] them. In most countries few Mahommedans will eat with a Christian; to salute him, even in error, is deemed unfortunate, and he is looked upon as unclean. Here none of the difficulties or feelings exist. The Christian is respectfully called a 'Kitabi', or 'one of the Book'.

The war changed all this: British and other foreigners were henceforth distrusted as potential aggressors and despised as infidel and immoral people. Xenophobia became ingrained in the national outlook and Afghanistan retreated into what has been described[5] as 'nearly a century of stultifying isolation'. The consequent setback for the country's development is unquantifiable, but must nonetheless have been considerable.

Shortly after the British force had retired through the Punjab, a small body of horsemen passed the other way, en route for Afghanistan. These were Dost Mohammed and his retinue, whom Ellenborough had released from exile. Following the annihilation of the Army of the Indus, dissension had again broken out between the Barakzai and the Popalzai, and a convoluted struggle for power had developed in Kabul. Against the odds, Shah Shuja at first survived, but in April 1842 was prevailed upon to leave the Bala Hissar in order to review a force being sent against Jalalabad. He was only a short distance from Kabul when he was, predictably, assassinated. Fateh Jang, his second son, was then proclaimed Amir, but the Barakzai refused to recognise him and insisted on putting forward as their candidate a Durrani chief, Nawab Zeman Khan. In May, civil war ensued and was only resolved with the arrival of Mohammed Akbar, who, after a period of renewed fighting and negotiation, reached an agreement under which Fateh Jang would remain on the throne, with himself as chief minister. However dissension continued and in September, Fateh Jang, realising the danger of his position, fled to Gandamak, where he met the British force on its way to Kabul, and the following month he left for India with the Army of Retribution. Another brother, Shahpur, took his place, but he too soon chose to go into exile. The Barakzais retook power and Mohammed Akbar established himself in Jelalabad, awaiting his father's return.

The country to which Dost Mohammed returned was suffering from severe economic disruption as well as political turmoil. He now reigned over an even smaller extent of territory than before the British invasion, and his rule extended little further than Kabul, Jalalabad and Ghazni. Kandahar reverted to the control of the 'Dil' brothers, while Afghan Turkestan remained split between a number of Usbek khanates. Herat also retained its independence under Kamran Mirza's former *wazir*, Yar Mohammed Khan, who had killed and supplanted him in 1842. Mohammed Akbar was in favour of capitalising on the British humiliation with an all-out attempt to recover the territories which had been lost since the days of Ahmed Shah Durrani, but Dost Mohammed was more cautious. There are also suggestions that Mohammed Akbar may have been actively disloyal to his father. It was therefore perhaps as well for the stability of the restored dynasty that he died within a few years, at the age of twenty-nine. He was to be long remembered as the young national hero who had defeated the Sikhs at Jamrud and annihilated the British army in the passes below Kabul.

For more than a decade, Dost Mohammed and the British held aloof, while the British debacle in Afghanistan and that of the Russians before Khiva postponed any likelihood of a confrontation between the two powers in Central Asia. In 1848 Dost Mohammed was prevailed upon to take advantage of the war between the Sikhs and the British by occupying Peshawar and ousting Sultan Mohammed, whom the Sikhs had reinstalled there. He then sent a force of cavalry to support the Sikhs, but only a headlong gallop for the Khyber Pass enabled them to escape with their lives following the battle of Gujrat, in which the Sikhs were finally defeated. In 1854, however, with the Crimean War about to break out after a decade of Anglo-Russian détente, the then Governor-General, Lord Dalhousie, decided to effect a rapprochement with Afghanistan as an insurance against possible Russian encroachments. Negotiations were opened and in 1855 a simple treaty[6] was concluded which stipulated that there would be peace between the Afghans and the British, that the East India Company would not interfere in Afghanistan, and that Dost Mohammed would be 'the friend of the Company's friends and the enemy of its enemies'. The Afghans had asked for firm assurances of support and for the reversion to them of Peshawar, but this the British were not prepared to concede. When the Crimean War came to an end, there were fears in both London and Calcutta that the Russians might wish to compensate for their defeat by again trying to extend their influence eastwards. Herat once more became the focus of attention and concern grew when the Persians briefly took it in October 1856. As in 1838, the British reacted by sending a force to the Persian Gulf, which went on to defeat the Persian army and forced a Persian withdrawal from the city. At the same time, a fresh initiative was taken with Dost Mohammed, who came personally to Peshawar to conclude a more detailed treaty[7]. This gave him some arms and ammunition and the equivalent of £10,000 a month to keep an army in the field against the Persians, and provided for three British officers to be stationed at Kandahar to supervise its disbursement. Dost Mohammed success-fully resisted a proposal to station the officers at Kabul, on the grounds that he could not guarantee their safety. When in 1857 the Indian Mutiny – or War of Independence – broke out, Dost Mohammed kept his part of the bargain. Although there was a call for a *jihad*, a holy war, and the temptation to take advantage of British weakness must have been considerable, particularly since the Punjab was denuded of troops in order to retake Delhi, he did not even reoccupy Peshawar. The view[8] of Lord Roberts was that 'Had Dost Mohammed turned against the British, I do not see how any part of the country north of Bengal could have been saved'. The British rewarded him by withdrawing his subsidy the following year.

With the conclusion of the Sikh Wars, a major change developed in the affairs of the north-western districts of the Indian sub-continent. British India now stretched to the Himalayan foothills and the Pushtoon territory between India and Afghanistan, where Peshawar was occupied and a treaty was concluded with the Khan of Kalat, bringing him under British influence. As there was no settled border, the British were now confronted by a mix of Pushtoon tribes whose lands were poor and whose traditional occupations were the imposition of tolls on travellers, cattle raiding, the capture of merchants for ransom, and other activities of a predatory nature. A pattern of warfare now developed, characterised by raids, looting and kidnapping on the part of the Pushtoon tribes, and punitive expeditions and retaliatory exactions on the part of the British. The latter also took hostages against good behaviour on the part of the tribes, and tried to play off one tribe against another. At the same time, efforts were made to prevent, so far as possible, the regime in Kabul from exercising its influence in the tribal areas. The chronically unsettled state of affairs on the Frontier was to be a recurring complication in the relationship between Britain and Afghanistan right up to 1947, and it had effect of deepening and prolonging the Afghans' distrust of the British.

Within Afghanistan, Dost Mohammed gradually re-established his authority and acquired territory. This he ruled through a number of his many sons, who enjoyed considerable autonomy over the provinces allotted to them. In 1845 he began to subdue Afghan Turkestan, but his major effort in that direction was not made until 1849, when he finally gave up hope of recovering Peshawar. His sons Mohammed Akram and Ghulam Haider then captured Balkh and Tashkurghan respectively, and Mohammedzai rule was progressively extended over the region in the course of the next decade, under the governorship of another son, Mohammed Azam. At the time of Dost Mohammed's death, only Maimana and Badakhshan retained a degree of independence.

Kandahar, meanwhile, remained for some years under the rule of the 'Dil' brothers, whose harsh and extortionate style of government was widely unpopular. No friend of his half-brothers, Dost Mohammed looked for an opportunity to move against them, but seems not to have had the resources to do so as long as he was actively engaged in Afghan Turkestan. However rivalries amongst the 'Dil' brothers grew as the next generation emerged and, when a power struggle broke out in 1855 between the last surviving brother, Ramdil Khan, and his nephew, Mohammed Sadiq Khan, Dost Mohammed saw his chance. Late in the year he marched on Kandahar and was successful in investing the city, but the fact that he remained there for nearly a year before handing it over to Ghulam Haider suggests that he had considerable problems in establishing control. His arrival also coincided with a severe famine, which caused great local distress, compounded by his need to find food and fodder for his army. Finally, in 1863, he conquered Herat, so completing the establishment of Barakzai rule over most of the territory that lies within Afghanistan's present day borders. He died at Herat two weeks later and was buried in the Gazargah, the peaceful and atmospheric shrine outside the city, which also houses the remains of the celebrated poet and mystic, Khwaja Abdullah Ansari.

Dost Mohammed's main achievement was to unify Afghanistan under his personal rule, but he achieved little else in the way of nation building. Despite his experience, while in exile in India, of British institutions and methods, he did little to reform or modernise either the Afghan economy or his own government. Education and health were neglected, as were industry and agriculture. His administration was rudimentary in the extreme and there were no government offices and few official records. He did, however, go to some lengths to build up a regular army and seems to have diverted most of his revenues in that direction, at the expense of his civil administration. Even so, his troops were more often than not expected to subsist on the proceeds of plunder or requisition. He was careful throughout to keep the reins of power in his own hands and those of his sons, who between them controlled virtually all the provinces. It seems, however, that they used their relative independence to keep most of the provincial revenues for themselves. Also, whereas his predecessors had relied heavily on their 'Indian' possessions for their income, he was forced to rely on the much poorer Afghan region. Revenue collection therefore tended to be a difficult and uncertain affair, and he was almost invariably short of funds. In general, his relationship with the Pushtoon tribes was more difficult than that experienced by his Saddozai predecessors, partly because he did not possess the legitimacy derived from descent from Ahmed Shah, and partly because of the pressures on him to collect revenues. While he could to some extent influence and control the closer tribes, and was in any case compelled to deal with those who dominated the routes to Kandahar and Peshawar, those at a greater distance tended to go their own way. He had to face repeated tribal insurrections, and his son Sher Ali Khan, as Governor of Ghazni, fought the Ghilzai no fewer than six times before they were finally subdued.

It was perhaps inevitable, given the provincial power bases which his sons possessed and the ambitions that many of them had for the throne, that civil war should have raged for half a decade after Dost Mohammed's death. To begin with, his chosen successor, Sher Ali, was successful in defeating his two elder half brothers, Mohammed Afzal and Mohammed Azam, and managed to repeat the process with his two full brothers, Mohammed Amin and Mohammed Sharif. However in 1866, aided by Mohammed Afzal's son Abdur Rahman, Mohammed Azam inflicted a series of defeats on

Sher Ali and the two placed Mohammed Afzal on the throne. The following year, however, Mohammed Afzal died, Abdur Rahman was estranged from his uncle and left for Russian territory, and in January 1869 Sher Ali wrested the throne back from Mohammed Azam. Now firmly in charge, his main preoccupation was to create a more effective army and, with British money and Turkish support, this eventually numbered some 50,000 men, part mercenary, part conscript. He also introduced some enlightened measures, creating an Advisory Council and a number of ministries, a postal system and Afghanistan's first public school, which was divided into civil and military departments and offered English language studies. He also created some small-scale industries and military workshops, and introduced some tax and monetary reforms. However his freedom of action was gravely hampered by his government's economic weakness in the aftermath of Dost Mohammed's conquests and the years of rivalry for the succession. Nor was he to be allowed to rule his kingdom in peace. Renewed British concern over Russian expansionism was, before many years were out, to result in yet another British invasion of Afghanistan.

While Sher Ali was contending with his brothers for the throne, British policy remained one of strict neutrality and non-intervention, and those in contention were only recognised *de facto* when it appeared that they were securely established in Kabul. However, once it was clear that Sher Ali was firmly settled on the throne, he was given a subsidy and a gift of arms, and in 1869, at his request, a conference took place in Ambala between him and the then Viceroy, Lord Mayo. At the conference, he argued for a revision of the treaties with Dost Mohammed, on the basis that they were one-sided, in that they committed him to be the 'enemy of the enemies' of the British without any reciprocal obligation on the part of the latter. Against the background of the prolonged strife with his brothers, he also looked for recognition not just for himself, but also for his dynasty. It was significant that at no point did he mention any threat from Russia and that his concerns appeared to be purely internal. Mayo was sympathetic in manner but cautious in practice: he made no commitment over the succession and promised what amounted to no more than moral support in the event of trouble. He also handed over a further substantial sum of money and gift of arms, which enabled Sher Ali to consolidate his rule in northern Afghanistan. Sher Ali's other concern, that no European officer should be posted as a British representative in Kabul, was also reaffirmed. This was an issue on which he had feelings which were both strongly held and, in the event, fully justified. In a despatch[9] to London, the Viceroy summed up the outcome of the conference in the following terms.

Firstly. What the Ameer is not to have –

No Treaty, no fixed subsidy, no European troops, officers or Residents, no dynastic pledges.

Secondly. What he is to have –

Warm countenance and support, discouragement of his rivals, such material assistance as we may consider absolutely necessary for his immediate wants, constant and friendly connection through our Commissioner at Peshawar, and our native agents in Afghanistan: he for his part undertaking to do all he can to maintain peace on our frontier and to comply with all our wishes on matters connected with trade.

British concern not to become entangled in Afghan affairs was, however, to be short-lived, as progressive Russian advances brought them to Bokhara in 1866 and to Samarkand two years later. At the same time they consolidated their gains by setting up a new Province of Turkestan, with Tashkent as its capital. Their control of Bokhara was seen as particularly significant, partly because its borders marched with those of Afghanistan, and partly because it had traditionally had close relations with the rulers at Kabul. In response to the Russian moves, the British government at first tried to reach a 'clear understanding' with the Russian Government as to its projects and designs in Central Asia, with the result that in 1872 letters were exchanged[10] designed to 'forestall any cause of disagreement between them' in that part of Asia. The two powers agreed to recognise Afghanistan as an 'intermediary zone' which would keep their 'respective possessions' from immediate contact. However, while the Government in London thus continued to adhere to what had become known as the 'stationary policy', a lively distrust of the Russians persisted and a school of thought developed which held that a clash between Britain and Russia in Central Asia was inevitable, and that steps should be taken to ensure that this took place as far away from India as possible. While there were some divisions of opinion between the more extreme and more moderate adherents of the 'forward policy' about the location of the 'scientific frontier' which they saw as desirable, the obvious place for it was along the line of the Hindu Kush, possibly with outposts at Kunduz, Balkh and Maimana. Herat, the hawks contended, should be occupied and a resident mission established in Kabul to control Afghanistan's foreign policy, and so pre-empt any move by the Russians to come to terms with Sher Ali and absorb Afghanistan in their sphere of influence[11].

As the 1870s progressed, further events occurred which strengthened the hands of the proponents of the 'forward policy'. In 1873, the

Russians mounted an expedition against Khiva and reduced it, like Bokhara, to the status of a vassal state. Some argued[12] that this action was not unreasonable, given that Khiva was a 'nest of brigands and slave traders', but the general view was that the move was a breach of faith on the Russian side and further evidence of their expansionist ambitions. At the same time, relations with Sher Ali became less easy. Persia and Afghanistan had agreed to submit to British arbitration a territorial dispute over the Sistan. The result of the arbitration, which was announced in 1873, was probably fair, but as was no doubt to be expected, it was disputed by both parties (and was still to be an issue between them a century later). Sher Ali was particularly affronted, as the dispute had arisen from Persian aggression and, unlike the Persians, he had co-operated with the arbitration commission. The Viceroy, now Lord Northbrook, proposed that he should send an emissary to Kabul to explain to Sher Ali both the Sistan award and the agreement with the Russians, but the Amir was as reluctant as ever to receive a British representative at his court. Instead, a conference was held at Simla in July 1873 between the Viceroy and Sher Ali's Chief Minister, Nur Mohammed, at which it became clear that the Afghans were now distinctly worried by the Russian advances and concerned to use the obvious British interest in the integrity of their country to try to obtain much more explicit assurances of assistance. The Viceroy recommended[13] that help should be given in the form of money, arms and, if necessary, troops, provided that Sher Ali was faced with unprovoked aggression and accepted any advice proffered to him. But the government in London were not prepared to sanction this, and all that Sher Ali received was another offer of money and arms, together with an assurance that the agreement between the British and the Russians meant that there was no threat to him from the north. Sher Ali was considerably put out at the lack of any British commitment, and his dissatisfaction was increased when the Viceroy wrote to remonstrate with him over his treatment of his eldest son, Yakub Khan, whom he had invited to Kabul under safe conduct, but had then imprisoned. He declined to receive the further British subvention, although he did, after a delay, accept the arms.

In London, Gladstone's Liberal government was then replaced by a Conservative administration led by Disraeli, and, as tension heightened in the Middle East, both the British and the Russians looked to Central Asia as an area in which pressure could possibly be brought to bear on the other in support of their objectives nearer home. Hawks in Russia advocated moves against India, while Disraeli seems[14] at one stage to have favoured a military initiative in the Persian Gulf and an attack on Central Asia from the direction of India. Even before the crisis developed, however, the new British government clearly felt that no reliance could be placed on the agreement with Russia over Central Asia, and that their sources of intelligence about Russian activity there were inadequate. In January 1875, therefore, a peremptory despatch[15] was sent to the Viceroy, instructing him to obtain Sher Ali's assent to the establishment of a British Agency in Herat. In response, North-brook argued[16] that there was no discernible threat from Russia, that Sher Ali was in no way insecure or disaffected, and that to insist on his acceptance of a mission would be in breach of previous understandings with him; and the issue was still unresolved when a new Viceroy, Lord Lytton, was appointed. A career diplomat and an impulsive, intolerant and intellectually arrogant man, Lytton was a convinced advocate of the 'forward policy' and had no hesitation in falling in with the government's wishes. He now concocted[17] the somewhat transparent stratagem of proposing the despatch of an envoy to Kabul to notify the Amir formally of Queen Victoria's assumption of the title of Empress of India, as well as of his own appointment as Viceroy. Sher Ali's reply[18] was entirely predictable: he was delighted to hear of the Queen's new title, as well as of Lytton's assumption of office, but he saw no point in receiving an envoy, especially since he believed that both partners were happy with the existing relationship and there seemed to be no need for further contact. If, however, the British had anything new to communicate, he would send an agent to learn of it. This politest of brush-offs provoked a response[19] from Lytton which reiterated the original demand and ended with the threat that if it were not accepted, Afghanistan would be regarded as 'a State which has voluntarily isolated itself from the alliance and support of the British Govern-ment'. In the exchanges that followed, Lytton remained categorical in insisting that the Amir must accept a resident British agent, and increased the pressure on him by making a number of military dispositions that could only be regarded as threatening. Sher Ali's position was straightforward[20]: he was completely satisfied with the existing relationship, and required only that the two treaties with Dost Mohammed and the assurances given in writing by the two previous Viceroys should be honoured. He referred frankly to his fears about receiving British envoys: not only would this 'scatter away former assurances', but would create among the Afghans the fear 'firmly fixed in their minds, and deeply rooted in their hearts, that if Englishmen, or other Europeans, once set foot in the country, it will sooner or later pass out of their hands'. Having no reply to these arguments, Lytton resorted to an ultimatum – there were to be no further discussions and the Amir must make up his mind whether or not to accept British officers. It seems that at this point, Sher Ali was prepared to accept all Lytton's demands, but the latter then pre-empted him by closing the negotiation.

There was then a lull until the summer of 1878, when the crisis in Afghan affairs finally developed. The Russians had for some years been corresponding with Sher Ali, but the content of their letters had been anodyne and the British, who had known of them, had at first made no serious objection. Then in 1876 and 1877 they had protested to the Russians about them, but with inconclusive results. Now, however, the Russians decided to 'create a diversion by way of Afghanistan' and raised the stakes. A mission was sent to Kabul under a General Stoliatov with a letter proposing a defensive and offensive treaty, the placing of Russian troops on Afghan territory, and permission to build roads and telegraph lines. At the same time, Russian troops were mobilised in Turkestan. Sher Ali, who realised well enough what the consequences might be, at first tried to bar Stoliatov from the country, but in the face of Russian insistence, gave way and reluctantly received him in Kabul. As a countermeasure, Lytton proceeded to insist on the reception in Kabul of a corresponding British mission and a message was sent to Kabul to inform Sher Ali that it was on its way. Both the latter and the government in London tried to avoid a confrontation, but Lytton pressed ahead in defiance of instructions[21], with the result that on 21 September 1878, Major Louis Cavagnari, a member of the proposed mission, rode forward to the Khyber Pass, where he was told by the local Afghan governor that if he proceeded further, he would be met with force. He turned about and rode back to Peshawar.

Feeling in London was that it would most unwise to be undertaking an adventure in Afghanistan, particularly as, by then, fences were being mended with Russia. But national prestige was now seen to be at stake, and the Cabinet decided on war[22]. As a preliminary step, Lytton was instructed[23] to seek an apology from the Amir and his acceptance of a permanent mission. Lytton gave Sher Ali just three weeks to comply and meanwhile went ahead with his military preparations. When no reply had been received in what was, given the state of communications, an impossibly short time span, he declared war. In this manner, the combination of a headstrong Viceroy and an irresolute Cabinet produced a second confrontation with Afghanistan which, in the outcome, was to be a no less costly failure than the first.

CHAPTER SIX

The Second Anglo-Afghan War

Sher Ali's response to the declaration of war and the invasion that quickly followed was to seek to leave the country and obtain support from the Russians. He found them profoundly unsympathetic and he was advised to make his peace with the British: no Russian troops, they insisted, could campaign in Afghanistan during the winter. Sher Ali then proposed that he should go to St. Petersburg to plead his cause personally with the Czar, but his request was politely refused. Broken in spirit, he died in Mazar-i-Sharif in February 1879, having left the capital in the hands of his less than favourite son, Yakub Khan.

During the preparations for the invasion, Lytton had a serious difference of opinion with the Commander-in-Chief, General Sir Frederick Haines, over the size of the invading armies. Haines and his staff insisted, despite Lytton's anxiety to keep expenditure down, on force levels that they considered adequate and refused to accept that Lytton or anyone else could overrule them. They eventually got their way (at the cost of being described by Lytton as 'a coagulation of mediocrities and inveterately obstinate stupidities'), but Lytton thereafter issued orders directly to the commanders in the field, an activity which improved neither tempers nor efficiency. As soon as the ultimatum expired, advances took place on three fronts. A column of 15,000 men under the command of General Sir Samuel Browne, who was to achieve a form of immortality through his invention of the military belt that still bears his name, advanced through the Khyber Pass. His campaign started badly, with a confused and mishandled attack on the fort at Ali Masjid, but the Afghans were finally forced to retire and Jelalabad was occupied on 20 December. A second column of 12,000 men, which was sent up via the Bolan Pass and Quetta under General Donald Stewart, arrived in Kandahar early in January to find that the Afghan garrison there had fled. In the Kurram Valley, a third column of 6,500 men under General Frederick Roberts (later Lord Roberts of Kandahar) met stiff opposition while trying to seize the Peiwan Kotal, the pass at the head of the valley. However a difficult flank march supported by a frontal assault eventually brought Roberts' troops into a position from which they could shell the Afghans' camp, and the latter withdrew in some confusion.

The rapid success of the military campaign left Lytton with the problem, which he seems to have left out of his calculations, of how to deal with Afghanistan. Costs were mounting and his forces, who were in barren country at the end of long supply lines, were being harassed by the tribes. To undertake a permanent occupation of Afghanistan, which could contribute little to the Indian exchequer, would be financially crippling. To restore it as a friendly neighbour would require an able and well-disposed leader, and none was in sight. It could perhaps be divided into a number of small principalities, but this would be a recipe for instability and render the country vulnerable to external intrigues. Following Sher Ali's death, however, Yakub Khan had assumed the throne, and the best option seemed to be to try to reach an accommodation with him, for all that he gave no sign of being a strong or capable monarch. Cavagnari was authorised to negotiate with him and, after some months of prevarication, he came out to meet General Browne's force, which was now advancing beyond Jalalabad. The upshot, in May 1879, was the Treaty of Gandamak[1], in which, in return for the restoration of Kandahar and Jalalabad, Yakub Khan ceded Pishin and Sibi, both on the road up through Quetta, and left the British in control of Kurram and the Khyber Pass. He accepted a permanent mission in Kabul and permitted the British to conduct his foreign policy, in return for a general amnesty, a subsidy for himself and his successors, and a promise of assistance in the event of unprovoked aggression. Both Lytton and the government in London preened themselves on what they saw as a military and diplomatic success and, defying strong parliamentary criticism, Disraeli congratulated[2] Lytton on having achieved the 'scientific frontier'. Cavagnari, now Sir Louis, was appointed envoy at Yakub Khan's court and, with a small contingent of cavalry, took up his appointment in July.

It had all been too easy. In the euphoria that prevailed, the majority seem to have noted neither the limited authority that the new Amir possessed in the country, nor that he was agreeing to a raft of unpopular measures which his father had steadfastly refused to accept. Of those involved, only Roberts, whose father had commanded Shah Shuja's contingent in the First Afghan War and who therefore had a better appreciation than most, seems to have had forebodings about what was in store. Nor was the debacle long in coming. Cavagnari had not been in post more than six weeks when the Afghan regiments which had arrived in Kabul from Herat and were commanded by Yakub Khan's brother, Ayub Khan, began to show worrying signs of insubordination. On 3 September they paraded at the Bala Hissar for their arrears of pay and rioted when only a portion was paid. It seems that it was suggested that they should go to the British Residency for the balance and that when they arrived there, the guards opened fire. They promptly went back to their quarters to collect their arms and within a short while returned and attacked the Residency. There they were joined by a city mob and the whole situation went out of control. Yakub Khan sent his Commander-in-Chief to try to restore order, but the latter was unhorsed and was lucky to escape with his life. Cavagnari was shot at an early stage and within a few hours, despite a desperate defence, his entourage were overwhelmed and killed almost to a man.

When the news of the massacre reached Simla forty-eight hours later, nobody had any doubt of the necessity of speedy revenge, but the army on the frontier was no longer on a war footing and transport had been scaled down. The only troops within reach of Kabul were Roberts' in the Kurram, and so he promptly left Simla and was back on the frontier by 12 September. By 1 October, having collected transport, his force of 7,500 men had crossed the Shutargardan Pass and was in the Logar Valley. There it was met by Yakub Khan, who evidently feared for his life if he had stayed in Kabul. He subsequently abdicated and was exiled to India, where he eventually died in 1923. He would, he said[3], 'rather be a grass-cutter in the English camp than be the ruler of Afghanistan'. As Roberts' units advanced on Kabul, they were opposed at Charasyab by a substantial force, supported by artillery and irregulars, and a vigorous battle had to be fought before the pass was cleared. On the 9th they entered Kabul.

Roberts proceeded to conduct in Kabul what can only be described as a reign of terror. Mass arrests were made and trials held under martial law. Almost certainly, many more hangings took place than the eighty-seven to which Roberts later admitted[4]: of those executed, only eleven were alleged to have been directly involved in the murder of Cavagnari. Lytton urged[5] Roberts on in uncompromising terms. 'Every Afghan brought to death I shall regard as one scoundrel the less in a nest of scoundrelism. ... Anyone found in arms should be killed on the spot like vermin. ... It is our present task to shed such a glare upon the last bloodstained page of Indian annals as shall sear the sinister date of it deep into the shamed memory of a smitten and subjugated people'. However, Roberts was to make haste 'before the political weathercock at home has shifted. ... There will be more clamour at home over the fall of a single head six months hence than over a hundred heads that fall all at once'. In this, however, Lytton was mistaken. What was happening was soon reported to London in letters from Roberts' officers and the Viceroy came under sustained attack in Parliament. Even some members of his own Council were moved to denounce the executions as 'judicial murders'. Lytton's reaction[6] was to try to shift the blame on Roberts and to insinuate that it was a case of the military having ignored his instructions and got out of control.

Roberts meanwhile announced Yakub Khan's abdication and his own assumption of supreme authority in Afghanistan, and a British military governor was appointed in Kabul. As an act of revenge for Cavagnari's murder, the Bala Hissar, already damaged by an explosion of gunpowder and ammunition, was largely destroyed. Roberts himself set up camp in the cantonment at Sherpur which Sher Ali had constructed for his army and which was consequently a much more defensible position than the cantonment used in the First Afghan War. This time the commissary was inside its walls, provisions and firewood were laid in, and there was sufficient shelter for the troops and animals. Here Roberts and his 6500 men settled in for the winter, masters, beyond Kabul and the cantonment, only of a tenuous line of communication through Gandamak to Jelalabad and Jamrud. He appointed four sirdars to represent him in the provinces, but of these, one was killed, two suffered various indignities, and the fourth never left the British camp.

Whereas some two years had elapsed in the First Anglo-Afghan War before Afghan resistance made itself effectively felt, this time the respite lasted only a few weeks. There were several reasons for this. On the earlier occasion, at least a Durrani prince was on the throne and Macnaghten had made good use of bribes and subventions to keep the tribal leaders quiet. This time the Afghan Amir had been spirited away, and the British were ruling alone and, to all appearances, permanently. Now that they were back in the country for the second time and were committing what were seen as atrocities, xenophobia and belligerency were that much more intense. Hardship was again being felt, as the army bought up food supplies. Popular feeling was also being roused by a call for a *jihad* by a Ghilzai mullah of great age and repute, Mir Din Muhammed, better known as the *Mushk-i-Alam*, 'Perfume of the Universe'. In early December, therefore, news began to reach Roberts that two separate forces, supported by tribesmen, were gathering to attack him. He decided to send out two columns, in an effort to defeat them severally before they could meet up and concert their attack. His plans, however, went awry, the Afghans eluded his main columns, and a small contingent of some three hundred cavalrymen and four field guns suddenly found themselves face-to-face with the entire Afghan army, some 10,000 strong. The guns were abandoned as the British force conducted a fighting retreat under intense pressure, and Roberts himself, who had ridden to the scene, narrowly escaped being cut down. The timely arrival of reinforcements prevented a total catastrophe, but the fact that the British had been outmanoeuvred encouraged thousands of Afghans to join the fighting. After a number of inconclusive engagements on the hills around Kabul over the following days, Roberts decided to abandon the city and retreat to the cantonment. The insurgents looted Kabul, concentrating on the Hindu and Qizilbash quarters, and then turned their attention to Sherpur.

National feeling was now intense. Yakub Khan's mother handed over her jewels and money to finance the resistance, grain was contributed to feed the tribesmen, and Yakub Khan's infant son was proclaimed Amir. Mohammed Jan, the commander of the Afghan forces, invited Roberts to retire to India, on the understanding that Yakub Khan would be restored and two British officers surrendered as hostages. Roberts, however, preferred to stay and defend himself in Sherpur, rather than risk a repetition of the winter retreat of 1842. He then received accurate intelligence of an imminent onslaught on the cantonment, and the defenders were ready and waiting when this came early on 23 December. The attack lasted for several hours but was driven back without much difficulty, with the attackers suffering, it was estimated, not less than 3000 casualties, against a British loss of 11 killed and 46 wounded. When the British cavalry reconnoitred the following day, they found that the Afghan force had dispersed to its villages and that the countryside was deserted. Roberts reoccupied Kabul and declared an amnesty which was accepted by a significant number of tribal chiefs.

Elsewhere in Afghanistan, all had been relatively quiet. Reinforcements arrived in Kabul and in the spring of 1880 General Stewart marched there from Kandahar and took over command from Roberts. His march was not uneventful: he was harassed by tribesmen and was accompanied at a discreet distance by masses of Hazaras, who burnt and looted the Afghan villages he passed. Then at Ahmed Khel, some 20 miles from Ghazni, he was confronted and attacked by a large tribal *lashkar*. A wild onslaught by several thousand *ghazis* threw the British force into confusion and at one point penetrated to within a few yards of General Stewart and his staff, who drew their swords and prepared to defend themselves. After the attack was finally repelled, some 1000 Afghan dead were counted on the field.

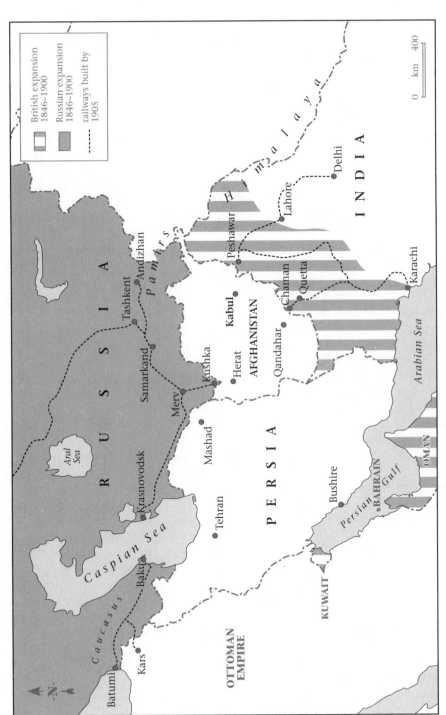

Map 7 British and Russian Expansion in Asia in the Nineteenth Century

Soon after Stewart assumed command in Kabul, the force left behind in Kandahar received news that an Afghan army under Ayub Khan was advancing from Herat. A British force went out to meet him and on 27 July the two armies met at Maiwand, where, for once, British fire power was not sufficient to repel the attacks of far greater numbers of Afghans. Also Ayub Khan out-generalled his British counterpart, General Burrows, and made good use of his 30 or more artillery pieces. In the ensuing rout, of an original force of some 2500, nearly 1000 British and Indian troops lost their lives. Many more would have undoubtedly become casualties if the Afghans had pressed home their pursuit. The survivors fell back on Kandahar, where they expelled the whole Afghan population and prepared for a siege. In Kabul, Roberts, who had been thoroughly discountenanced by his supercession by Stewart, eagerly accepted the task of going to the relief of Kandahar and, with a picked body of 10,000 troops, made his famous forced march between the two cities, covering the 300 odd miles in just twenty days, an average of fifteen miles a day in the height of the summer. Although he was unopposed along the route, this was a remarkable feat of organisation and discipline. Having reached Kandahar, he and the garrison of the city marched out and inflicted a decisive defeat on Ayub Khan.

In terms of hostilities, that was the end of the Second Anglo-Afghan War. On the political front, meanwhile, good progress had, against all the odds, been made towards a settlement. At the time of Yakub Khan's abdication, the chances of this had seemed so remote as to be almost non-existent, and in the last quarter of 1879 the British were again envisaging little more than the dismemberment and abandonment of the country. By the turn of the year, unwilling to incur continuing expenditure on the occupation of the country, Disraeli's government were insisting on a complete withdrawal by the end of the following summer and there seemed at that point little hope of leaving behind a coherent state. In Kandahar, Sher Ali Khan, the son of one of the 'Kandahar Sirdars' whom Dost Mohammed had driven out of that city, was confirmed as governor, with assurances of permanent British protection. Herat was offered to the Persians, but no progress was being made in negotiations over it, while no prospective ruler was in sight for Kabul, and equally none for the territory north of the Hindu Kush. In a total *volte face*, Lytton, faced with the necessity of abandoning the 'forward policy', now argued[7] that a British withdrawal might prevent the Russians being provoked into a further advance, whereas the fear that the British might march north from Kabul might induce them to make a pre-emptive attack into the Afghan territory which lay between the Amu Darya and the Hindu Kush. If there were any Russian move, it would be for the government in London to bring pressure to bear.

Early in 1880, however, a new factor entered the equation, with the arrival in Northern Afghanistan of Sher Ali's nephew, Abdur Rahman, who, following his departure from Afghanistan twelve years earlier, had been living in Tashkent as a Russian pensioner. During that time, the Russians had prevented him from meddling in Afghan affairs, but they now saw their opportunity and sent him on his way with a gift of 200 rifles and a modest sum of money. The gamble that Lytton then took shows the depths of his desperation. There was the obvious risk of Afghanistan falling under Russian influence, he did not even know precisely where Abdur Rahman was and still less did he know what his intentions were. Nevertheless, as soon as he heard of his presence he telegraphed[8] to London to urge that he should be given public recognition as Amir. The government in London had doubts, but agreed that Lepel Griffin, the political officer who had been appointed to Kabul, should establish contact with Abdur Rahman and assure him of British interest and goodwill. In April 1880, a messenger was sent north and contact was made; and in response to a friendly, if guarded, reply, a further deputation was sent and a firm offer conveyed. Abdur Rahman was invited to accept the Amirship, no conditions were attached, and an assurance was given that a withdrawal from Afghanistan was intended. In this manner, all the negotiating cards were handed to Abdur Rahman even before the negotiation began.

At that point, an election took place in Britain, in which Afghanistan featured as a major issue. The Conservative Government fell and Gladstone and the Liberals again took over. Lytton was recalled and replaced by the Marquis of Ripon, and the abandonment of the 'forward policy' was confirmed. Abdur Rahman meanwhile played hard to get: he asked questions about the extent of the territory he would rule, whether he would have to accept a British agent at his court, and what material help he could expect to receive. At the same time he proceeded to gather support among the tribal leaders and to amass sufficient strength to give him the option of starting hostilities, if negotiations should fail. This apparent ambivalence caused Stewart and Griffin to recommend that negotiations should be broken off; and Ripon[9], who had his own doubts about Abdur Rahman, 'the most Russian of all the candidates', and who preferred Yakub Khan, was tempted to agree. But Yakub Khan was clearly a broken reed and Abdur Rahman could not now be rebuffed without the risk of driving him into the arms of the Russians. Also the amount of support he was gathering was becoming an increasing threat to the British position in Kabul. In July, he arrived in Charikar and on the 22nd of that month Stewart held a formal durbar in Kabul at which he was formally recognised as Amir. Griffin then went out to meet him and was favourably impressed. He was given most of the assurances he wanted: Britain would not interfere in Afghan internal affairs, no British envoy would be stationed at Kabul, and aid would be provided to repel unprovoked aggression. In return, he undertook not to have any political relations with any country other than Britain, while Kandahar would remain independent and the territories ceded in the Treaty of Gandamak would remain under British control. On 11 August, two days after Roberts had left for Kandahar, Stewart and the Kabul garrison marched away to India, leaving Abdur Rahman on the throne at Kabul, if not yet in control of the country as a whole.

The cost to British India of the Second Anglo-Afghan War was of the same order of magnitude as that of the first. In monetary terms, it eventually amounted to at least £17 million, as against the £5 million that had been originally estimated. Due to dilatory and defective accounting and auditing, it was not until very late in the day that this huge discrepancy came to light. There is also considerable uncertainty about the tally of British and Indian casualties, and no reliable figure was ever produced. Yet again, the stock of transport animals, a necessity for the commerce of north-western India, was decimated. Afghanistan, for its part, also suffered severely. Its economy was badly disrupted and both the populations and the wealth of the cities sharply declined. In May 1880, the view[10] of Lord Hartington, the Liberal Secretary of State for India, was that

> As the result of two successful campaigns, of the employment of an enormous force, and of the expenditure of large sums of money, all that has yet been accomplished has been the disintegration of the State which it was desired to see strong, friendly and independent, the assumption of fresh and unwelcome liabilities in regard to one of its provinces, and a condition of anarchy throughout the remainder of the country.

That it was soon possible to amend this assessment for the better was due to the emergence, more by luck than judgement, of an able and dependable neighbour in the person of Abdur Rahman.

CHAPTER SEVEN

Abdur Rahman, The 'Iron Amir'

L epel Griffin[1] described Abdur Rahman as

> a man of about forty, of middle height, and rather stout. He has an exceedingly intelligent face, brown eyes, a pleasant smile, and a frank, courteous manner. The impression that he left on me and the officers who were present at the interviews was most favourable. He is by far the most prepossessing of all the Barakzai Sirdars whom I have met in Afghanistan, and in conversation showed both good sense and sound judgement. He kept thoroughly to the point under discussion, and his remarks were characterised by shrewdness and ability. He appeared animated by a sincere desire to be on cordial terms with the Indian Government.

It is not difficult to discern Abdur Rahman's motives in choosing the British connection. His position, he said, was that he had been a guest of the Russians for some twelve years and had 'eaten their salt'. He would not want to appear ungrateful to them and would wish to be the friend of both powers. This was not, however, a practical proposition. The British, who were actually in occupation and therefore had to be dealt with, were insistent that he should have no relationships except with themselves. The Russians, on the other hand, had accepted that Afghanistan was outside their sphere of influence. Their rejection of Sher Ali, without even the support to enable him to establish himself in Afghan Turkestan, was a clear indication how matters stood. More than this, however, it seems that, although Abdur Rahman often exasperated the British and was always concerned to keep them at arm's length, he genuinely held the view expressed in his autobiography[2], that the British were 'really anxious to see Afghanistan a strong independent Government – a true ally and barrier', whereas the Russians wished 'to see Afghanistan divided into pieces and very weak, if not entirely cleared out of their way to India'. He may have manoeuvred to extract as much as possible out of the British, but he also reckoned that he knew his Russians. Lytton's gamble therefore paid off, Abdur Rahman came to rely on the British for his protection and, despite difficulties from time to time, the relationship was maintained throughout his reign.

Abdur Rahman's immediate concern was lack of money. There was none in the treasury: indeed, as he says in his autobiography, there was no treasury[3]. When he arrived in Kabul, he records, there was no palace, and he and his court had to live in mud huts and tents. However a large British subvention helped him on his way and he was, throughout his reign, to receive regular British subventions and gifts of arms. Indeed, the British reaction to any problem tended to be to buy his acquiescence by throwing money at him. His other main concern was to establish his authority across a country which was yet again split into a constellation of independent fiefdoms. Kandahar was the first object of his attention, in the wake of considerable controversy in both India and Britain over the desirability of retaining it. In Calcutta, military opinion was divided: both Roberts and Haines were opposed[4] to withdrawal, believing that the city was needed as a base from which to oppose any 'enemy in the interior of the country'. Others of the military argued that a base at Quetta, from which a move could be made towards Kandahar if such were needed, would suffice. Counsels were no less divided in London, and fierce debates[5] took place in both the Lords and the Commons. Queen Victoria, who regarded Russia as Britain's principal enemy, was highly reluctant to include mention of a withdrawal in her 1881 Speech from the Throne, and it took all Gladstone's powers of persuasion to bring her round. Eventually, with opinion largely divided along party lines, the policy of withdrawal was adopted, and it was put diplomatically to Wali Sher Ali that he would be well advised to abdicate, notwithstanding the commitment he had earlier received from the British Government. It turned out that he was by no means reluctant to go, and he agreed without much demur to retire to Karachi on a British pension.

When, therefore, the city was offered to Abdur Rahman early in 1881, he had little option but to accept it, despite the problem that he did not have immediately available the military strength to hold it against his cousin Ayub Khan, now recovering in Herat from his earlier defeat. The balance of strength, indeed, was such that it was well on the cards that Ayub Khan might be able not only to capture Kandahar, but also go on to take Ghazni and even Kabul. In April

1881, the last British troops left Kandahar and Afghanistan; and in July, as feared, Ayub Khan advanced from Herat, defeated a force led by Abdur Rahman's Commander-in-Chief, Ghulam Haider Charki, and took the city. Realising that he was in a 'make or break' situation, Abdur Rahman mobilised Ghilzai support, marched on Kandahar and, having bought over a part of Ayub's army, inflicted a severe defeat on him outside the city. At the same time, he sent an army from Northern Afghanistan against Herat which in October succeeded in occupying that city. Ayub fled to Persia and eventually to India, and, in little more than a year, Abdur Rahman was, in name at least, master of the greater part of the country.

To establish his authority, Abdur Rahman did what no previous Afghan Amir had done except marginally, he claimed that his rule was based on divine sanction rather than derived from the consensus of the tribal *jirga*. As one commentator put it[6], he 'always held somewhat inflated notions as to the divine right of kings'. As he himself expressed it in his autobiography[7], the people had full authority to choose their king, but 'the throne is the property of the Almighty King of kings, our Creator, who appoints kings as shepherds to guard his flock, and into whose care He confides the creatures of his herds. ... Kings stand to their countries as the vice-regents of God'. There is no doubt that this was, for him, an article of faith, apparently reinforced by an element of mysticism, and he took very seriously what he saw as his responsibility as an 'assistant to the Almighty King in temporal affairs'. At the same time, however, it served him well in bringing religious sanctions to bear against his opponents and in helping to break the power of the mullahs, whom he saw as dangerous subversives and whom he mostly held in contempt. 'Every priest, mullah and chief of every tribe and village', he wrote[8], 'considered himself an independent king and for about 200 years past the freedom and independence of many of these priests was never broken by their sovereign. ... The tyranny and cruelty of these men were unbearable'. He characterised the venerable Mushk-i-Alam as the Mush-i-Alam, the 'Mouse of the Universe' and stigmatised the mullahs as 'ignorant priests' whose teachings were 'entirely contrary to the principles and teachings of Mahomed'. To bring them under government control, he took over the *waqf*, the religious trusts, so destroying their economic independence and relegating them to the status of government functionaries. He also instituted examinations, to test their religious credentials and to determine, depending on the results, the amounts of their stipends. He himself took control of judicial processes, established a unified system of *sharia* courts, personally authorised, and even wrote, religious handbooks, assumed the role of the guardian of Islam against 'infidel domination' and reserved for himself alone the right to call a *jihad*. Ultimately he managed to rally the bulk of the clergy to his side and in 1896, after his conquest of Nuristan, they conferred on him the title of *Zia al-Millat-i wa al-Din* (Light of the Nation and Religion).

It was not, however, merely the religious establishment that Abdur Rahman had to bring to heel. His reign was characterised by a series of tribal revolts, more than forty in all, some only marginally threatening, but several, for example those by the Ghilzai in 1886, the Usbeks in 1888 and the Hazaras in 1891–93, of major consequence. To counter them, he raised a conscript army, which he recruited on the *hasht nafari* ('one in eight') system and for which he received British assistance in the form of money and armaments, and he was totally ruthless in eliminating his tribal opponents, often in exceedingly unpleasant ways[9]. As he put it[10], his task was

> to put in order all the hundreds of petty chiefs, plunderers, robbers and cut-throats ... This necessitated breaking down the feudal and tribal system and substituting one grand community under one law and one rule.

To reinforce brute suppression, he played off traditionally hostile tribes against each other, made astute use of arranged marriages between key tribal families and his own, razed fortresses and villages, made extensive use of subsidies and took hostages against good behaviour. He also implemented policies of forced migration, moving, for example, some 10,000 Ghilzai families north of the Hindu Kush, thereby both weakening that tribe and diluting the tribal structures in the areas of settlement. Otherwise Afghans were forbidden to move around the country without government consent, a restriction that remained in force until 1964. To suppress the Hazaras, he proclaimed an anti-Shia *jihad,* invaded the Hazarajat with Ghilzai support, settled the latter on much of the land and reduced thousands of the former inhabitants to slavery. In the mid-1890s, he conducted a campaign in Kafiristan and followed up his conquest with forcible conversions, the region thenceforth being known as Nuristan, the 'Land of Light'. To extend his control over the country, he appointed governors to act as his agents and collect taxes, with firm instructions to put down any incipient revolts. The provincial boundaries which he established often divided tribes, and gradually the network of governors began to replace tribal authority, particularly in areas where officials dealt in lands which had previously been in collective ownership. Nearer to home, to guard against disaffection in his own family, he provided members of the Mohammedzai with generous allowances. At his court, he formed an elite of relatives, leading Mohammedzai, *ghulam bacchas* (literally 'slave boys') and young hostages from prominent families, to form the nucleus of an administration. This he filled out by creating a number of ministries and an advisory council, which had, however, no formal authority. He also established a national *loya jirga*, which did no more, however, than approve the measures that he chose to put before it. Its usefulness lay rather in the fact that it conveniently isolated its members in the capital, well away from their power bases. With the help of British subsidies, he established a state administration and a strong army, and, by the end of his reign in 1901, this 'Iron Amir' had established effective control over virtually the whole country, underpinning the system with an extensive network of spies and informers.

To preserve his independence in the face of the imperialist pressures that surrounded him, Abdur Rahman relied on two props, extreme isolationism and the British connection. The economic stagnation that persisted during his reign was in great measure due to his reluctance to bring in more than a very few foreign experts to help modernise the economy, while he was also adamantly opposed to the extension to Afghanistan of the railway and the telegraph. He objected strongly to the programme of railway construction that the British undertook beyond Peshawar and Quetta, and he was clear that, at least while Afghanistan was, from a military point of view, relatively weak, he was not prepared to put in place what he saw as an easy means of moving troops into his country. He described[11] the line driven through the Khojak tunnel to New Chaman on the border facing Kandahar, as a 'knife thrust into my vitals', and ordered a boycott of the line and its terminus. He also regarded foreign residents and investors as potential sources of trouble, inviting external intervention if problems involving them should arise. He kept the British agent in Kabul totally isolated and did not permit him even to meet the British who were resident there.

Throughout his reign, Abdur Rahman adhered scrupulously to his agreement with the British that they should conduct his external relations, recognising that their protection was his only defence against Russian incursions. It was not long after the final British withdrawal from Kandahar that tensions arose on the northern frontier. In the early 1880s, the Russians, after an initial reverse, overwhelmed the Tekke Turkmen, who lived to the south of the Kara Kum desert, between the lower reaches of the Amu Darya and the Caspian Sea. The British sought assurances in St. Petersburg over Russian intentions in the area, but for more than two years received no more than evasive replies. Then, early in 1884, the Russians announced the annexation of the Merv oasis, nearly three hundred miles south of Khiva and a mere two hundred north of Herat. This *fait accompli* aroused in London what the Duke of Argyll called, in what is possibly one of the worst puns ever coined, an acute bout of 'Mervousness'[12]. The British were in no position to challenge the Russian move, but both sides, realising the risks inherent in the situation, decided that it would be sensible to negotiate a precise frontier along the indeterminate stretch of territory lying to the south of Merv between the Amu Darya and the Afghan border with Persia along the Hari Rud. It was agreed that a joint demarcation commission should be set up, and in late 1884, the British sent out a Commissioner. However the Russians could not resist the temptation to delay the despatch of their own Commissioner, allegedly on grounds of ill health, while pushing their forces southwards from Merv. As they approached the most northerly Afghan outpost, at Panjdeh on the Murghab river, the British delivered a strong warning. Drawing a distinction between an occupation of the Panjdeh oasis and an advance on Herat, they made it clear[13] that while the former might have 'the most disastrous', but unspecified, consequences, the latter would be regarded as an act of war. The Russians nevertheless pressed on and in March 1885 Russian and Afghan forces duly met at Panjdeh. The Russians had the better of the engagement and it was assumed that their advance would continue. The two empires were at last on the verge of the confrontation which had for long seemed all but inevitable. This otherwise totally unremarkable oasis for a brief time shot into the headlines and was the focus of a crisis that might well have developed into a full scale Anglo-Russian war.

Abdur Rahman had some grounds for claiming sovereignty over Panjdeh, which had traditionally paid tribute to Herat. In both India and London, therefore, the Russian move was seen as an act of aggression, and the emotional temperature quickly rose. Troops were mobilised in India, war credits were voted in London and officers were sent to Herat to assess the state of the city's fortifications. Abdur Rahman, however, who happened to be on a state visit to India at the time, was relatively relaxed, and made it clear that while he did have views about the alignment of a Russo-Afghan frontier, he was resigned to the loss of Panjdeh. The government in London, who were at the time preoccupied with a crisis in the Sudan, took their cue from him and within a short while accepted a Russian suggestion that the affair should be referred to the King of Denmark for arbitration. In Russia itself, counsels were divided, but the Emperor was eventually persuaded to align himself against the military hawks. Early in May, the two sides began direct negotiations in London, and in September a protocol was signed laying down the general line of the frontier. The actual demarcation, however, was not to be easy. The Joint Commission convened and by June 1886 had managed to complete it to within some fifty miles of the Amu Darya. At that point, however, the Russians seem to have realised that the grass was, literally, greener on the Afghan side of the fence than on their own, and tried to obtain territory south of the Amu Darya. The Commission became deadlocked and it was not until the summer of the following year, after difficult negotiations in St. Petersburg, that final agreement was reached. Doubts about Russian good faith were such that the outcome was greeted with considerable scepticism in London, and a common view was that the agreement would be no more than temporary and that the British and Russian empires were bound at some point to meet along the Hindu Kush. In the outcome, however, the agreed frontier was to be honoured by both sides for the best part of a century. Had it not been for British sensitivities and their eventual determination to challenge the Russians over Panjdeh, it is highly likely that northern Afghanistan would have become part of the Russian Central Asian empire.

Eastwards from the line demarcated in 1887, there was little difficulty in agreeing that the frontier should lie along the Amu Darya, but the British continued to be nervous over the mountainous areas beyond, where the Russians had also been advancing and were approaching Chitral, which the British had claimed some years earlier. The British were determined that at no point should they have a common frontier with the Russians, and so in 1895 they negotiated an agreement which left a long finger of Afghan territory, the Wakhan, stretching between the two empires from Badakhshan to the border with China. Abdur Rahman had no wish to assume responsibility for the administration of this remote area, but his objections were overcome by the offer of an annual subsidy to cover the cost.

Abdur Rahman's visit to India in 1885 had been a considerable success and he held the then Viceroy, Lord Dufferin, in high esteem. In 1888, however, Dufferin was replaced by Lord Lansdowne, who was much less forbearing in his dealings with the Amir. He started[14] by lecturing him about the 'barbarities' he had inflicted on the Usbek rebels, repeatedly pressed him to accept British officers on his northern frontier, urged him to have a telegraph line laid to Kabul, and advised him, in less than tactful language, not to do anything to provoke the Russians. Abdur Rahman liked none of this and his attitude grew noticeably less friendly, and he tried in 1892 to bypass Calcutta and open a direct link with the British Government. He also proposed that he might himself visit London and put his grievances before Parliament. Eventually he was invited to London, but instead sent his son Nasrullah, who, if he was not already anglophobe, was certainly so after the visit, which only made matters worse.

Meanwhile the intrigues that Abdur Rahman was pursuing among the frontier tribes were causing the authorities in India increasing concern, and raised doubts both about his trustworthiness and over their own ability to keep the tribes in check. In response, they reverted to a form of 'forward policy': in 1889 and 1890 they mounted military expeditions against some of the more troublesome of the tribes, and in 1892 took under their protection the Turi tribe of the Kurram Valley. All this provoked a Pushtoon backlash and some intense fighting took place. Lansdowne had repeatedly failed to respond to several invitations addressed to him by the Amir to send a representative to Kabul to sort out points of difference, but he now came to the conclusion that the only way to deal with the persisting problems on the frontier was to negotiate a line that would mark the limits of British and Afghan influence and authority. After some difficulty he prevailed on Abdur Rahman to accept a mission headed by Sir Mortimer Durand, the Indian Government's Foreign Secretary, and an understanding[15] was reached, supported by a map, over the areas each side should hold. The Amir was reluctant to accept the agreement, which detached of many of the eastern Pushtoon tribes from his dominions, but was persuaded to agree when his annual subsidy was increased from 1.2 million to 1.8 million rupees and he was assured that he could freely import arms and ammunition.

The demarcation of the Durand Line caused incessant difficulties. It took until 1897 for the task to be completed, and even then there were still some stretches that had not been covered. In its final form, the Line took little note of ethnographic, and sometimes not even topographical, factors. Tribes, sometimes even villages, were divided. From the Afghan point of view, it had serious drawbacks. It put a final end to any hopes of stretching Afghanistan's frontiers to the sea and, as the British held the main passes, they were in a position to block the migration routes used by the considerable population of nomad *kuchis*. Both disadvantages were to tell against Afghanistan after British rule had given way to that of Pakistan. Any hopes of creating a state that would include the totality of the Pushtoon nation were also dashed. The British, for their part, had to deal almost immediately with a major Pushtoon uprising, as the latter realised that they were being committed to British sovereignty. The Pushtoons were encouraged by Afghan agents and were inspired by a number of mullahs, the most notorious of whom were the Hadda Mullah, the Mullah Powindah and Sahdullah Khan, the 'Mad Mullah', and it took the deployment of 35,000 troops and two years of heavy fighting before the rising was suppressed.

Towards the end of the century, Abdur Rahman became increasingly plagued by gout and his strength visibly declined. To the end, however, he was firmly in charge. While there can be no doubt about his capacity as a ruler, his achievements were variable. He preserved Afghanistan's independence, keeping both Britain and Russia at arms' length while not provoking either to attack him. Internally, he circumscribed the power of the tribal and religious leadership, consolidated the Afghan state and created a unitary kingdom with settled frontiers. However this was at the cost of social and economic development, and Afghanistan remained, during his reign, a backward, impoverished, isolated and xenophobic country. He established a number of small factories, mainly for the purpose of manufacturing armaments, but Afghanistan's trade stagnated and its communications were little improved. Levels of literacy and medical services remained minimal, while, apart from setting up a *madrassa*, a religious school, in Kabul, he did little or nothing to develop an educational system, and Sher Ali's tentative experiment was not continued. Any Afghans who wanted anything other than a traditional education had to find it outside the country, so effectively condemning themselves to exile. Despite the few constitutional changes and the administrative and legal reforms, essentially his rule remained absolute and he was notorious for his ruthless brutality and suppression. Opponents, actual or potential, were murdered or exiled, while torture and execution were commonplace as a means of preserving law and order. He was never a popular figure in his own country, and the Afghans never forgave him for accepting the Durand Line.

CHAPTER EIGHT

Habibullah and the Politics of Neutrality

Almost uniquely in Afghan history, there was no contest for the succession when Abdur Rahman died. He had groomed his eldest son, Habibullah, for the task and had wisely kept all his sons in Kabul, allowing none of them to acquire a power base in the provinces. Although Habibullah was the son of a slave girl, and his father's senior wife, Bibi Halima, undoubtedly had ambitions for her own son, both the army and a sufficient number of tribal leaders, thanks in part to the judicious matrimonial alliances that Abdur Rahman had arranged, gave Habibullah their support.

In character, Habibullah was the antithesis of Abdur Rahman. A tolerant and good-natured man, he was uxorious by nature and fathered a considerable number of children on his four wives and thirty-five or so concubines. As with so many Afghans, his other main pleasure was hunting, and he also took to photography and motor cars. He was fortunate that, largely as a result of his father's repressive policies, there was little or no internal unrest during his reign, but he was careful to placate the tribal leadership, setting up a State Council for tribal affairs, easing the system of compulsory conscription and giving the *khans* more freedom to conduct their own affairs. He also dismantled Abdur Rahman's spy apparatus and put an end to some of the latter's more brutal forms of punishment. At the same time, the religious establishment regained influence, although, following his father's example, Habibullah was at pains to ensure that they accepted the religious legitimacy of his rule. Also influential were several of the prominent Afghans whom Abdur Rahman had forced into exile and who were now allowed to return. Among them were the 'Peshawar Sirdars', the descendants of Sultan Mohammed Khan, who, as the 'Musahiban' family, were to play a key role in Afghan affairs in the first half of the twentieth century. The eldest of the five Musahiban brothers, Nadir Khan, was before long appointed commander-in-chief. During the latter years of Abdur Rahman's reign, the former commander-in-chief, Ghulam Haider Charki, had found it advisable to be away from Kabul as much as possible, but two of his sons, Ghulam Nabi and Ghulam Sidiq, now also rose to prominence in the military.

Also among the men of influence at Habibullah's court was Mahmud Beg Tarzi[1], a descendant of one of the 'Kandahar Sirdars', whose father had been exiled to Damascus by Abdur Rahman and who now returned to Kabul with his Syrian wife. An intellectual, a nationalist and a modernist, Tarzi was much influenced by the 'Young Turk' movement, and was allowed to start Afghanistan's first newspaper, the *Siraj-al-Akhbar*, which took a strongly pan-Islamist and anti-imperialist stance. He was not afraid to draw attention to what he saw as Afghanistan's failings under Habibullah's rule, in particular its economic and social backwardness, and he was critical of religious traditionalism. He felt strongly that Afghanistan and other Islamic states had to adopt new ideas and modernise their economies, if they were not to remain in a position of permanent inferiority to the more developed world. From the example of Japan, he believed that this could be achieved while preserving indigenous social and religious structures. Tarzi tutored two of Habibullah's sons, Inyatullah and Amanullah, who each married one of his daughters, and it was he who was to be the principal architect of the modernising and liberalising tendencies which were to be a dominant feature of Afghan policy during the first three decades of the 20th century.

While Habibullah could afford to be relaxed about Afghanistan's internal affairs, her external relations were to be a cause for concern throughout his reign. In India, the feeling that was shared by the Viceroy, Lord Curzon, and others at the time of Habibullah's accession was that they had received very little in return for the subsidies and undertakings they had given Abdur Rahman. There had also been, shortly before the latter's death, renewed Russian pressure, in the shape of a formal request[2] for a direct relationship with Afghanistan 'not of a political nature'. Given that the two countries now shared a lengthy frontier, this request was not unreasonable, but the British could hardly fail to assume that any direct relationship would inevitably develop a political content. While they managed to avoid giving a direct reply, the move reinforced their anxiety to establish a more influential relationship with the Afghan Amir. Curzon therefore invited[3] Habibullah, with increasing insistence as the months went by, to come to India for a personal discussion.

This Habibullah was highly reluctant to do. He no doubt took little pleasure in the prospect of meeting Curzon face to face and there was also the question of *amour propre* – was it right that a monarch should go to meet a mere Viceroy? He insisted, credibly, that he could not leave Kabul so early in his reign and that he was perfectly content with the treaties concluded with his father. Curzon responded by insisting that the treaties had been personal to Abdur Rahman and stepped up pressure on the Amir by preventing the transit of arms deliveries and withholding the payment of subsidies. Habibullah, who had inherited a healthy balance in the subsidy account, continued to stall, and asked the awkward question whether, if the treaties were personal and the undertakings in them for the subsidies and freedom to import arms had lapsed, this did not also apply to the agreement over the Durand Line and British control of his foreign relations? To emphasise the point, he announced the despatch of twenty-four envoys to countries around the world. By this time, Curzon was recommending a declaration of war and invasion of Afghanistan, but was firmly overruled by the Cabinet in London, who decided, a little belatedly, that they desired no more than a resumption of the relationship Britain had had with Abdur Rahman. While Curzon was back in England for leave and consultations, the Indian Government proposed the despatch of an envoy to Kabul to renegotiate the relationship. Habibullah, who had now stalled for three years and probably had a keen sense how far it was safe to go, was not slow in agreeing.

The man chosen as envoy was Sir Louis Dane, the Indian Foreign Secretary, who duly arrived in Afghanistan late in 1904 with a draft treaty in his pocket. The atmosphere was cordial, but the discussions were long and difficult, the main point in contention being whether any treaty should be personal to the Amir. The latter eventually countered Dane's draft treaty with one of his own, which merely confirmed the arrangements made with Abdur Rahman. Curzon objected strongly and recommended that Dane should be withdrawn, but the government in London was more concerned with the situation on the frontier and the potential threat from Russia than with trying to browbeat the Amir into submission. Dane was instructed to sign the treaty[4], Habibullah received the arrears of subsidy due to him and no limitations were placed on his right to import arms. His prestige in Afghanistan was much enhanced by this emphatic diplomatic success, although there was nothing in the wording of the treaty to suggest that it was other than personal to himself. This rapprochement in Anglo-Afghan relations was reinforced two years later, when Habibullah accepted an invitation to visit India. Curzon having been replaced by Minto, the visit went off well, although the Amir brought with him a considerable entourage and overstayed his welcome. He shot the inevitable tiger, and spent much of the time in sight-seeing, socialising and proposing marriage to various English ladies. More seriously, he was impressed by the relatively advanced state of India's technology and economy, and became more receptive of Tarzi's urgings of the need for Afghan development. He was also inducted as a Freemason by Kitchener, the Commander-in-Chief, and the hostile reaction to this in Afghanistan only ceased when, after his return, he had several mullahs executed.

Very soon afterwards, however, relations with Britain were again soured by the signing in 1907 of an Anglo-Russian Convention[5]. This had its origins in the growing desire of the two countries to put an end to the 'Great Game' and minimise the risks of conflict between them. Following the humiliation Russia had suffered in the Russo-Japanese war of 1904–05, nationalist self-confidence and militarist influence had waned in St. Petersburg, and both countries were becoming nervous at the rise of German power. As far as Afghanistan was concerned, the Russians again confirmed their 1873 declaration that the country was outside their sphere of influence and undertook to conduct their political relations with it through the British, while the latter guaranteed not to interfere in Afghan affairs and not to occupy or annex any part of the country. During the fifteen months of negotiation that led to the Convention, there was no consultation whatever with the Afghans, yet the stipulation was made that Habibullah's 'approval' was required for it to come into effect. Predictably, the Amir refused to have anything to do with it, and eventually the two signatories agreed to ratify it without Afghan participation. The backlash created in Afghanistan at this high-handed treatment strengthened what was to become known as the 'war party' centred around Mahmud Tarzi, and, under the latter's influence, pro-Turkish, anti-imperialist and pan-Islamic sentiment continued to spread within the royal family and the Afghan elite. With traditionalists and modernists joining forces, Inyatullah and Amanullah, were, together with the Amir's brother, Nasrullah, prominent in the 'war party', as were the Musahiban and Charki families. With Afghan encouragement, masterminded by Nasrullah, hostile activity on the frontier increased significantly between 1907 and 1909, matching British efforts to adopt a renewed 'forward policy' in tribal territory. Under pressure at court to come out in support of the tribes, Habibullah kept silent, but seems to have placed no restrictions on Nasrullah's activities and to have agreed not to prevent any of his subjects from participating in the conflict. The result was that a number of religious leaders declared a *jihad* and led forays across the frontier.

The outbreak of the First World War was at first treated with indifference in Afghanistan, and Habibullah announced that the country would remain neutral. However feelings changed as soon as Turkey became a belligerent. The Caliph's call for a *jihad* received wide approval, which was reinforced by reverberations from the anti-British agitation which was aroused in Muslim circles in India. With *Siraj-al-Akhbar* in the lead, anti-British and anti-Russian feeling became more articulate and support grew for Afghanistan's participation in the war. To begin with, Habibullah had little difficulty in containing these pressures, but he found himself in a much more difficult position when, in September 1915, a Turko-German mission, which had managed to travel overland from Baghdad, arrived in Kabul. The Amir called a *jirga*, at which there was general support for an anti-British *jihad*. Nevertheless he was clear that he should adhere to his policy of neutrality: he was reluctant to risk a military confrontation with the British and Russians, and he was not, in any case, a belligerent man. He also no doubt saw himself as bound by treaty obligations and retained some of the goodwill engendered by his visit to India. He therefore devised a careful balancing act, by expressing pro-Islamic sentiments and giving *Siraj-al-Akhbar* its head, but urging caution until such time as the war had weakened the British and it could be seen which way the struggle would go. To the Turko-German mission, he professed a readiness to attack India, provided that he was supported by a substantial Turkish or German army, and he eventually signed a totally unrealistic draft treaty in which he pledged support for the Central Powers in return for no less than twenty million pounds in gold, 100,000 rifles and 300 cannon. Rather more seriously, the mission tried to promote unrest on the frontier, but again, without the active support of the Amir, their efforts largely failed in the face of effective British counter-measures and a substantial increase in the subventions paid to the tribes. At the same time, while conceding as little as possible to the 'war party', Habibullah was quietly assuring[6] the British agent in Kabul that there was nothing to worry about – the British should watch his actions rather than his words. He too received an increased British subvention, and eventually, in January 1916, he again declared his neutrality in uncompromising terms at a public durbar.

The outcome of the war justified Habibullah's policy, but failed to placate either the 'war party' or the religious and tribal leaders in the east of the country. There was a widespread belief that Afghanistan had betrayed her Islamic principles and had failed to grasp the opportunity to become fully independent that had been presented to her, particularly after the Russian revolution of 1917. Realising his danger, Habibullah asked[7] the British, as a reward for his constancy, to grant him independence in his external, as well as internal, affairs. The British, however, with an eye to the Bolshevik state now threatening to the north, failed to give him a quick reply, so probably signing his death warrant. In February 1919, he was murdered in his sleep while away from Kabul on a hunting trip.

Although hindered by lack of financial resources, Habibullah managed to initiate a slow process of economic and social reform. He also gave the country two decades of internal peace and increased commercial activity, under a relatively relaxed style of government. During his reign, communications were improved, Afghanistan's first hospital and hydro-electric plant were built, and a number of factories were established. However his major achievement was in the educational field, with the foundation of the Habibia High School on the model of a French lycée, a military academy and a teacher-training college. These institutions began to give the sons of the Afghan upper classes an educational grounding, in part at least in tune with the requirements of a twentieth century state. They also marked the beginning of Afghanistan's critical social divide, between the traditional Afghan society of the tribe and the countryside and that of an increasingly westernised, urban elite.

CHAPTER NINE

Amanullah and the Drive for Modernisation

The responsibility for Habibullah's murder was never satisfactorily established, although Nasrullah was formally accused of having instigated it and an unfortunate army officer, who was alleged to have committed the actual deed, was duly tried and executed. One theory was that the assassination was an act of revenge by a local villager who had survived the suppression of a revolt that had taken place in the area some years previously. Another, favoured by many British, on the basis of no evidence whatsoever, was that it was the outcome of a Bolshevik plot. Yet another, put about by the Russians and echoed by the Afghans themselves, was that the British were behind it, although why they should have wished to remove a reasonably well disposed ruler and create a recipe for instability on the Frontier was not explained. The altogether more probable explanation is that it was the work of one or more of the 'war party', either out of simple ambition for the throne, or of impatience at Habibullah's *immobilisme* and failure to adopt a wholehearted anti-British stance. On this theory, the most likely regicide was Amanullah, possibly with the support, or at the instigation, of his formidable mother, the Ulya Hazrat, Habibullah's principal wife. As Habibullah had failed to nominate a successor and the principle of primogeniture was, as we have seen, not admitted in Afghanistan, there was an immediate contest for the succession. Nasrullah, who had been a member of the hunting party, promptly assumed the title, and was supported by Inyatullah, by many of the clergy and by those army units that were near at hand in Jalalabad. However it may have been no accident that stronger cards were held by Amanullah, who had stayed behind in Kabul and who therefore controlled the arsenal and the treasury and was able, by means of judicious pay increases, to

86

buy the support of the Kabul garrison. He was also able to attract religious and tribal support, as well as that of Tarzi and the 'modernists'. Nasrullah and Inyatullah submitted within a few days and were imprisoned, as also were the Musahiban family, although the latter were soon declared innocent and released. On 27 February 1919, Amanullah was formally crowned.

One of Amanullah's first acts was to send a letter[1] to Lord Chelmsford, the Viceroy of India, informing him of Habibullah's death and his own succession. Afghanistan, he declared, was 'independent and free', but he would be prepared to consider concluding such commercial treaties with India as would be to their mutual advantage. This put Chelmsford in something of a quandary, since the British position had been that the treaties they had negotiated with the Amirs Abdur Rahman and Habibullah had been of a personal nature and they could not consistently regard Amanullah as being bound by them. In a belated reply[2], the Viceroy ducked the question of independence and merely noted, somewhat disingenuously, that he took it from Amanullah's message that the latter intended 'to act upon the treaties and engagements concluded with the British Government' by the previous Amirs. 'Subsidiary' commercial treaties could be considered later, after 'this period of mourning' was over. Amanullah, meanwhile, had announced[3] to a durbar in Kabul that Afghanistan was now 'entirely free, autonomous and independent, both internally and externally'. He then issued a decree[4], the tone of which was described in Delhi as 'as bad as possible', in which he referred to 'great unrest in India' and declared that 'the Indians, in rising and creating disturbances, are right. . . . Excepting themselves, no one is considered a human being by the British'. Early in May 1919 reports[5] reached Peshawar of a further durbar in Kabul in which he had declared that the time had come for a *jihad* against the British. At the same time, Afghan troops were deployed towards the frontier and a small force occupied a village near the Khyber Pass, from which they could control the water supply to the British garrison at Landi Kotal. If there was one thing about which the authorities in Delhi were clear[6], it was that unless very prompt and decisive action was taken, the tribes might well rise *en masse* and the whole situation get out of hand. British troops were therefore committed and the Third Anglo-Afghan War began.

The British were in no doubt about Amanullah's motives in provoking the war. 'It is clear from reports from our Agent in Kabul', Chelmsford reported[7] to Montagu, the Secretary of State for India, 'that the Amir's enquiry into the circumstances of the murder of the late Amir has caused deep dissatisfaction among the populace.' Finding his situation impossible to maintain and under encouragement derived from accounts of Indian disturbances, grossly exaggerated, he has been led to proclaim a Holy War, coupled with promises of easy conquest of India, in order to avert a rebellion against himself'. More specifically, the Government of India believed that by imprisoning Nasrullah, Amanullah had seriously antagonised the Afghan army and religious leaders. A later theory was that, in order to distract the army, Amanullah sent it towards the frontier, but without any intention of commencing hostilities. These, on this theory, were the result of the local commanders exceeding their instructions. However there was certainly more to it than this. Amanullah was nothing if not a patriot and had imbibed anti-British sentiments from his mother, as well as from Mahmud Tarzi, whom he now appointed Minister for Foreign Affairs. Amanullah not only wished to compel the British to recognise Afghan independence, but also had ambitions to recover the territory between the Durand Line and the Indus that had been part of the Afghan kingdom in the time of Ahmed Shah Durrani. He also harboured strong pan-Islamic sentiments and saw himself as the champion of the Muslim population in India. As it seemed to him, moreover, the circumstances were favourable and the prospects good. There was much anger among the Muslim population of India at the defeat of Turkey, the seat of the Caliphate, in the World War. The principle of self-determination was part of the contemporary *zeitgeist*. Russia was in turmoil and presented no threat from the North. Within India, there was famine and an influenza epidemic, while there was also considerable disaffection, as the British seemed not to be living up to the promises of constitutional advance that they had made during the war. On the contrary, the widely hated Rowlett Acts, which among other things provided for internment without trial, were in force and had led directly to riots in Northern India and the infamous Jalianwala Bagh massacre. While the Indian exiles in Kabul doubtless exaggerated the prospects for an Indian uprising, they were not wholly without foundation, as indeed the official British report on the war admitted. The Southern Punjab, it recorded[8], 'practically rose in rebellion'.

At the same time, the Indian Army had suffered appalling casualties during the World War, its morale was low and much of it was still in Mesopotamia. The British units stationed in India, for their part, were relatively few and were short of stores and transport. They had lost many of their most experienced men, were in the throes of demobilisation and included a large number of Territorials, temporarily posted to India. On the Frontier, the religious leaders made great efforts to raise the tribes and a general conflagration there was entirely possible. The Mahsuds and the Wazirs did indeed rise, while the Khyber Rifles, composed of Afridis, had to be disbanded. However British efforts, master-minded by the Chief Commissioner of the NWFP, Sir George Roos-Keppel, kept the bulk of the tribes uncommitted.

The Afghans were also tactically inept. The Afghan Army was in no state to conduct a sustained offensive, yet it neither attacked on all fronts simultaneously nor co-ordinated its moves with an expected uprising in Peshawar. This in any case failed to develop, as the efforts of the Afghan postmaster to stir up trouble were forestalled by effective British intelligence and decisive pre-emption. The day before the uprising was due to take place, British units sealed the gates of the city and turned off the water supply until the prospective insurgents were surrendered. The British were thus able to stabilise the position in the Khyber area and were later to capture the Afghan fort at Spin Baldak, on the road between Quetta and Kandahar. However they were greatly embarrassed by events in the central region of the frontier, where Nadir Khan gathered tribal support and attacked the British fort at Thal. A number of forward posts had to be evacuated, with appreciable casualties. Nadir Khan did not, however, press home his attack and withdrew when a relieving British force arrived.

By this time, however, Amanullah had started to make overtures for peace, no doubt influenced not only by the poor showing of his army and the absence of an Indian uprising, but also by the air attacks[9] that the Royal Air Force mounted into Afghanistan. Although they possessed only a few antiquated aircraft in India, Jalalabad was an easy target and was hit by one-and-a-half tons of bombs in a single day, while a Handley Page V–1500 had just sufficient range to reach the Afghan capital, where it hit the palace, an armaments' factory and Amir Abdur Rahman's tomb. Amanullah's message[10] to the Viceroy talked of 'misunderstandings' and of 'a war forced on us', and complained, rather plaintively, if not without some justification, that:

> It is a matter of great regret that the throwing of bombs by Zeppelins on London was denounced as a most savage act and the bombardment of places of worship was considered a most abominable operation, while now we can see with our own eyes that such operations were a habit which is prevalent amongst all civilised peoples of the West.

Overall, the Viceroy judged[11] that the message displayed sufficient 'climb-down' to merit a positive response. There was some surprise in London at the Viceroy's willingness to grasp the olive branch, but there was no wish in India to prolong the war. A decisive outcome could not be foreseen, while the tribes were still unpredictable, the hot weather of 1919 was particularly intense and cholera was rife among the troops. Hostilities ceased less than a month after they had begun, neither side having gained any significant advantage.

There then followed an inconclusive exchange of messages between Amanullah and Chelmsford, until at the end of July an Afghan delegation was invited to Rawalpindi to negotiate a peace treaty. There the Afghans astounded the British not only by accusing them of having started the war but also by asking for military support and proposing a readjustment of the frontier to give them control in the tribal areas, together with a subsidy to repay them for their trouble. However their bluff was duly called and within a few weeks they accepted a treaty[12] that was heavily weighted in the British favour. It stipulated that 'to mark their displeasure', the British would withdraw their concession allowing the Afghans to import arms through India, that the arrears of subsidy owed to Habibullah would be 'confiscated' and no further subsidy paid, and that the existing frontier would stand, subject to final demarcation. The Afghans were put on probation for six months, at the end of which time, provided their 'acts and conduct' remained friendly, further negotiations could be held. Amanullah thus had, on paper at least, to accept the Durand Line and abandon his claim to the tribal areas beyond, but he was more than compensated by a letter attached to the treaty by the chief British negotiator, which stated explicitly that Afghanistan was now 'officially free and independent in its internal and external affairs', the war having 'cancelled all previous treaties'. This left Amanullah triumphant, with his prestige immensely enhanced, both internally and on the international scene. He could – and did – present the outcome as a defeat for British arms and, more accurately, as marking the birth of an independent Afghan nation. Conversely, on the British side there was a good deal of recrimination. The government in London complained that they had given no authority for the concession, which they described as a 'surrender of prestige', and Curzon, then Foreign Secretary, dissociated himself from it. But Delhi had read the situation better: as Chelmsford put it in a report[13] to London,

> We have to deal with an Afghan nation, impregnated with the world-spirit of self-determination and national freedom, inordinately self-confident in its new-found emancipation from autocracy and in its supposed escape from all menace from Russia, impatient of any restraint on its absolute independence. To expect the Afghanistan of today willingly to accept a Treaty re-embodying our old control over her foreign policy is a manifest impossibility. If we were to impose it at the point of the sword, to what end? The Treaty would have been torn to shreds the moment the point of the sword was withdrawn.

Thus in Delhi at least, the constraints governing any dealings with Afghanistan had at last been understood. However there remained the lingering feeling that it might be possible to maintain the reality, if not the letter, of control. As the Viceroy went on to say,

> Afghanistan's economic and geographical dependence on India justifies the hope that we may exert our control in the substance, provided always that we do not drive her elsewhere for that help of which she stands in real need.

There was, therefore, a residue of belief in British circles that they could keep Afghanistan in a state of dependency, where they considered her still properly to belong. However Chelmsford's initial hope that it might be possible to regain Afghan confidence and resume the role as her protector was not to be realised. When the substantive treaty was eventually signed some two years later, after long and difficult negotiations, it failed to dispel a continuing atmosphere of mutual distrust. The negotiations themselves were hardly forwarded by Curzon's refusal[14] to concede to an Afghan delegation visiting London that the Foreign Office had any respon- sibility for them: Afghanistan was, he insisted, the sole concern of the Government of India. Under the terms of the treaty, diplomatic missions were exchanged, but, in the face of continuing unrest along the frontier, the British felt compelled to make increasingly aggressive attempts to subdue the tribes, while Amanullah continued to try to stir them up. In 1923 he went in person to Jalalabad and held a tribal *jirga* at which he gave money and encouragement to disaffected leaders from the Indian side of the Durand Line, and it took more than a year and the threat of severance of diplomatic relations before this support ceased. At the personal level, too, few fences were mended. Amanullah sensed Britain's continuing ambivalence and his sentiments remained strongly anti-British, while Sir Francis Humphrys, who was the British Minister in Kabul for most of Amanullah's reign, allowed his personal dislike of the Amir to stand in the way of a genuine attempt to improve relations[15]. This lingering antagonism was to be to Amanullah's disadvantage when crisis finally overwhelmed him.

On his assumption of power, Amanullah also applied himself to the relationship with the Soviets. One of his first acts was to send a message[16] to Lenin expressing a desire for friendly relations, and he followed this up by sending a personal representative to Moscow to propose an alliance. This initiative was manna to the Bolsheviks, who were having at the time to fight for their survival and were facing widespread unrest among their Muslim minorities in the territories immediately north of Afghanistan. Initially, they had little choice but to appease these minorities, which they did partly through bogus promises of autonomy or even independence, and their efforts were bolstered by their ability to point to a cordial relationship with the Afghans, to whom at one stage they even offered to restore Panjdeh. But the honeymoon did not last. The two governments signed a treaty[17] in September 1920 in which the Bolsheviks undertook that both Bokhara and Khiva would be independent, and that they would give Afghanistan a large subsidy and military assistance. However on the one hand these promises of support went largely unfulfilled, while on the other, the Bolsheviks did not hesitate to reassert their authority over the khanates. Amanullah for his part extended assistance to the Amir of Bokhara, who was resisting this Soviet take-over, as well as to the rebels, known as *basmachi*, who were doing likewise across Turkestan. However the Amir was soon forced into exile in Afghanistan, while, despite the presence of Nadir Khan in northern Afghanistan with orders to assist the *basmachi*, their revolt virtually collapsed in 1922 and they were thereafter able to make no more than a spasmodic nuisance of themselves. Thousands of Tajiks, Usbeks and Turkmen from Soviet Central Asia fled to Afghanistan as the Soviet grip was reimposed, bringing with them an appreciable carpet industry and their flocks of karakul sheep which, as so-called 'Persian' lambskin, were subsequently to be one of Afghanistan's major foreign exchange earners.

In the early 1920s, therefore, Amanullah's pan-Islamic credentials began to wear thin both within and outside Afghanistan, as he not only appeared to have abandoned his fellow Muslims to the north and in India, as well as the Pushtoon tribes to the east of the Durand Line, and as he entered into treaty relationships with their perceived oppressors. He also had problems when in 1920 numbers of Indian Muslims decided to conduct a *hijra*, an exodus from British 'infidel' rule to the Islamic kingdom of Afghanistan. Thousands of Muslims from Sind and the Frontier Province moved into Afghanistan, to the point where Amanullah was wholly unable to support them and was compelled to prohibit their entry. Soon, however, he was more concerned with internal affairs and, again under the influence of Mahmud Tarzi, had already begun to develop his programmes for the reform, secularisation and modernisation of the Afghan state and Afghan society. There were essentially two stages in this reform programme. The first lasted from his accession up to 1927, when he departed on a 'Grand Tour' of Europe and the Middle East, while the second covered the very short time that was left to him between his return in 1928 and his overthrow some six months later. The main focus has generally been placed on the latter period, when, with a fresh realisation of Afghanistan's backwardness in comparison with the countries he had visited, he tried to push through measures that were, in Afghan terms, of extreme radicalism. However the earlier period is the more significant, if only because he was able to put into effect many of the reforms he proposed then, whereas he did not have the time to implement those he announced on his return from his international tour.

Amanullah's reform programme covered the range of national affairs. For the first time, a written constitution[18] was drawn up and promulgated. In it, he tried to create, on the Turkish example, a secular framework within which the monarchy and government could operate, and to define the relationship between religion and the state. However, the modernists were unhappy with the concessions to religious concepts which it incorporated, while the traditionalists took exception to the idea that the state might have a partly secular basis, rather than exist purely as an expression of divine will. At a public meeting, the head of the venerated Mujadidi family and the acknowledged religious leader of the country, the Hazrat Sahib of Shor Bazaar, threw the text of the constitution to the ground, denouncing it as a communist publication. Amanullah also took steps to reform the legal structure, creating an independent judiciary, a system of courts and a secular penal code. He placed particular emphasis on education, established a number of secondary and other schools, including some for girls, and started to send young Afghans abroad for higher studies. He introduced secular and vocational curricula and brought in teaching staff from France, Germany and India. He enacted provisions to enhance the legal rights of women and issued decrees abolishing domestic slavery and forced labour. On the financial side, his reforms were extensive. He instituted a government budget, reorganised the tax system and established a customs tariff. He collected taxes in cash where previously they had been levied in kind, and set up a livestock census and a land survey for tax purposes. He introduced identity cards (with limited success) and enforced conscription by means of a lottery system. He abolished a host of titles and sinecures, curtailed stipends and campaigned actively against corruption and nepotism. The reaction within the country to these and other measures, and their relevance to his eventual downfall, have occasioned much debate. The controversial nature of some of his social reforms, in particular those affecting women's rights and education, has led many to argue that they were so universally repugnant to the rigidly conservative society of that time that they were in themselves the direct cause of his losing his throne. A dissenting view is that the damage was done not so much by the reforms themselves, limited as they probably were in their effects across the country at large, but rather because in promoting them, Amanullah took on the traditional power brokers, the tribal and religious leaders, and threatened them with a serious loss of wealth, status and privileges. In fact the truth lies in both directions. The educational and judicial reforms in particular undermined the position of the religious leadership, including, significantly, the mullahs whose power derived from the influence they possessed at tribal and village level. At the same time, many of the secular measures affected the tribal leaders, whose status and perquisites were, for example, much reduced by the tax reforms and the change in the conscription system from one of local selection to one of lottery. However the mullahs and tribal leaders would not have been able to arouse the degree of opposition that Amanullah had to face, had there not been also the widespread popular belief that most of what he was trying to do was incompatible with Islam.

It was not long before Amanullah was in trouble. His withdrawal of support from the trans-Durand tribes in the face of British insistence had done his reputation no good, and in 1924 the Mangal and Jaji tribes of the Khost region rose in revolt, led by local mullahs, notably the notorious *Mullah-i-Lang*, the 'Lame Mullah'. The army was unable to deal with the uprising and Amanullah had to call on other tribes to help quell it. The process took all of nine months, during which time the rebels came close to Kabul and Amanullah used two aircraft supplied by the British and piloted by Germans to attack them. This use of 'infidel' pilots caused widespread resentment, as did the eventual execution of the *Mullah-i-Lang* and some fifty of his followers, while the Government's perceived dependence on tribal support created dangers for the future. There were many casualties on both sides and the cost of subduing the revolt amounted to the equivalent of some two years' governmental revenues. Amanullah's prestige was further weakened when a *loya jirga* which he held in 1924 to review the causes of the revolt insisted on watering down some of his reforms, notably those relating to the rights and status of women and the concept of equality of citizenship, irrespective of religious faith. Over the following two years, Afghanistan was relatively peaceful and reasonable relationships seem to have been restored with the tribal and religious leaders.

In 1927, therefore, Amanullah left on his 'Grand Tour'. He visited India, Egypt, Italy, France, Germany, Britain[19], the Soviet Union, Turkey and Iran. In all these countries, he and Queen Soraya made a considerable impression, if only because Afghanistan was a relatively unknown country and it came as a pleasant surprise to find it ruled by an engagingly amiable and outgoing king, accompanied by an attractive consort. Amanullah treated the whole tour very seriously, and worked hard to interest his hosts in the development of his country and to obtain equipment, finance and technical assistance. Having seen the extent of European civilisation and culture, as well as the advances achieved in Turkey and Iran, his concern to modernise Afghanistan was now overwhelming. But he had also lost all conception of the bounds of the acceptable and when he returned to Kabul in July 1928 (driving his newly acquired Rolls-Royce all the way from Teheran), he promptly set in train the events that were to lead to his early downfall. His first act was to call another *loya jirga*[20] of some thousand tribal leaders, whom he humiliated by insisting that they should appear with beards and hair cut, and dressed in black coats, waistcoats and trousers, shirts and ties, black boots and homburg hats. Before this thoroughly uncomfortable and unhappy audience, he described his tour and stated his determination that Afghanistan should catch up with the more advanced nations he had visited. His announcement that a new, yet more liberal constitution would be promulgated aroused relatively little interest, but the social measures he proposed – monogamy for government employees, a minimum age limit for marriage, the further education of women, the abolition of *purdah* and the wearing of western dress in public throughout Kabul – caused rather more of a stir. Other measures, notably the further curtailment of the powers of the mullahs, an increase in land revenue and the lengthening of the period of conscription from two years to three, increased his unpopularity. When the Hazrat Sahib of Shor Bazaar organised a petition against these reforms, he was summarily jailed, while other mullahs, including the chief *qazi* of Kabul, were charged with treason and executed. Wild stories were soon being put about, that Amanullah had renounced Islam and embraced Catholicism, and that he had become deranged through drinking alcohol and eating pork. There was also much talk of Queen Soraya having appeared unveiled in western gatherings and having been photographed in that state (and in fact a contemporary photograph[21] shows her in a dress that left her shoulders and arms almost completely bare).

The precise events that triggered Amanullah's fall are uncertain, but the trouble began among the Shinwari tribe in the Khyber area, possibly as a protest against tax levies, and soon resulted in the capture of Jalalabad and the sacking of the town, the royal palace and the British consulate. Amanullah showed the extent of his desperation by the fact that in the weeks that followed, he twice summoned[22] Sir Francis Humphrys and asked his advice. The latter was outspoken about the widespread alienation from the regime and advised that the tribes should be conciliated as a matter of urgency. However little had been done when another revolt broke out in Koh-i-Daman, north of Kabul, led by a Tajik by the name of Habibullah, also known as the Bacha-i-Saqao, the 'son of the water carrier'. The latter was apparently an army deserter who, as leader of a gang of bandits, had acquired something of a reputation as a 'Robin Hood' through his harassment of oppressive government officials and support of the poor. In December 1928 he attacked the 900-man government garrison at Jabul-us-Siraj, which surrendered without firing a shot, and then marched on Kabul, where a battle took place across the grounds of the British Legation on the outskirts of the city. For some ten days, the Legation lay in no man's land and sustained extensive damage, mainly from government artillery[23]. The Bacha was forced to withdraw, but shortly afterwards successfully ambushed and annihilated a government force sent out in pursuit.

Kabul was now at the Bacha's mercy. Amanullah freed the Hazrat Sahib of Shor Bazaar and rescinded most of the reform measures he had implemented or proposed. However the concessions came too late and in January 1929 he formally abdicated and fled from Kabul in his Rolls Royce, leaving his half-brother Inyatullah as Amir in his place. The Bacha's cavalry nearly caught him when the car stuck in a snow drift, but he managed to extricate it just in time. Inyatullah for his part lasted no more than three days and was saved only by the joint efforts of the Hazrat Sahib and Sir Francis Humphrys, who arranged for aircraft to fly in under a guarantee of safety and evacuate the remaining members of the royal family. The two half-brothers joined up in Kandahar, where Amanullah formally cancelled his abdication and took the field against the Bacha's forces. He had some limited success in rallying support, but a combination of tribal antagonisms and suspected treachery within his own ranks undermined his confidence, and it was not long before he retired to Kandahar, collected his family together and fled to India, cutting the telegraph wire behind him as he went. He finally sought asylum in Italy, where King Victor Emmanuel had been unwise enough during the world tour to invest him with the Collar of the Annunciation, so accepting him as a 'cousin'. The request could, therefore, hardly be refused and Amanullah eventually died in Italy in 1960.

As there had been over Habibullah's murder, there was, again, much speculation about the British role in these events. This extended not just to the Soviet and European press, but also to several British papers, where it was given a sensational slant by suggestions[24] that T. E. Lawrence, the 'Lawrence of Arabia', who was at that time serving on the frontier as an aircraftsman in the RAF, might have had his finger in the pie. Many Afghans subsequently ascribed Amanullah's overthrow not to any internal rejection of his reforms, but to the effects of external intrigues. In an environment in which undercover operations were traditional and commonplace, there can be no certainty that these allegations were entirely false, but again it is hard to see what advantage the British stood to gain from

Amanullah's fall, whatever official feelings about him may have been. What, however, is certain is that they at least maintained a posture of strict neutrality and that this included strenuous efforts to dissuade any of the Frontier tribes who were so inclined from joining in the fray. This in effect meant depriving Amanullah of support that might have tilted the scales in his favour.

Amanullah was, according to contemporary accounts, an energetic and dedicated man, hard working, sincere in his beliefs and modest in his life style. His flamboyant and extrovert personality antagonised many, but he was not unintelligent, and he possessed a good measure of charm and courage. Although his attempts to achieve social progress were the more eye-catching, his pioneering economic and financial reforms might also, had he survived, have contributed substantially to the development of his country. There has been much criticism of his expenditures, on diplomatic representation abroad, on his tour, on uncoordinated and unproductive industrial and other ventures, and on a grandiose new capital at Darulaman. Undoubtedly there was much that he did that was ill-considered and wasteful, and he lacked the clean and competent administration that he needed if his various projects were to succeed. Partly as a result of his loss of British subsidies, his financial resources were also inadequate for the purposes he had in mind. However during his time, Afghanistan was, however poor, an economically viable country, largely self-sufficient and free of public debt, and it is certainly an exaggeration to allege, as some of his detractors have done, that he succeeded merely in bankrupting it. On the contrary, he did manage to take the first tentative steps towards a modern, monetised economy, and his tax reforms in particular were both sensible and badly needed, although the widespread resentment they aroused contributed to the growing pressures against him.

Amanullah's tragedy was that he was a man who was long on reformist zeal and short on worldly wisdom. Despite his many attractive qualities, he was arrogant, impatient and impulsive, and increasingly surrounded himself with incompetents and sycophants. While he was concerned to root out corrupt practices, these were, paradoxically, increased through his creation of a bureaucracy that was, inevitably, susceptible to corruption and nepotism. His naivety was also such that he appeared to think that the inherent reasonableness of his reforms would ensure their acceptance and that little 'selling' of them, let alone any forcible imposition, would be necessary. As the grandson of Abdur Rahman and the son of a strong-minded woman whose father had been one of the most prominent tribal leaders of the country, he should have been well aware that control of Afghanistan required a strong central authority, as well as a Machiavellian ability to handle the tribes and manoeuvre them towards an acceptance of rule from Kabul. Following the Third Anglo-Afghan War, he did realise how weak his army was and he tried to put it in better shape. However the means he employed, the centrepiece of which was the introduction of Turkish military advisers, were counterproductive in that they antagonised the army leadership without introducing effective reforms. Nadir Khan and his brothers, who were probably the most competent of the men whom Amanullah had around him, were antagonised both on personal grounds and as a result of the Turkish presence, and Nadir Khan chose to retire. He went first to be Minister in Paris and then, after a serious illness, lived privately in the South of France. The Turks recommended a reduction in army pay and its substitution by free quarters and rations. However incompetence and corruption meant that both were inadequate, to the extent that half-fed troops had to live in tents during the worst of the Afghan winter. The army under Amanullah was, therefore, an ineffective force and so he never had the clout to impose his will on rebellious tribes[25]. This was a key factor that led to his failure to ensure the survival of his regime and the permanence of the reforms he was concerned to introduce.

CHAPTER TEN

The Rule of the Brothers

T he Bacha-i-Saqao's nine months' rule in Kabul was characterised by anarchy, pillage and terror. He formed a government composed of relatives and friends, the majority of whom were illiterate. Adherents occupied Herat and Kandahar, while opposition in the north, initiated by Ghulam Nabi Charki and supported by the Soviets, melted away, and the Pushtoon tribes, much as they disliked seeing the kingdom in the hands of a Tajik, were unable or unwilling to combine to drive him out. Amanullah's reforms were comprehensively rescinded, schools were closed and young women whom Amanullah had sent to Turkey for education were recalled. The Bacha's sole support came from the religious leaders, to whom he returned the responsibility for justice and education. With an empty treasury and no means of raising funds through taxation, he resorted to extortion and plunder, and many of Amanullah's officials and adherents were murdered, along with numbers of people of wealth and position, including two of Amanullah's half-brothers.

With their habitual suspicions now sharpened by ideological antagonism, neither the British nor the Soviets relished this situation, each fearing that the other might be able to exploit it. The British adopted an arms' length policy. They withdrew their diplomats and, while according the Bacha *de facto* recognition, acknowledging that he held effective power, they withheld *de jure* recognition, which would have signalled that they regarded his rule as legitimate. The Soviets, on the other hand, retained a Legation in Kabul, but were nervous of the influence that the Bacha, as a Tajik, might assert in Soviet Central Asia. They mounted a barrage of hostile propaganda against him and accused the British of having supported him against Amanullah. Their calculation, after some internal debate, evidently was that the Pushtoon tribes would never accept him and that he must sooner or later fall.

As soon as the news of the Bacha's take-over reached Nadir Khan and his two brothers, Hashim Khan and Shah Wali Khan, who were with him in the south of France, the three immediately left for India and by March 1929 they had crossed the frontier to Khost, where they were joined by a fourth brother, Shah Mahmud. They received overtures from Amanullah and from the Bacha, but rejected both and set about gathering a tribal *lashkar* for an advance on Kabul. The authorities in India recognised that they probably represented the best prospect from the British point of view, but there was difficulty about giving them overt support, as this would be likely both to alienate them from the Pushtoons and to risk intervention by the Soviets. Under a flag of neutrality, therefore, the Government of India adopted some rather quixotic ground rules, under which they would prevent nobody from proceeding from India to Afghanistan, but would intern as a combatant anyone who, having done so, later returned to India. They also banned recruitment from the tribes on the Indian side of the border. For several months, the brothers made little or no headway. Many of the tribes were enjoying their new independence from Kabul and Nadir Khan had no funds with which to buy their support. Several times his attempts to put together an effective force were frustrated by defections and tribal antagonisms, while Hashim Khan, who was fighting on a separate front, was driven back into India and interned. At one point, after the Bacha's forces had captured Gardez and were also in control in Kandahar, Herat and the north, it seemed as if the cause might be lost. But the brothers eventually managed to recruit clandestinely among the 'British' tribes and in September 1929 a force under Shah Wali Khan launched a successful assault on Kabul, which was taken in early October.

It is doubtful whether Nadir Khan seriously wanted the throne. Consistently during the campaign, he denied any desire for it and, although he also refused to endorse Amanullah's claims, it is reasonable to suppose that to have done so would have wrecked altogether his chances of putting together an anti-Bacha coalition among the tribes. He was also by no means a fit man. Once in Kabul, however, the tribal leaders who had accompanied him pressed him to accept the kingship, and this request, which he accepted with a show of reluctance, was later endorsed by a full-scale tribal *jirga*. The Bacha gave himself up, possibly under Nadir's guarantee of safety, but was publicly executed with a number of his immediate followers: it is said that Nadir was unable to make good his promise in the face of tribal demands for vengeance. Nadir was also in no position to pay off his tribal supporters, and had no means of preventing them from going on the rampage in Kabul and looting everything on which they could lay their hands.

When the brothers arrived in Kabul, they had virtually no assets, apart from their tribal support. They were almost totally without financial resources[1], the treasury was empty and the army had ceased to exist. There were few people around whom they could trust, while there were many who contested their right to supplant the 'Kabul Sirdars', who, as the descendants of Dost Mohammed, had held the throne for more than a century. Amanullah and his supporters decried what they saw as a 'snap vote of a victorious *lashkar* and servile Kabulis' and did not abandon hopes of reinstatement. Moreover, as Richard Maconachie, the new British Minister in Kabul reported[2],

> Throughout the country the advantages of anarchy seem to have been better appreciated than its drawbacks, and the tribes were asking themselves why they should resign the freedom which they had enjoyed for the past year, and submit again to a central authority which would inevitably demand payment of land revenue, customs duties and bribes for its officials, and possibly the restoration of the arms looted from the government posts and arsenals.

The response of Nadir Shah, as he now was, to all these problems was a combination of conciliation and brute repression. During 1930, the Shinwaris rose against him and he had to buy off their leaders, and there was also trouble with the Ghilzai. In Kohistan, there was some hard fighting over a period of several months before a fresh rising there was subdued, with tribal support and the use of aircraft. The repression that followed was particularly brutal and many Kohistanis were rounded up and executed. While declaring himself in favour of 'progress and reforms', in practice Nadir Shah went to some lengths to appease the religious establishment. He annulled all Amanullah's secular legislation and confirmed the Bacha's enforcement of Islamic law through religious courts. He also endorsed the latter's cancellation of all of Amanullah's more liberal social measures, including those governing women's rights. He reintroduced *purdah* and enforced the wearing of the *chadri*. In 1931 he promulgated a new constitution[3] which, although it was mostly based on Amanullah's and was by no means well or even consistently drafted, lasted, with minor amendments, for more than thirty years. Parts of it contained elements of democracy, and there was provision for consultation with the tribal leaders by means of a bi-cameral parliament, 105 of whose members were selected as a consultative National Council. But in practice the King was supreme, and Nadir and his brothers governed the country more or less as a family concern. Hashim Khan became Prime Minister and Shah Mahmud Minister of War, while Shah Wali and Mohammed Aziz, a fifth brother who had taken no part in the 'liberation', were sent as envoys to Britain and the Soviet Union respectively. While there is no reason at all to doubt Nadir Shah's patriotism and determination to remain independent of Britain and the Soviets, he was careful to maintain friendly relations with both. There was a difficult moment when a Soviet force invaded northern Afghanistan in pursuit of Ibrahim Beg, a prominent *basmachi* leader. This stimulated the Afghans to hasten to restore their authority in the north, and Ibrahim Beg was soon driven across the border and captured by the Soviets. A Treaty[4] of Neutrality and Non-Aggression was signed by the two governments in June 1931. From the British, Nadir accepted a subsidy of £175,000, together with a gift of 10,000 rifles and accompanying ammunition, which he used to re-equip the Kabul garrison. This was the only external aid he received and, while no specific conditions were attached, it is noteworthy that, unlike Amanullah, he refrained scrupulously from interfering with the tribes in British India, even though the incentive and opportunities were considerable. During the 1930s, the British had continuous trouble along the Frontier and had to go to great lengths to deal with it, employing a three-pronged strategy of aerial bombardment, substantial subsidies and the construction of roads and forts ever deeper into the tribal areas. At one point, when the Waziris rose in revolt under the leadership of the notorious Fakir of Ipi, three British divisions were operating there. At another, the Ghilzai crossed the Durand Line from India at the instigation of a mullah who was popularly known as the Shami Pir ('Syrian Saint'), with the aim of restoring Amanullah to the Afghan throne. The Pir, who in fact came from Damascus, was eventually given a substantial sum of money by the British, on condition that he returned whence he had come. An additional problem was posed by Abdul Ghaffur Khan and the 'Red Shirt' movement, the *Khudai Khidmatgars*, which was devoted partly to social reform, but partly also to the cause of national liberation, and whose activities dominated the frontier scene for most of the decade. On the occasions when the British became suspicious of Nadir Khan's role and raised the issue with him, his response[5] was that he never invited tribal leaders to Kabul and that, as and when they came of their own accord, he never encouraged them but sent them away with the minimum present that was demanded by the Pushtoon rules of hospitality. In the event, the British found no reason to doubt his word: indeed he seems to have been genuinely nervous of the Soviets, whom he believed still to favour Amanullah, and he tried to obtain secret guarantees[6] from the British of protection in case of Soviet aggression. The British were not unsympathetic, but failed to offer anything concrete.

It was inevitable that, particularly after news of the British subsidy and gift of arms became public, Nadir Shah's 'hands off' policy would arouse strong suspicion in Kabul. There also remained a core of reformists who were loyal to Amanullah and persisted in regarding Nadir Shah as a usurper. The first serious manifestation of opposition, in July 1933, was the assassination of Mohammed Aziz, then Ambassador in Berlin, by a student who declared that he had committed the deed as a supporter of Amanullah and in specific protest against the government's links with the British. Shortly afterwards, another young Afghan entered the British Legation with the aim of killing the Minister, but failed to find him and instead shot three of the staff. But it was probably a personal vendetta, rather than any political motivation, which led to the assassination of Nadir Shah himself in November 1933. In 1932, he had had a meeting with Ghulam Nabi Charki at which the long-standing antagonisms between the Musahiban and Charki families had come to the fore. Nadir formally accused Ghulam Nabi of complicity in an uprising in the east of the country and, when the latter responded truculently, Nadir, in a fit of rage, ordered his immediate execution. After the event, Nadir quickly summoned a *jirga* and produced proofs of Ghulam Nabi's treasonable activities, but he failed to allay the considerable misgivings that the execution had aroused. On the anniversary of the confrontation he was shot dead during a public appearance by a young man who was variously described as Ghulam Nabi's natural, or adopted, son, but who may merely have been the son of one of his retainers.

Nadir Shah did much to stabilise Afghanistan and help it recover from a long period of strife and upheaval. He began to restore and industrialise the economy, enlisting for the purpose the skills of a small number of Afghan entrepreneurs, under whose management cotton became an important export crop, in addition to fruit and karakul. State revenues came increasingly from the export/import trade, with the advantage that less had to be levied from politically sensitive taxes on land and agriculture. Nadir Khan also reformed the currency and established the Bank-i-Milli, Afghanistan's first bank. He began to improve communications, building the first motorable road through the Hindu Kush. He regrouped and enlarged the army, which gradually became more competent and professional. While his regime was authoritarian and his social policies regressive, this was inescapable if stability was to be assured; and he did reopen schools and continue to send young Afghans abroad for higher studies, so reintroducing a gradual expansion of secular education.

At Nadir Shah's death, the three surviving brothers rallied round his nineteen-year old son, Zahir Shah, and continuity of rule was assured. Hashim Khan remained Prime Minister, and over the next twenty years he and Shah Mahmud exercised what was in effect a regency. For the most part, this was an era of peace and stability. As under Nadir Shah, their recipe for stability was to do nothing to arouse religious antagonism, to give the tribal and religious leaders a role in government through the National Council (which, like Abdur Rahman's *loya jirga*, had the advantage of keeping them away from their power bases), and to placate progressive opinion with a limited show of democracy and reform. With the execution or incarceration of those held responsible for the assassinations of 1932 and 1933, there was minimal residual support within the country for the restoration of Amanullah. External relations expanded and in 1934 Afghanistan joined the League of Nations. In the late 1930s, the Afghans purchased some aircraft and rifles from Britain, but were still chary of allowing either Britain or the Soviet Union to enhance their presence or influence within the country. They therefore turned to Germany, Italy and Japan for economic and educational assistance. During the 1930s, German influence grew, despite an uncharacteristic lack of competence in their engineering work: the dams and bridges they constructed during this time had an embarrassing habit of being washed away at the onset of the spring rains. However they were more successful in helping Afghanistan expand its meagre output of electrical power and Siemens managed to establish a useful presence. Lufthansa also started an air service between Kabul and Berlin. A concomitant to this was that many top Afghans became distinctly pro-German or even pro-Nazi, encouraged by the myths of racial superiority and brotherhood that the Germans propagated. Much was now heard of the idea that the Afghans were of true Aryan blood, and little, conversely, of the myth[7] that had previously been current, that they were one of the lost tribes of Israel.

Also in the 1930s, some modest economic progress was achieved, although Afghanistan remained preponderantly an agricultural and pastoral nation. Companies, known as 'Shirkats', were progressively floated by the Bank-i-Milli, each enjoying a monopoly in a particular sector of the economy, with both private and governmental participation. Given their monopoly status, these companies tended to do well, to the benefit of the members of the royal family and other notables who held shares in them. Further roads were also built, although the traditional caravans continued to carry the bulk of the country's trade. Education, including higher education, was expanded, although it still reached only a tiny minority of the school-age population. Four secondary schools functioned in Kabul, Habibia and Istiqlal with French assistance, Nejat with German assistance, and Ghazi with staff from British India. Later the Americans took over the running of Habibia from the French, while the British Council helped to run Ghazi. This variety of teaching methods and media of instruction did nothing for the coherence of the educational system, and was perpetuated among the faculties of Kabul University, which was founded in 1932.

During the Second World War, despite their pro-German sentiments, the Afghan Government again adopted a policy of strict neutrality, and this was confirmed by a *loya jirga* in 1941. At one point in the early war years, the Germans were considering the instigation of a coup in Kabul and the restoration of Amanullah; at another they were, with the Italians, looking for ways to create trouble for the British on the Frontier. In October 1941, the British and Soviet governments delivered parallel ultimatums to the Afghan government, demanding the expulsion of the two hundred or so German and Italian citizens from the country. This caused much resentment among the Afghans, particularly in view of their policy of neutrality, but they had no realistic alternative but to comply: only a few months previously, the British and Russians had jointly invaded Iran when there had been a hesitant response to a similar demand.

Following the war, Afghanistan was confronted by wholly new challenges. She was now financially buoyant, as she had been able to spend little during the war years, while still selling abroad her karakul and agricultural produce. The former went mainly to America, the latter mainly to India, where large armies had had to be kept provisioned. The means thus seemed to be available to fulfil the desire, which existed in Afghanistan no less than in other countries emerging from wartime stringency, for a faster tempo of economic development. It was also natural that, again as in so many countries in a post-war environment, there should have been a climate favourable to political liberalism and reform. Early in 1946, Hashim Khan retired, deferring to the feeling among the royal family that however desirable his conservative and authoritarian style might have been after the traumas of the 1920s and early 1930s, it was out of tune with the requirements of the post-war age. He was succeeded by the youngest Musahiban brother, Shah Mahmud, a less polished but much more tolerant and liberal man, who went on to release political prisoners, allow a measure of press freedom and permit the entry into the 120-member parliament of some fifty relatively radical members, who proceeded to examine and criticise ministerial activities. Among the intelligentsia, a small reformist movement, the *Wikh-i-Zalmaiyan* ('Awakened Youth') was permitted to appear, while an embryonic student movement came into being at Kabul University. Shah

Mahmud also set in train a policy of economic development, mainly based on the idea of harnessing the power and irrigation potential of the Helmand River, where he hoped to bring about the 'greening of the desert' through large-scale irrigation, agricultural settlement and hydro-electric power.

Internal developments were, however, quickly to be overshadowed by quite novel problems in foreign relations. The Soviet Union had emerged victorious from the war and was now, to all appearances, a powerful, self-confident major power. Beyond the Amu Darya, the indigenous populations continued to be diluted by an influx of migrants from the Russian heartland and Soviet control was becoming progressively tighter. Against this, it was clear that the British would soon be withdrawing from India, which meant that the traditional counterpoise was about to be removed. The Afghans were as surprised as anyone to see the British go and leave behind them two independent nations, and they were dismayed to find that there was no influence that they could bring to bear on the process. The North-West Frontier Province and, more particularly, the Pushtoons in the Tribal Areas should, they insisted, have the right of self-determination, to the extent that, if they so decided, they should be allowed to form an independent state, the soon-to-be-notorious Pushtoonistan. In 1944, the Afghans reminded the Indian government of their interest, but received the blunt reply that the Durand Line was an international frontier and that what happened on the Indian side was none of their business. In this, the British were less than consistent, since in the context of the Anglo-Afghan Treaty of 1921, the British negotiator had explicitly conceded[8] that ' the conditions of the frontier tribes of the two governments are of interest to the Government of Afghanistan'. The British had also long conceded, as the Simon Constitutional Commission of 1928–30 put it, that 'the situation of the [North West Frontier] Province and its intimate relation with the problem of Indian [political] advance are such that special arrangements are required. ... British India stops at the boundary of the administered area'. It could, moreover, be plausibly argued, as the Chinese did over the McMahon Line, their frontier with India, that the Durand Line was imposed by an 'unequal' treaty and therefore had no valid status. Nevertheless, in July 1947, when a referendum was held in the NWFP, the British offered the sole choice of joining one or other of the successor powers, India or Pakistan, and rejected Afghan representations that there should also be the choices of independence or union with Afghanistan. There was not even the option, which had been granted to the Indian Princely States, of choosing temporary independence until a decision might be reached about the territory's ultimate allegiance. The referendum was boycotted by the Congress Party, but in the Settled Areas of the NWFP, of the more than half the electorate who voted, less than a quarter of one per cent were against joining Pakistan. Consultations with *jirgas* in the Tribal Agencies showed a similar overwhelming consensus. The Afghans protested vigorously and, when their protests went unheeded, achieved the distinction of being the only country to vote against Pakistan's admission to the United Nations.

Following Partition, the Pakistan Government, with the advantage of the common Islamic faith, found itself able to govern the Tribal Agencies much more lightly than its British predecessors. The regular army was withdrawn, amnesties were declared and the Agencies were treated as virtually autonomous entities. This did not, however, prevent the growth of the demand that was first articulated by the 'Red Shirt' movement in June 1947, that the NWFP should be given independence as the state of 'Pushtoonistan'. In supporting this demand, the Afghan government could reasonably point to the inconsistency between the Pakistanis' demand for a plebiscite in Kashmir and their refusal to hold one in 'Pushtoonistan'. But their contention that their only concern was for an independent homeland for the tribes rang rather hollow, and there was a strong suspicion within the international community that they were engaged in straightforward irredentism, their ultimate aim being the incorporation into Afghanistan of the Tribal Agencies and perhaps the whole NWFP. (Sometimes they even appeared to include Baluchistan, which was not a Pushtoon area, but would give them an outlet to the sea). Moreover, if, as they contended, the Pushtoons were a 'nation', ought there not also to be a plebiscite among the tribes on the Afghan side of the frontier? Also working against them was the general concern, on both legal and political grounds, for the inviolability of international frontiers, and the view, which was generally held, that the Durand Line was one of them.

As Pakistan, contrary to many expectations, survived and consolidated itself, so the Pushtoonistan issue became effectively a lost cause. But this did not prevent the two countries becoming increasingly at loggerheads over it. A fierce propaganda war developed, and from 1947 onwards the Pakistanis engineered delays in the transit of Afghan goods from Karachi. In 1949, the Afghans convened a *loya jirga* in Kabul which declared its support for Pushtoonistan and repudiated all the frontier treaties which previous Afghan Governments had concluded with the British. At the same time, across the border, the Fakir of Ipi, still very much in evidence, was declared by a tribal gathering to be the 'President' of an 'Independent Pushtoonistan'. In 1950 and 1951 tribal incursions took place across the frontier, diplomatic relations were severed and, at one stage, Pakistan imposed a blockade on petroleum products destined for Afghanistan. This gave the Soviet Union the opportunity to step in, and in 1950 a trade agreement was concluded, on terms favourable to the Afghans, under which Afghan wool and raw cotton were bartered for petroleum and other commodities. As a result, Soviet influence in Afghanistan registered its first major advance. Within two years trade had doubled and soon the Russians were supplying Afghanistan not only with petroleum but also with such commodities as cement and cotton cloth that had previously been delivered through Pakistan. Russian prospecting for oil and gas also began in Northern Afghanistan.

On the wider economic front, matters had also not been going well for the Afghans. Their instinct in the immediate post-war period had been to turn to the Americans for assistance, partly because they had a genuine admiration for a country which appeared to have sound anti-colonial credentials and was now a strong and influential global power. Partly, also, they saw the Americans as replacing the British in providing a counterpoise to the Russians. The Americans had for years shown minimal interest in Afghanistan: a Treaty of Friendship had been concluded in the mid-1930s, but it was not until 1943 and 1944 that diplomatic missions were exchanged. Nor, following the war, was the American Government at all enthusiastic over providing economic assistance, and the Afghans were compelled to negotiate an agreement with a private American company, Morrison-Knudsen, for the implementation of the Helmand Valley scheme. Almost immediately, however, serious problems appeared. Costs quickly escalated, way beyond the Afghans' ability to pay from their accumulated reserves, and the negotiation of loans to cover the shortfall, which entailed official American involvement, gave rise to much acrimony. When the Afghans' initial request for a loan of $118 million from the US Export-Import Bank was pared down to a mere $21 million, their resentment was extreme. To save money, Morrison-Knudsen started to cut costs and some essential preparatory surveys were neglected. Little thought was given to the potential problems of salinity and waterlogging, and even less to the 'cultural' aspects of the project: it seems to have been assumed without question that both existing communities and new migrants, not to mention the nomads whom the Afghans wished to settle as agriculturists[9], would be able to adapt without difficulty to the new ways of living and cultivation that would be entailed. There were also problems in that neither the American company nor the Afghans knew how to deal acceptably with the other. The Americans were technically efficient, but had little regard for Afghan sensitivities, while the Afghans had neither the technical nor the administrative capacity to undertake much of the work for which they had agreed to be responsible, but were too proud to admit their inability to cope. The disruption to supplies of equipment coming in through Pakistan also caused serious problems for the project. The two dams required for it were completed in 1951 and, after much controversy, an integrated Helmand Valley Authority was eventually set up in 1952. But it was by then all too clear that the scheme, in which American prestige was closely bound up, had serious drawbacks and would fail by a long way to meet the over-ambitious aspirations that had initially inspired it. It was, in fact, to be one of the first of the economically, socially and environmentally disastrous big dam projects with which the world has subsequently become depressingly familiar.

From 1948 onwards the Afghans also approached the Americans for supplies of arms, but, despite a personal visit by Shah Mahmud to Washington in 1951, they did no better than they had done on the economic front. The Americans saw Afghanistan as strategically unimportant and doubted whether, even if provided with arms, it would be able to resist a Soviet invasion. They were also suspicious that the real reason for the request was to bolster the Pushtoonistan campaign and were inclined to see Afghanistan as a potential aggressor against Pakistan. The Afghans were thus able to make little or no headway in strengthening their antiquated armed forces, and their sense of vulnerability, vis-à-vis both the tribes and their more powerful neighbours, went unrelieved.

On all fronts, therefore, Afghanistan's prospects were by the early 1950s the cause of much disappointment and concern to the royal family. They were particularly worried that Shah Mahmud's moves towards political liberalisation were destabilising the country, and he accordingly reverted to press censorship and a clamp down on 'liberal' critics, a number of whom were jailed. Economic development was stalling, the hoped-for new relationship with the Americans had not materialised, and the Pushtoonistan issue was not only unresolved, but was seriously damaging the country's trade and foreign relations. Again the family took counsel among itself, with the King, now in his early forties, playing a role in the deliberations. In September 1953, Shah Mahmud gave way as Prime Minister to Mohammed Daoud Khan, the eldest son of the assassinated Mohammed Aziz, and hence the King's first cousin.

CHAPTER ELEVEN

Daoud: The First Decade

D aoud was a man of considerable force of character, possibly, after Abdur Rahman , the most dynamic leader that Afghanistan has seen. Following his father's assassination, he and his able brother, Mohammed Naim (who became his Foreign Minister), were brought up by Hashim Khan, who gave them a thorough political and administrative training. Daoud was educated at Habibia College and the Afghan Military Academy, which he attended alongside King Zahir. The two men became close friends and associates, and Daoud married the King's sister. Under Shah Mahmud, Daoud had been Minister of War and the compiler of the request for arms which, much to his annoyance and frustration, the Americans had turned down. To pursue what he and his following of 'Young Turks' in the royal family saw as Afghanistan's essential interests, he proposed more energetic action over economic development and modernisation, together with a more robust approach to the Pushtoonistan issue. He had no time for political liberalism and his conduct of affairs was invariably autocratic and often harsh. He would probably have preferred that Afghanistan's primary alliance should have been with the Americans, but once they had shown themselves unwilling to make a commitment, he had no hesitation in seeking a close relationship with the USSR. Despite the departure of the British from the Indian sub-continent, he did not see that the Russians would be tempted to act aggressively towards Afghanistan, since he believed that they would find it not only daunting militarily, but also damaging both economically and to their international reputation (a calculation which would, in the course of time, be amply borne out). He was by no means blind to the risk of Communist subversion, but, in his view, Communism had no appeal within Afghan society: both the traditional and educated classes had a stake in the existing social order, while the people at large, with their adherence to tribal, Islamic ways, were far removed from the proletariat which was the accepted vehicle of a Communist revolution. He was, in any case, confident that his security apparatus could keep any subversives well under control.

In many ways, therefore, the advent of Daoud marked a watershed in Afghan affairs, which was given emphasis by its coincidence with the spread of Cold War repercussions to the Middle East and South Asia. Early in 1954, the United States reached an agreement for the supply of arms to Pakistan and later in the year the latter country joined the South East Asia Treaty Organisation, one of the ring of military alliances which were being created at United States' initiative around the periphery of the USSR and Communist China. A year later, Pakistan joined the Baghdad Pact (later the Central Treaty Organisation), which also included the USA, Britain, Turkey, Iraq and Iran. It is doubtful if Pakistan was in fact much exercised by the spectre of a military threat from either of the Communist powers, with whom she had a minimal common frontier. Rather, her main objective was to strengthen her hand, both militarily and diplomatically, against the possibility of a confrontation with India and, to a lesser degree, Afghanistan. A further near coincidence was the death of Stalin in 1953 and a consequent change in Soviet policies towards the Third World. Whereas Stalin had shown little or no interest in the Third World and had dismissed its leaders as 'lackeys of imperialism', the new Soviet rulers saw economic and strategic advantage in strengthening their relations with Third World countries and in trying to supplant Western influence with their own. In the mid-1950s, Afghanistan became one of the first countries to receive Soviet attentions of this nature: some observers, indeed, have speculated that, with its convenient geographical location, the Russians may have seen it as a test case.

All these developments stimulated Daoud's aspirations for his country. He again tried to negotiate an arms deal with the Americans, but, when negotiations broke down at the end of 1954, he almost immediately turned to the Soviet bloc. It is not entirely clear what passed between the Afghans and the Americans at this point[1]. One suggestion is that the Americans made it a condition of an agreement that the Afghans should sign a Mutual Security Treaty or join the Baghdad Pact, but that the Afghans were unwilling to do this. Another is that the Afghans were not wholly negative, but that the Americans felt unable, primarily for strategic and logistical reasons, to respond to an Afghan request that, as part of the deal, they should guarantee the security of Afghanistan in the event of a Soviet attack or internal subversion. A variation on this theory is that, but for their insistence on a guarantee, the Afghans would have received American military assistance with no political strings attached. Whatever the truth of the matter, the outcome was that by the middle of 1955, the Afghans had concluded an agreement with Czechoslovakia for the supply of $3 million worth of arms, and that later in the year Daoud managed to persuade a *loya jirga* to approve the concept of a thoroughgoing military relationship with the Soviets. The tribal leaders had strong misgivings over dealings with 'infidel' countries and the likely strengthening of the government's power to their own disadvantage, but Daoud was able to play on the emotions raised by the Pushtoonistan issue, as well as to point to the rebuff, whether real or alleged, received from the Americans. In the middle of 1956, the USSR extended a $32.5 million loan for military aid, a move that set Afghanistan on a course of military dependence on Moscow. Among the arms supplied were T34 tanks, MIG 17s, Ilyusin 28s and helicopters. More significant is that Russian military training started in earnest and that a succession of Afghan officers and other ranks began to go to the USSR for this purpose.

On the economic side, the Russians started early in 1954 with a loan for the construction of two grain silos, a flour mill and a bakery, and additional loans were extended later the same year for road building equipment and for the construction of gas storage facilities and a gas pipeline in northern Afghanistan. The Czechoslovaks also stepped in with provision for cement plants and other projects. If the bakery, which produced bread which the Afghans despised by comparison with their indigenous *nan,* was no great propaganda success, the same cannot be said of the paving of the streets of Kabul, which the Russians also financed. This was all the more a public relations triumph as the Americans had earlier refused to have anything to do with it. From then on, a succession of barter and project agreements were a feature of Afghanistan's relationship with the Soviet Union and her European satellites. Some of the projects were less than successful, but others made a positive contribution to Afghanistan's infrastructure and economy.

The Russian foot was therefore already well in the door when in 1955, a further crisis occurred in Afghan-Pakistani relations. In March of that year, for credible internal reasons, Pakistan amalgamated the provinces of West Pakistan into 'One Unit'. The idea was to strengthen national cohesion by giving the West and East Wings of the country equality of representation in the National Assembly. Afghan eyes, however, were on the consequent demise of the North West Frontier Province. Even though the Tribal Areas were not involved in the amalgamation, they chose to see it as a deliberate move to prevent the emergence of 'Pushtoonistan'. Rioting broke out in Kabul, Jalalabad and Kandahar. In Kabul the flag was burnt at the Pakistani Embassy, and in the two other cities the Pakistani consulates were sacked. The Afghan consulate in Peshawar was then attacked in retaliation, diplomatic relations were broken, the border was closed and the two countries prepared for war. Happily, the worst outcome was avoided through the intervention of five Middle East governments, who put together an international mediation commission. This did not resolve the underlying problem, but, after the border had been closed for some five months, the Afghans backed down and formally rehoisted the Pakistani flag over the Embassy and consulates.

This again provided the Soviet Union with an opportunity. They negotiated another transit agreement with the Afghans and once more provided essential supplies of petroleum and cement. Politically, too, they seized their moment to weigh in. Towards the end of 1955, fresh from a triumphal visit to India, the Bulganin/Khruschev travelling circus arrived in Kabul and gave the Afghans explicit support over Pushtoonistan. The two men announced the gifts of a hospital and buses for Kabul and promised a $100 million credit, on the very soft terms of a 30 year repayment period and 2% interest. Some of the projects to which this loan was applied were significant for their strategic value: they included a new air base at Bagram north of Kabul and an all-weather road from Kabul to the Soviet border. The latter was an impressive piece of engineering, crossing the Hindu Kush at over 11,000ft, through a 3km tunnel below the Salang Pass. Primarily on the strength of this assistance, early in 1956 the Afghans launched their first five-year plan, with advice from Russian planning experts. From the Soviet point of view, wearing their Cold War blinkers, all this was a wise investment. As Khruschev put it[2],

> It was clear to us that the Americans were penetrating Afghanistan with the obvious purpose of setting up a military base. ... The amount of money we spent in gratuitous assistance to Afghanistan is a drop in the ocean compared with the price we would have had to pay in order to counter the threat of an American military base on Afghan territory. Think of the capital we would have had to lay out to finance the deployment of our own military might along our side of the Afghan border.

At that point, late in the day, the Americans reacted. They now concluded that their interests dictated that Afghanistan should not be left as an exclusive Russian preserve and they too went into serious business there. In the military field, they began to offer courses at US defence colleges, while American advisers from Columbia University became engaged on the reform of the educational system. But more of their effort was concentrated on economic assistance and non-military education. American teachers arrived in Kabul and Afghan students started to go to American colleges. To match the Soviet road-building programme south to Kabul and through Herat to Kandahar, the Americans took responsibility for the road from Herat to the Iranian border, the road between Kandahar and Kabul and the roads from these two cities to the Pakistan frontier. In civil aviation, they managed to gain an inside track and developed the national airline, Ariana, in collaboration with Pan-American Airways. Whether or not as part of this deal, they also embarked on the construction of an international airport at Kandahar. The odd thing about this project is that while it was ostensibly designed to be a stop-over for piston-engined aircraft passing between the Middle East and South Asia, by the time it was completed in 1962 longer range jet aircraft had taken over. The airport was thereafter barely used for international flights and was, on the face of it, a total white elephant. There have, however, been suggestions in Washington that far from there having been any lack of foresight, the real purpose of the airport was military and strategic, to offer an alternative haven for American aircraft launching a nuclear strike on the Soviet Union. On the wider scene, before many years had passed, the Russians and Americans found themselves not merely competing in Afghanistan, but often dove-tailing their projects and even indulging in a measure of co-operation. Several power and irrigation schemes were constructed, as were a number of small industries, specialising in the processing of agricultural produce, such as sugar and cotton. Agriculture itself started to pick up, as the results of the Green Revolution found their way into the country, and the Russians advised on the creation of a collective farming project near Jalalabad. Irked by the predominance of American and other Western educationalists at Kabul University, the Russians also pressed for 'their own' institute of higher education and were allowed to set up a polytechnic.

Notwithstanding these developments, the late 1950s were not without difficulty for Daoud. The Helmand Valley scheme still failed to prosper and in some areas, due to salinity and waterlogging, crop yields were eventually to be less than half those achieved in its initial years. In 1959, inter-tribal fighting broke out in Paktya province, initially over the ownership of trees, and, following the killing of an Afghan army officer who had been trying to negotiate a truce, several thousand tribesmen fled to Pakistan. The Afghan army's intervention was unprecedentedly swift and effective and, partly as a result, Daoud was encouraged to take a strong line with tribal leaders in Kandahar. Since the time of Ahmed Shah Durrani, these had been exempted from paying land tax, but this time Daoud decided to enforce payment. Riots ensued, but were once again quickly suppressed by the army. Daoud had also asserted his authority earlier in the year, when, without warning, the wives and daughters of the royal family and other notables appeared unveiled at the annual *Jeshn,* the ceremony marking Afghanistan's independence under Amanullah. This caused total stupefaction and, as was inevitable, the mullahs were outraged. A delegation promptly formed up on Daoud, but he was well prepared theologically and insisted that *purdah* and the veil were not required by Islam. When the mullahs, who were less than convinced, continued their campaign, Daoud had some fifty of them arrested and thrown into jail. They were then charged with treason and heresy, since under the constitution and in accordance with the principle established by Abdur Rahman, the king ruled with divine sanction, and to oppose him was to be guilty on both counts. Contrary to many expectations, the mullahs received no public support and Amanullah's fiasco thirty years earlier was not repeated. On the understanding that each family would have the choice whether or not to observe *purdah,* the mullahs caved in and were released.

As the 1960s dawned, therefore, Daoud's regime was riding high. He had seen off challenges from the tribal and religious leaders, and the state was noticeably stronger. The army was becoming more mobile, better trained and better equipped, and had shown that it could operate effectively in an internal security role. Albeit with some hiccups, his ambitions for an increased tempo of economic development were being realised. Educational opportunities were continuing to expand, women were becoming emancipated and were beginning to play a role outside the family. On the international scene, Afghanistan was gaining a reputation as a non-aligned nation and its *bi-tarafi* (without sides) policy was paying off. Substantial assistance was coming from both the Communist and Western blocs, amounting to some 80% of total developmental expenditure, and Afghanistan's infrastructure was being expanded and modernised. In 1957, King Zahir paid a state visit to Moscow, while towards the end of 1959, President Eisenhower came to Kabul. But for the obsession with Pushtoonistan, this relatively happy state of affairs might well have continued. However Daoud now tried to force the issue. In September 1960 he sent a tribal *lashkar,* stiffened by regular soldiers, into the Bajaur area of West Pakistan, but far from rising in sympathy, the local tribesmen repulsed the incursion without difficulty. In May the following year he tried again, following a request from the Nawab of Dir and the Khan of Jadul for assistance in a tribal dispute. This time the fighting was fiercer, with the Pakistani air force joining the battle, but the Afghans were again defeated by a combination of Pakistani tribesmen and the local tribal levy, the Bajaur Scouts. During the summer, however, small scale incursions continued and there were a steady stream of casualties on the Pakistani side, while Pakistani consulates were subjected to a campaign of harassment.

In August 1961, the Pakistanis, now under the energetic leadership of President Ayub Khan, himself a Pushtoon, finally chose to act. They closed their consulates in Jalalabad and Kandahar and demanded the closing of the Afghan consulates and trade missions in Pakistan. While this might have dislocated the Afghans' trade to some extent, the damage would not have been extensive and they would have been well advised to let matters rest there. Instead, they broke diplomatic relations and closed the frontier. The Pakistanis asked that Britain should officially represent their interests in Afghanistan, but, in a move that was virtually unprecedented, the Afghans refused to agree to this. Such was the obsession about Britain still prevalent in Kabul that many there continued to see a British hand behind the Pakistanis' actions. The latter therefore had to make do with the Saudi Arabians.

The closure of the border had a variety of damaging effects. It not only hit the Afghans' trade, but also stopped the annual migration of the nomad *kuchis* to and from Pakistan, a restriction that caused them much hardship. It also prevented the transit of supplies needed for American aid projects. Yet again the USSR was the only country to benefit. It gained considerable political and economic advantage by mounting a massive airlift of Afghan grapes and other fresh fruit to the Soviet Union, while Ariana airfreighted further quantities to India. In 1962, a long and difficult route was opened to Khorramshah in the Persian Gulf and was used primarily for the transport of American aid supplies. The Afghans chose to resent American attempts to persuade them to open the border with Pakistan for the release of the aid supplies stranded there, but eventually they agreed to an eight week respite. More generally, however, the closure began seriously to damage the Afghan economy. Because, in consequence of a long-standing policy of placating the tribes, government taxation was by now only minimally derived from land and livestock, it was particularly vulnerable to the interruption of its commerce. Some 45% of government revenues came from customs dues, and three quarters of this was being lost. Financial pressures were also intensified by heavy expenditures on developmental projects, which were becoming more than the economy could bear. Before long, the government was short of some £7 million worth of revenue and its foreign exchange reserves were exhausted. Inflation and shortages became permanent features of the economy. In July, the Shah of Iran offered his good offices to try to resolve the dispute and travelled to both capitals in quest of a solution. However his initiative foundered on the rocks of Afghan insistence that a condition of any settlement must be a total return to the status quo ante. As the months went by, and although in the autumn of 1962 there were further massive airlifts of Afghan fruit to India and the Soviet Union, it became increasingly clear that the Afghan economy could not sustain indefinitely the strains being put on it. An IMF Mission which arrived in the autumn of 1962 pulled no punches in setting out the problem[3]. In March 1963 the landslide occurred: on the 9th of the month it was briefly announced on Radio Afghanistan that Daoud had resigned and that a commoner and graduate in physics at Gottingen University, Dr Mohammed Yousuf, had been asked to form a new government.

It was not just the need to find a solution to the impasse with Pakistan, crucial though this was, that brought about Daoud's downfall. For a year or more the royal family had been debating the future of the country and wider considerations had come into play. Partly, they were nervous of the increasing dependence on the Soviet Union that Daoud's policies were entailing. More fundamentally, however, there was the realisation that, particularly with the emergence of an assertive educated class, Daoud's excessively autocratic rule was becoming increasingly resented. There was, in fact, a growing incompatibility between the policies of social, educational and economic advance that he was, with some success, pursuing and his determination to keep the levers of power in his own hands. The royal family had taken note of developments in several Middle East countries, where traditional rulers had in recent years been overthrown and replaced by revolutionary regimes. Particularly shocking had been the murder in 1957 of the Iraqi King Feisal and his Prime Minister Nuri Said, but upsets had also occurred elsewhere, most recently in the North Yemen. The general feeling in the royal family was that a move towards a constitutional monarchy and a more democratic style of government was a necessity if they were not to suffer a similar fate. To achieve these objectives, the first requirement was the removal of Daoud, but this was only achieved when he provided the opportunity. In the course of the royal family's debates, he himself put forward proposals for a constitutional monarchy, with a parliament in which a single political party would be allowed to function. However the King and others feared that this would not be a genuine move towards democracy, but that, as the inevitable leader of that party, Daoud would merely acquire increased power. When the King declined to study Daoud's proposals, the latter offered his resignation. This the King accepted.

An enigma remains about the motives underlying some of Daoud's policies. Why did he persist so long with an obviously unwinnable confrontation with Pakistan? Was he, in the manner of so many despots, merely pursuing an external quarrel in order to divert attention from internal dissatisfactions? Or was he, as some have contended, deliberately playing on the emotions of the tribal leaders and the country at large, in order to persuade them to acquiesce in the acceptance of large-scale Soviet military aid? In other words, was he primarily concerned, in an era of unsettling economic and social change, to ensure the predominance of the centre's power in relation to that of the tribes? Or was he personally so emotionally involved in the Pushtoonistan issue that he was blind to the realities? Was his personal ascendancy and quick temper such that none dared to open his eyes to the fact that the issue aroused very little enthusiasm among the Pushtoons and Baluchis across the border? It remains uncertain where the balance of the truth lies.

Daoud's position was inherently strong. His association with the armed forces extended back over many years, he paid meticulous attention to promotions and appointments, and he had close personal relations with officers at senior and middle level. There can be little doubt that he could have relied on the army's support in any showdown with the rest of the royal family. That he agreed to go peacefully was probably due partly to the royal family's tradition of talking through their problems and acting by consensus. However it must also have stemmed from his own – eventual – realisation that his policies, particularly over Pushtoonistan, were leading nowhere and that his departure was the only means of making the fresh start that was urgently needed. He may also have felt that there would soon be a place for him in a democratised system. In any event, he retired into private life and bided his time.

CHAPTER TWELVE

King Zahir and Cautious Constitutionalism

According to diplomats in Kabul, there was a very noticeable easing of tension there as soon as the news of Daoud's departure had sunk in. Afghans were now prepared to talk freely to foreigners, safe from the attentions of his security apparatus. A cosmopolitan society began to develop, in which Afghans mixed with diplomats, UN personnel, aid workers and foreign residents. The business and aid community were particularly encouraged, expecting that the border with Pakistan would soon be opened and normal trade and developmental activity resume. For the longer term, following indications given by Dr Yousuf in a broadcast delivered a few days after his appointment, there was the expectation of an increased role for private enterprise, a more liberal political system and a freer society generally.

It was far from easy for the new government to live up to all these expectations, but some quick successes were achieved. It so happened that a number of economic and aid measures were in the pipeline, and so capital could be made out of their announcement. Among them was an agreement with the IMF, new road construction agreements with the Soviet Union and the United States, the purchase of new aircraft for Ariana and an American grant for the expansion of Kabul University. Prompt diplomatic moves also were made to resolve the impasse with Pakistan, with the result that by the end of May, delegations from each country had met in Teheran at the invitation of the Shah of Iran and had agreed to re-establish trade and diplomatic relations, as well as to reopen the frontier. Although the Afghans continued to pay lip service to 'Pushtoonistan', the agreement put the issue firmly on the back burner. While it continued to cause tension from time to time, it never again gave rise to a serious confrontation between the two countries.

Equally important, although they took longer to effect, were the moves the government made to introduce a new, more democratic, constitution. To advise on its preparation, Dr Yousuf announced the formation of a seven-man constitutional committee, which included at least one prominent liberal, Mohammed Siddiq Farhang, who had been active in the political ferment of the late 1940s and early 1950s. The committee began to meet at the end of March 1963, and, assisted by a French constitutional adviser, worked steadily for nearly a year, when it produced a draft which was then exhaustively examined by a 32-member Constitutional Advisory Commission. Finally, in September 1964, a *loya jirga* was convened to consider the draft constitution and formally approve it. Considerable efforts were made to give this body a membership that was as representative as possible of the whole nation (although, of its 452 members, just four were women), and indirect elections were held across the country to produce delegates from each province. Perhaps not surprisingly, therefore, the *jirga* was anything but a rubber stamp. Many of its members were practised in speaking in tribal *jirgas* and the level of oratory was often impressive. The bulk of the controversy centred round the role of the royal family and the nature of the judicial system. As it was drafted and finally passed, the constitution[1] declared that the royal family should consist solely of the descendants of Nadir Shah and set out rules for the succession. However the *jirga* showed its independence by amending the section defining the family's role. Whereas the only restrictions contained in the draft were that members of the royal family could not hold the offices of Prime Minister, Minister, Member of Parliament or Justice of the Supreme Court, the *jirga* insisted, no doubt with a view to preventing the return to public life of Daoud and Naim, on including a provision that the royal family should 'not participate in political parties'; and a proposal that they should be barred from participating in political activities more generally failed only because of the difficulty of defining what such activities might be. There was also a vigorous debate about the legal system and the judiciary. Here, there was a clear divide between the traditionalists and modernists which ended, after 'a combination of flattery, cajolery and partly veiled threats'[2], with the balance favouring the latter. The final text showed a clear preference for a secular legal system, albeit within an overall Islamic context. Strong feelings were also expressed over the questions of internal banishment and forced labour, evils to which Afghans had not infrequently been subjected in the past. Under the constitution, there was provision for a bicameral parliament (the *Shura*), with a fully elected 216-member lower house, the *Wolesi Jirga*, elected by secret ballot, and an 84-member upper house, the *Meshrano Jirga*, partly elected and partly appointed by the King.

However the question of the formation of political parties was deferred for further consideration, until such time as a specific political parties law could be prepared. Also deferred for later consideration were measures to establish elective provincial and municipal councils.

Within less than a fortnight, the *loya jirga* had completed its work, and the King signed the new constitution into effect on 1 October 1964. This was perhaps the high point of consensus between the traditional and educated sections of Afghan society, the latter urbanised, the former overwhelmingly rural. The intelligentsia's primary concerns were for reform, democracy and modernisation, as well as power for themselves. The traditionalists were prepared to tolerate this because they had several axes of their own to grind. Partly, they had suffered under Daoud and were prepared to make concessions in the hope of bringing into existence a watertight system that would make it difficult for him to make a comeback. They had also suffered from the corrupt and arbitrary activities of the provincial legal, administrative and police authorities and were thus in favour of a reformed judiciary and provisions governing human rights. An additional factor was that they were beginning to realise that power was likely to shift irrevocably from them to the modern sector if they did not make their influence felt. Their tolerance of reform was therefore at an unprecedented level, buttressed by the realisation that only through active participation could they ensure that they would attract development to their areas and block measures that were contrary to their interests.

Elections under the new system were duly held in August and September, 1965. Particularly in the provinces, the levels of participation were low. The membership of the *Shura* was heavily weighted in favour of the rural leadership and its supporters, who were best able to afford the relatively high costs of standing as candidates, while religious stalwarts, led by the Mujadidi family, were also well represented. There was some official intervention to prevent the election of extremist members, whether of the left or of the right, but in general the results were found acceptable. However trouble began as soon as the *Shura* assembled. Partly this was because, in the absence of political parties from which a government might be formed, there was an immediate 'them and us' situation, particularly in the *Wolesi Jirga*. Few members had any incentive to give the government their support and, when Dr Yousuf and his ministers appeared to give a report on their activities as an interim government, they were subjected to a barrage of vituperative criticism. Some members also criticised the royal family and, in veiled terms, even the King himself. A few days later, when Dr Yousuf again appeared to present his new administration, a unprecedented phenomenon occurred, a demonstration by students from Kabul University and the capital's high schools. The students occupied the public gallery and even some of the seats in the chamber itself, and refused to leave until their 'rights were satisfied'. Such was the disorder that the *Wolesi Jirga* was forced to adjourn its proceedings.

Essentially, the students' grievances were not so much against the government or the political system as over their own prospects. For many years, such was the shortage of educated manpower that the government and other state bodies had been able to absorb as many school and university graduates as presented themselves for employment. Now, however, the numbers of students had been increasing fast, thanks partly to American and other aid to the educational sector, while official ranks were becoming full and the prospect of graduate unemployment ever more threatening. Moreover, even if employment was obtained, graduate jobs were miserably paid. Even so, only a minority of students joined the demonstrations, which erupted onto the streets of Kabul on 25 October (the *Sehum-i-Aqrab*, thereafter to be commemorated as a 'martyrs' day'), the day after the fiasco in the *Wolesi Jirga*. Towards the end of the day, the army were called in and opened fire, with the result that two students and a bystander were killed, and many more injured. In the aftermath, Dr Yousuf resigned and was succeeded by Mohammed Hashim Maiwandwal, a former Ambassador to London and Washington, who eventually managed to exert the government's authority and, by appearing personally at the university, calmed the students. However precedents for obstructive parliamentary opposition and student militancy had alike been established. It was against this background, and with the opportunities provided by a more open political system, that the foundations of a communist party were quietly laid. Among its leaders were three men who were to be future Presidents of Afghanistan, Nur Mohammed Taraki, Babrak Karmal and Hafizullah Amin.

Taraki was born in 1917 and came from a semi-nomadic *kuchi* family. However his father managed to send him to an elementary school and in 1931 he became a clerk in a trading company in Kandahar. There he did so well that the company sent him to their office in Bombay, where – although nothing is known for certain – it is likely that he was cultivated by the Communist Party of India. In 1937 he returned to Afghanistan and, after some time in higher education, worked in the Department of Press and Information, first in Badakhshan and then in Kabul. Later, he moved to Kabul Radio and the Bakhtar News Agency. In 1948 he joined the *Wikh-i-Zalmaiyan* and started to gain a reputation as an author and political activist. In 1949 he published the bi-weekly *Angar* (Embers), with an anti-authoritarian and anti-aristocratic outlook. In 1953 he was sent to Washington as Press Attaché, but denounced the Daoud government when it was formed and was promptly recalled. He was not, however, jailed and he spent the next decade running his own translation agency, while still writing and remaining politically active. Among other things, he did translation work for the US Embassy. He was unsuccessful in the 1965 election, but the same year, at a meeting in his house attended by just thirty 'comrades' drawn from a number of pre-existing 'study groups', he founded the Peoples Democratic Party of Afghanistan (PDPA), of which he became the General Secretary.

If Taraki was of humble birth, the same cannot be said of Babrak Karmal, who was the son of a respected Major-General who had been Governor of Paktya Province. Accordingly, he received an 'upper crust' education and was a student at the German language Nejat High School. Twelve years younger than Taraki, he was an activist at an early age and was at one stage barred from taking up a place at Kabul University. However he was subsequently admitted to the Faculty of Law and Political Science, only to be imprisoned for three years when Shah Mahmud suppressed the liberal movement in which Taraki had also participated. It seems to have been while Karmal was in prison that he became a committed communist. When he was released, he completed his degree, did his compulsory military service and took a government job. In 1965 he was elected to the *Wolesi Jirga,* and it was he who was the prime mover in instigating the student demonstration which wrecked its initial session. A man of intense ambition, he was a compelling orator and dominated the *Wolesi Jirga* from session to session. He had no qualms about flaunting his Russian connections and was a frequent guest at the Soviet embassy.

Meanwhile Hafizullah Amin, who was around the same age as Karmal, had been trained as a teacher. In 1957 he went to the USA to study for his MA and in 1962 for his PhD. A capable organiser and administrator, by the early 1960s he was Principal of the Kabul Teachers Training College. While in America, he became President of the Union of Afghan Students, and his activities, combined with the 'progressive' views he was now expressing, led to his recall to Afghanistan in 1965. Like Taraki, he did not gain a seat at the election. He joined the PDPA, but continued to work in the Ministry of Education. In 1969 he was elected to the *Wolesi Jirga.*

The PDPA, of which Taraki and Karmal were founding members, was, in all but name, the Communist Party of Afghanistan, and was regarded by its adherents as such. Its membership, like that of many other communist parties in the Third World, was overwhelmingly intellectual and middle class: not that there was much alternative, since the industrial working class were few in number and mostly illiterate, and there was no way of reaching the population in the countryside, where the way of life was still overwhelmingly tribal and Islamic. Where the PDPA inevitably made inroads was among the disaffected youth at Kabul University and other educational institutions. It would be naive to suppose that it did not, from the outset, have close links with the KGB, and it is likely that many of its leaders were on the latter's books. Amin may have been recruited while in America, and it seems that Taraki was supported at an early stage by the payment of 'royalties' on the supposed translations of his writings into Russian. As he had relinquished his translation work in 1963, he could hardly have supported himself, as he was supposed to have done, on the proceeds of the writings themselves, and it is likely that it was these 'royalties'[3] that enabled the PDPA to finance its 1965 election campaign. The closeness of Taraki's relationship with the Soviet Union is shown by the fact that during 1965, he not only went there for medical treatment but was also given an extensive tour of the country. His own view[4] was that he had been treated as if he were a Head of State. In 1966, the party was briefly encouraged by the passage through parliament of a press law which opened the way for the publication of a variety of papers and journals, many of them critical of the government. Among them was 'Khalq' ('The People') which was produced by Taraki in April of that year. Its language fell short of being openly communist, but would have been unmistakable to any student of communist propaganda. It was banned within a few weeks, having published just six issues.

It was not long, however, before the PDPA's initial impetus was lost and it lapsed into factionalism. In 1966, Taraki and Karmal fell out, and in 1967 the latter went off to found his own party, which he called 'Parcham' ('The Banner'). The split clearly had its roots in personal rivalry, in which class differences were no doubt a major factor. While Karmal had many friends and relatives among the upper-middle class, Taraki came from a lower-class, rural-orientated background. However there were also differences of emphasis in the strategies adopted by the two. The more sociable and outgoing Karmal, who had his platform in parliament, seems to have been in favour of 'working the system', by expressing loyalty to the King, by taking temporary allies, and by recruiting and influencing officials and others in public life. The more retiring and unworldly Taraki, on the other hand, insisted that the Party should retain its ideological purity and confine itself to pursuing the class struggle. Compounding the personal animosities and policy differences, the two parties also became more tribally orientated, Karmal attracting supporters from a variety of ethnic groups, and Khalq, formed by Taraki, becoming more exclusively Pushtoon. *Khalq* was thus more concerned with the Pushtoonistan issue, *Parcham* more indifferent. Hafizullah Amin remained loyal to Taraki and before long was playing an influential organising role within *Khalq*, as well as recruiting from among the teaching profession and, later, in the armed forces.

Khalq and *Parcham* were by no means the most active, nor even the largest, of the semi-clandestine political groupings that came together during the 1960s and early 1970s. There were other left-wing parties, more extreme and even 'Maoist' in character, notably the pro-Chinese *Shula-i-Jawed* (Eternal Flame), founded by the Mahmudi family, and the *Setem-i-Milli* (Against National Oppression), founded by Taher Badakhshi, a Tajik who had previously been a founding member of the PDPA. On the right, the Mujadidi family were prominent among religious-orientated groups, some, based in the Law Faculty of Kabul University, of a extreme Islamist outlook. In the centre, Maiwandwal formed a mildly socialist party, the Progressive Democratic Party. Another party of the centre-left, *Afghan Millat*, succeeded in publishing a newspaper by that name for most of the constitutional period. In the absence of legitimacy, however, none of these groupings were able to play an overt role in the nation's affairs, which fell into increasing disarray. In 1967, Maiwandwal became seriously ill and was succeeded as Prime Minister by Nur Ahmed Etemadi, also a former diplomat, who had to deal with a *Wolesi Jirga* that was no less vituperative than that faced by Dr Yousuf. A number of bills were passed, but more were left in limbo, while the *Shura* indulged itself in obstruction and witch-hunting. A typical incident occurred in 1967, when the government abolished an important livestock tax rather than face a storm in the *Shura*, with the result that the budgetary situation took a marked turn for the worse.

If it did nothing else, all this demonstrated that there was substance in the *Democracy-i-Nau* (the 'New Democracy', as it was familiarly called) and that the *Shura* possessed power, if only of a negative character. Accordingly, when fresh elections were held in 1969, the traditional tribal and landowning leadership exerted itself country-wide, with the result that when the new *Shura* assembled, it was found to represent a major shift to the right. Only sixty members of the former *Wolesi Jirga*, most of them of a conservative outlook, survived. Farhang and Maiwandwal were among the casualties, although Karmal retained his seat and was joined by Hafizullah Amin. Etemadi was reappointed Prime Minister and lasted until 1971, when he was replaced by Dr Abdul Zahir, formerly the Speaker of the *Wolesi Jirga*.

Outside the *Shura*, the university remained in a state of chronic unrest, with major disturbances occurring in 1968, 1969 and 1970.

Several were ostensibly in support of strikes by industrial workers, which also became a feature of the national scene (although there is nowhere any suggestion that either *Khalq* or *Parcham* took the slightest interest in them, or in the working class more generally). In 1970, a religious backlash occurred, when large demonstrations took place in protest at an allegedly sacrilegious poem[5] which had appeared in *Parcham*, the weekly journal published by Karmal's party. The government responded by imprisoning or expelling from Kabul a number of the provincial mullahs who had joined the demonstrations, and then had to use the army to suppress the resulting disturbances in the provinces. There was also an ugly outbreak of acid attacks on women who were wearing western dress, which in turn provoked a public demonstration by some 5,000 women, following which the culprits were given long prison sentences. Conflicts between religious and leftist groups also became increasingly prevalent at schools and the university, leading to several fatalities. All this unrest reflected growing divisions within society, not just of a religious/ideological nature, but also as between the successful members of the urban, educated middle class and those who were increasingly alienated because they could not now aspire to their ranks, as well as between that elite and the majority of the nation, still cocooned in a traditional, rural background.

The economy, too, was going from bad to worse. Foreign aid, which had been the government's main source of financial support, began to slow down, while earlier loans were falling due and the country's ability to earn foreign exchange was at best stagnant. With over half their trade dependent on the Soviet Union, the Afghans were forced to accept standards and terms which were generally inferior to those which might have been obtained on the world market. With little control of imports, much of Afghanistan's earnings were devoted to the acquisition of western-style consumer goods. The major construction and industrial projects having been completed, the need was for efficient maintenance and management, but local expertise remained in very short supply. Most industries were running considerably below capacity, while, with a limited taxation base, the armed forces were a constant drain on resources and budgetary deficits were piling up at an unsustainable rate. The government machine remained corrupt and excessively bureaucratic, and proved itself wholly unequal to the task of managing the economy. The country's plight became even worse when the rains failed in the years between 1969 and 1972. By 1971 there was widespread famine and, with relief operations hampered by incompetence and corruption, probably as many as 100,000 people – some say more – died. In 1972, there was yet another change of Prime

Minister, the incumbent this time being a young American-educated technocrat, Moosa Shafiq, who had played a major role in the drafting of the 1964 constitution. His vigorous approach was in marked contrast to the ineffectiveness of his predecessors, and, with the King's active support, he made great efforts to improve government performance, stifle corruption and get development moving again. A measure of his success was that the budget, which had been delayed in the *Wolesi Jirga* for months, was promptly passed. He also managed to resolve the long-standing dispute with Iran over the waters of the Helmand Basin. But he was only a short way down the road when he was stopped dead in his tracks. On 17 July 1973, when the King was in Italy for eye treatment, Daoud re-emerged and took over the country in a virtually bloodless coup.

CHAPTER THIRTEEN

The Return of Daoud and the Saur Revolution

Writing to the Foreign Office shortly after Daoud's resignation in 1963, the British Ambassador in Kabul, Michael Gillett, ventured the forecast[1] that

If the relaxation in the control of the press and the gradual introduction of a liberal political system should lead to an upsurge of anti-government sentiment and a factious opposition, there is certain to emerge a group with supporters among the royal family urging a return to strong government under Prince Daoud and, possibly, the suspension of the Constitution.

Gillett would probably have attached a shorter time span than the ten years that it took for his forebodings to be realised, but Daoud's return fully bore them out. Daoud himself said[2];

For more than a year, the subject was being considered by some friends, and various plans discussed. Only when anarchy and the anti-national attitude of the regime reached its peak was the decision for taking action made.

During his ten years of enforced idleness, Daoud never ceased to discuss affairs with his cronies, and he had probably been planning a come-back for a much longer period than a year. The trigger may well have been, not the anarchy that he alleged, but rather the fact that Moosa Shafiq was beginning to look as if he might be able to turn the country round. Daoud may have believed that if he did not move when he did, there might no longer appear to be any justification for his action. As it was, the King's democratic experiment was reckoned to have failed, and Daoud was able to muster sufficient support for his move.

In large measure, responsibility for the failure has to be laid at the door of the King. He was generally seen as a decent, well-intentioned man who was a genuine patriot and had the best interests of his country at heart. For most of his reign, however, he had done little more than occupy the throne, while the country was run by his uncles and cousins, and he seems never to have learnt the art of leadership. In the early 1960s, he saw the need to exert himself, but he lacked the courage and decisiveness to follow through his reforms and ensure their success. He needled his Prime Ministers, but rarely gave them the support they needed in successive crises. The nub of his failure was his refusal to pass into law the political parties, provincial councils and municipalities legislation, which would have given his governments, as well as the provincial and municipal councils, the political support they needed in order to function effectively. His concern seems to have been that the passage of these acts might have opened the door to extremism and factionalism. In particular, his cousin and son-in-law, General Abdul Wali, who in the early 1970s became the power behind the throne, is said to have advised him that there was a real danger of a left-wing electoral victory if political parties were allowed to operate legally. Given the left wing's minority status among the educated elite, itself a small minority in the country as a whole, such a development was, to say the least, improbable. A more realistic view would have been that the danger lay with the traditionalist right, who, if they had been allowed to organise themselves, might have been able to form a reactionary party and run the country in their own interests. But there is at least a chance that a moderate, responsible coalition of parties would have emerged. The essential need was for a mechanism that would have created a mutual dependence between the executive and the legislature, and this the King refused to permit. Instead, the continuing stand-off between the two arms of government led to the ineffectualness of both. Other areas in which the King did not have the courage to permit democratic practices were the judiciary and the press. The judiciary was never reformed in accordance with the provisions of the Constitution and a Supreme Court was never convened, while, although a Press Law was passed in 1965, censorship and arbitrary closures were the order of the day. When finally the King appointed Moosa Shafiq and gave him his unqualified backing, it was too late.

The King's final shortcoming was in the field of security. Abdul Wali, who was responsible both for the palace guard and the key army units based around Kabul, as well as for the royal family's security apparatus, seems not to have learnt what Daoud and his supporters were up to until it was too late. Given that Daoud was the main – indeed the only serious – threat to the regime, and that he had apparently discussed his plans not just with trusted supporters but also with Karmal and his *Parcham* associates, this failure was an amazing dereliction of duty. Throughout the whole of the constitutional period, neither the King nor his government seem to have taken sufficiently seriously the subversive threat posed by Daoud and his supporters on the one hand, and the Marxist movement on the other.

It took little effort for Daoud and his supporters to carry through their coup. On 17 July 1973, a few hundred troops, led by a handful of officers, seized the palace and other key positions in Kabul. Abdul Wali briefly resisted, but surrendered when a tank put a shell through the wall of his house. He was kept under house arrest for two years before he was allowed to join the King in exile. Almost immediately, another plot was discovered, also originally aimed at deposing the King. Among those implicated was Maiwandwal, who, with forty-four military officers and civilians, was arrested just two months after Daoud's assumption of power. There had been the expectation that Maiwandwal, who had returned from abroad after the coup, might join Daoud's cabinet, and the general dismay at his arrest turned to shock when it was learnt that he had been strangled while under interrogation. This was a major setback for the reputation of the new regime, which had at first been welcomed by many who wished to see a return to firm government. Another coup attempt was foiled the same year, and several more in the years following. Soon the country's jails began to fill with political prisoners, and stories of torture and executions made the rounds. Some executions were, indeed, publicly announced.

Once the coup was complete, Daoud assumed the offices of President, Prime Minister, Foreign Minister and Minister of Defence, and a Central Committee, composed mainly of army officers, was briefly formed. Possibly because he was not personally in touch with officers in the middle and junior ranks of the armed forces, Daoud seems to have relied on Karmal and the Parchamis, who in the early 1970s had begun to recruit supporters from among the officer corps. Little is known about Daoud's relationship with Karmal, but it is possible that the two men had been in touch for some years and that Daoud had provided Karmal with funds. Certainly a number of Parchamis were active participants in the coup, their calculation no doubt being that, once in the government, they would be able to expand their influence and forward their political objectives. A republic was a step in the right direction and Daoud, now an elderly man, was unlikely to last long. Karmal, however, did not join the government; and soon Daoud was quietly relieving of their posts men of leftist sympathies, both in the government and in the military. He also sent a number of young Parchamis to provincial administrative posts, where their reformist zeal was quickly stifled by local inertia and hostility. Before long *Parcham*, frustrated by progressive exclusion from effective power, lost its sense of drive and purpose, while *Khalq*, which was in principle in favour of Daoud's take-over but had refrained from active support, now found its overtures ignored. At the other end of the spectrum, Daoud also clamped down on Islamist religious groups, which were increasingly showing subversive tendencies. In 1974, Mohammed Niazi, the leader of the *Ikhwan-i-Musalamin* (Muslim Brotherhood), was jailed, along with some two hundred of his associates, while some fifty others fled to Pakistan, where they set up opposition movements. They included two men of whom much more would be heard, Gulbuddin Hekmatyar, an engineering student and activist at Kabul University, and Burhanuddin Rabbani, a lecturer in Islamic law. The Pakistan government gave them asylum, valuing them for the counterpoise to Pushtoonistan agitation that they represented. They took up residence in Peshawar and, until restrained by an agreement between the two governments, organised incursions across the frontier. However they achieved little success and many of their supporters were captured. Their most significant attempt was in the Panjshir Valley, where a group led by another former student, Ahmed Shah Massoud, briefly took some government posts before being forced to withdraw. Later in 1974 Hetmatyar and Rabbani split, the former establishing the *Hezb-i-Islami* (Islamic Party) and the latter the *Jamiat-i-Islami* (Islamic Society).

Meanwhile in Kabul, an increasing number of men of conservative outlook, who were trusted by Daoud and had served him during his earlier tenure of office, were placed in positions of responsibility. He restricted contacts with foreigners in Kabul and closed down the press, which was replaced by anonymous *'shab-namah'* (evening news-sheets), distributed clandestinely by opposition groups. In 1975, he founded his own party, the *Hezb-i-Inqilab-i-Melli* (National Revolutionary Party), and in early 1977 he convened a *loya lirga* which approved a fresh constitution[3] and elected him as President for a six year term. The constitution provided for a unicameral parliament and a one-party state, with the *loya lirga* as the 'supreme manifestation of the power and will of the people'. After nomination by parliament, the President was to be elected by a two-thirds majority of the *loya jirga*. However any impression that the system would be democratic was rapidly dispelled when it became clear that the *loya jirga* would be largely composed of Presidential nominees and representatives of the armed forces, the Party and the government, and that candidates for the parliament would be nominated by the

Party. The constitution contained a good deal of socialist and revolutionary rhetoric, and called for 'economic and social reform', 'the elimination of exploitation', land reform and nationalisation. In practice, however, it did no more than formalise what was already in existence, an extremely autocratic, centralised and repressive regime, which drew its strength from the armed forces and the bureaucracy.

While Daoud was trying to consolidate and legitimise his regime, his efforts were progressively offset by economic troubles, due partly to a continuing fall in aid receipts. As a result, the Third Five Year Plan had to be cut back to some 40% of the previous Plan, in contrast to the 200% increase that had been planned. The United States was increasingly cutting back its aid programmes and focussing on South-East Asia, while there can also be little doubt that the Soviet Union was profiting at Afghanistan's expense. The karakul market had been moved from London to Leningrad and its earnings were being applied to servicing Afghanistan's debt, while, despite the rise in international oil prices, those paid by the Russians for Afghanistan's gas remained at rock bottom levels[4]. Internally, agricultural production was barely keeping pace with population growth, while fortunes were being made by a few and inflation was hitting the many. Disaffection was also continuing to grow among frustrated graduates and school leavers. Daoud had meanwhile begun to institute measures of land reform, which, although he was careful to introduce them gradually, were, with other impositions, causing much discontent in the countryside. To restore his economic fortunes, Daoud tried to take advantage of the new influences that were emerging on the international scene. The Shah of Iran, now replete with oil money, was, with American encouragement, intent on building up a regional sphere of influence. Negotiations soon began between the two governments and an understanding was reached in 1974 whereby Afghanistan would receive as much as $2 billion in aid over the following decade. A number of projects were mooted, including a railway link across Afghanistan from Iran and the USSR on the one side to Pakistan on the other. By 1977, however, it was becoming painfully obvious that the Shah's pretensions were running far ahead of his financial resources, and a humiliating process of backtracking took place. Smaller pledges of aid were also made by other oil-rich countries, including Saudi Arabia, Iraq and Kuwait. Afghans went increasingly to work in Iran and the Gulf, and remittances began to help the country's balance of payments. Inevitably, Daoud was tempted to try to revive the Pushtoonistan issue, and a propaganda campaign was mounted in the early years of his second period of rule, encouraged by the problems the Bhutto regime was experiencing with Baluch dissidents. However the Shah and others urged restraint and by 1975 relations had improved, with Daoud and Bhutto exchanging official visits. There was even talk of Afghanistan being given transit rights to Gwadur, a small port on the Indian Ocean.

Daoud's relationship with the Soviet Union during his second period of office has several features of interest. There can be little doubt that, if only through their *Parcham* associates, the Russians must have known that his coup was in prospect, and it has even been suggested that they were in touch with him before it took place. However this may be, it is understandable that they should at least have done nothing to expose it. Their official relations with King Zahir's regime were friendly enough, but they were not over happy with it. They mistrusted its relatively liberal outlook and good working relationship with the United States, even though the latter's developmental assistance had been declining for some time. Had Moosa Shafiq managed to ensure the success of the 'democratic experiment', this might well have satisfied the bulk of the intellectuals and the politically conscious and left the PDPA sidelined. Daoud had earlier shown himself to be well disposed and it seemed as if their *Parcham* allies would play a role within the government. Also they were keen to muster support for their current anti-Pakistan policy and were confident that they could rely on Daoud to provide this. They therefore started by giving Daoud considerable support, granting a moratorium on earlier debt and promising substantial new aid. However, by the time he paid his first official visit to the Soviet Union a year after he had seized power, relations had already begun to cool, and by 1977 they were in bad shape. The Russians had several grounds for concern. Daoud had by then purged the Parchamis from his government and the armed forces. He had reduced the numbers of Russian military advisers in the country and was turning to countries other than the Soviet Union, in particular India and Egypt, for military training. He was also negotiating with Iran and Middle East states, no friends of the Soviet Union, for financial aid and developmental assistance, and was mending fences with Pakistan, now a close associate of Communist China. During a visit to Moscow in the course of 1977, it seems that Brezhnev took him to task for the number of foreign experts who were working in Afghanistan and that he retorted angrily that his government would employ whom it pleased and would not be dictated to. He then walked out of the room and broke off the talks. Some have reckoned that it was this confrontation that sealed his doom the following year[5].

The Soviet Union was now coming face to face with the contradictions inherent in its two-track policy towards Afghanistan. Ever since the mass emigration of Usbeks and others following the 1917 revolution and the protracted problems with the *basmachi*, the

Russians had been highly sensitive over their frontier with Afghanistan. Along its length, they maintained an 'iron curtain'[6], complete with watchtowers, wire fences and cleared strips, and no settlement was allowed within 70 kilometres. As Khruschev revealed in the 1950s, they saw a continuing threat of American penetration and were prepared to go to considerable lengths to ensure that their influence in Afghanistan remained securely predominant. In practice, if only for reasons of geography, they had little to fear, and could well have achieved their objective by confining themselves to cultivating close official relations, backed by military and economic assistance. An independent Afghanistan, non-aligned but within their 'sphere of influence', would have served them well. However they also had their ideological convictions and were in the 1970s reverting to the Stalinist concept that more could be achieved through Marxist-Leninist parties in the Third World than through non-communist national leaders, many of whom had proved to be unstable and unreliable. The American set-back in Vietnam was also encouraging them in the arrogant belief that Communism was achieving an unstoppable world-wide momentum. In the Afghan context, this caused them to shift their support away from Daoud and towards the Afghan Marxist movement, while continuing to try to subvert young Afghan officers whom they accepted for military training in the Soviet Union. All the latter, amounting to several thousand in the years between 1955 and 1978, were routinely indoctrinated. Probably only a minority became committed Marxists, but a significant number were sufficiently disaffected to respond to *Parcham*'s approaches. More were dissatisfied at their poor pay and prospects, since, with their Russian background, they tended to be discriminated against when promotion was being considered, and their loyalty to the Musahibans was dubious.

In assessing the events leading to Daoud's overthrow and the immediately subsequent developments, the problem is that all concerned were comprehensively mendacious. History was constantly rewritten as each leader assumed power and tried to present himself in the best possible light. In many cases, the facts are quite obscure, despite the confidence with which many commentators have presented them. However it seems that in preparation for a coup, the PDPA decided to start recruiting in the armed forces, particularly among Pushtoon officers. Hafizullah Amin was put in charge of this exercise and was soon receiving an encouraging response. Incredibly, while Daoud's security apparatus had certainly penetrated the PDPA and must have known much of what was going on, nothing effective was done. Relations between *Khalq* and *Parcham* remained acrimonious until 1977 when, in response to Soviet pressure, exercised though the intermediacy of Ehsan Tabari, a leading member of the Tudeh party of Iran, they again formed an uneasy united front. The Russians in all probability reckoned that it would be many years before the overwhelmingly tribal and feudal Afghanistan would be ready for a Communist revolution, and it is likely that their sights were set no higher than to ensure that Daoud would fall and that his regime would be succeeded by a stable, pro-Soviet successor. In doctrinal terms, as one Soviet academic put it[7], it was 'absolutely foolish', indeed 'impossible', to try to do in a few years what would realistically take at least twenty and possibly half a century. The transformation of a traditional society could only be achieved extremely slowly, and certainly not by wrecking its existing structure and relationships. Even in the Soviet Union, there had been the 'great mistakes' of the 1920s and 1930s. As a Soviet official in Moscow was also reported[8] as saying, 'If there is one country in the world we would like not to try scientific socialism at this point in time, it is Afghanistan'. This was not, however, the PDPA's attitude. They saw themselves as the pioneers of Marxism in the Third World, whose task it was to achieve a direct transition from a feudal to a communist society. In Afghan conditions, the 'mobilisation of the working class' would simply take too long to achieve. As Hafizullah Amin put it in the *Kabul Times*[9],

> If we had waited to follow the same class pattern of working-class revolution through a national democratic bourgeoisie, then we would have followed such a long and thorny road that it would have required not only years but centuries.

The PDPA therefore had their own agenda, and the subversive tendency, both civilian and military, which grew in strength, with active Soviet involvement, from the mid-1950s onwards, by the 1970s had acquired a content of its own. A coup was planned, but all concerned were taken by surprise by the events that triggered it.

The crisis began with the murder on 17 April 1978 of Mir Akbar Khyber, a prominent Parchamist ideologue and organiser. The responsibility for the murder remains unclear, the most likely possibilities being that it was the work either of Daoud's secret police or of Hafizullah Amin and the *Khalq*. Popular opinion, however, took it that the American Embassy and the CIA were the culprits, and a large anti-American demonstration packed the streets of Kabul on the day of Khyber's funeral. Daoud took alarm at this evidence of support for the PDPA and decided to arrest its leaders, who were rounded up and jailed on the night and early morning of 25/26 April. What then happened is a matter of some uncertainty. Hafizullah Amin's account was that when the police came to arrest him, he was given time and opportunity to send messages to his military associates, telling them what was happening and giving them detailed instructions for a military take-over the following morning, 27 April. It is, however, equally possible that the associates knew well enough what was happening and realised that they were also at risk, and that they needed no instructions what to do. In any event, on the morning of 27 April, the tanks began to roll.

As with Daoud's earlier coup, the attacking forces were small, probably no more than a few hundred men and some 40–50 tanks[10]. However luck favoured the rebels as their tanks manoeuvred through the capital's traffic and among crowds of workers leaving their offices for the Muslim weekend. For some curious reason, instructions had been given to the armed forces to celebrate the arrests of the PDPA leadership, and so there was a certain lack of good order and military discipline at the time. Accordingly, when Daoud, who was holding a cabinet meeting to decide the fate of the arrested PDPA leaders, sent his Chief of Staff to rally support, the latter had very limited success. He broke an arm when his staff car jumped a traffic light and hit a taxi, and he was in considerable pain for the rest of the day. The first unit he approached, the 8th Division at Kargha, was without its commanding officer, and the junior officers were unable to persuade it to march on Kabul. Eventually, the 7th Division at Rishkor, also on the outskirts of Kabul, was successfully mustered, but it disintegrated as a fighting force when it was attacked from the air while marching (in column of fours!) towards the capital. The rebels failed to cut Daoud's communications and aircraft were summoned from the Shindand air base, but they were very low on fuel when they arrived and were unable to identify the attacking force in the few minutes available to them over Kabul. There was, therefore, little to hinder the assault mounted by the rebel 4th Armoured Brigade, led by Major Mohammed Aslam Watanjar, who had also been prominent in Daoud's own coup five years previously. Watanjar first secured the airport, where the other coup leader, Colonel Abdul Qadir Dagarwal, left by helicopter for the Bagram air base. There he took charge and organised air strikes on the royal palace, where Daoud and the presidential guard were conducting a desperate defence. Fighting continued the whole day and into the night, when the defenders were finally overwhelmed. Daoud and almost all his family, including women and children, died in the fighting. Altogether, there were possibly as many as two thousand fatalities, both military and civilian.

Essentially, therefore, this was a military coup, albeit by men of left-wing sympathies, carried out when the civilian PDPA leadership were all behind bars. However it was not long before the civilians asserted their authority. The Revolutionary Military Council which was immediately formed was disbanded within forty-eight hours and power was handed over to a joint military/civilian Revolutionary Council of the Democratic Republic of Afghanistan, with Taraki at its head as President and Prime Minister. This too declined in importance, while power increasingly rested in the Cabinet which was formed within a few days of the coup. It is interesting to note[11] that, of the first PDPA cabinet, only the three military men had been educated in the Soviet Union. Of the civilians, ten had been educated in the USA, two in Egypt, two in Western Europe and four in Afghanistan. One wonders whether the politics of the civilians would have been the same had they had the privilege of an education at Lumumba University in the USSR.

CHAPTER FOURTEEN

Khalq Rule and Soviet Invasion

O nce the new PDPA government had been put together, it had two immediate concerns. The first, while it was still unsure of its grip, was to reassure the nation about its intentions, the second was to settle its internal rivalries. While there was a good deal of relief at the disappearance of Daoud, there were also immediate doubts about his successors, of whom very little was known in the country at large. To begin with, therefore, Marxism was soft-pedalled and catch-words such as 'nationalist', 'democratic', and 'reformist' were employed, while lip-service was paid to Islam. All 'progressives' and 'victims of Daoud's repression' were invited to help in the country's development. The Soviet government were quick to recognise the regime, but denied that they had any hand in its formation, while the American government, for their part, were hesitant about branding it as communist. The reason was partly that they did not wish to burn any boats by causing the invocation of the Foreign Assistance Act, which prohibited aid to communist countries. If the regime's initial camouflage was not quickly penetrated, it was only because it made little immediate impact on the country at large. Well before the year was out, however, it emerged in its true colours, not only as overtly communist, but also as unremittingly brutal and determined to revolutionise Afghan society from the grass roots up, by terror if necessary.

An internal power struggle, however, had first to be settled between *Khalq* and *Parcham*. At the outset, the PDPA cabinet was almost equally divided between the two factions, with Karmal, Amin and Watanjar serving as Deputy Prime Ministers to Taraki. Thanks partly to Hafizullah Amin's considerable organisational capacity and recruiting successes, however, *Khalq* was by some margin the stronger partner and soon had the upper hand. Personal and ethnic differences no doubt played their part in the break-up. Karmal and Amin were at daggers drawn, and there was also no love lost between Karmal and Taraki. Policy disagreements, however, were more important. The Parchamis continued to favour a gradualist approach, but the Khalqis, and Amin in particular, were determined on a root and branch social and economic revolution. The Soviet Communist Party sent out an official to try to reconcile the two factions, but without success. Within a few weeks six leading Parchamis were exiled as ambassadors, Karmal to Czechoslovakia. Two months later they were summoned home to face trial, but all took the wiser course of disappearing from view, with Soviet connivance as it turned out. Meanwhile a thoroughgoing purge of Parchamis took place in Kabul. In August, Abdul Qadir and others were arrested, allegedly for plotting a coup. Further arrests, of military and police officers and of government officials, followed, and many were tortured and killed. Several hundred more were dismissed from their posts and replaced by Khalqis. By July, Amin was the sole Deputy Prime Minister and in charge of the *Khalq's* security apparatus (then known as ASGA – in English translation, the Organisation for the Protection of the Interests of Afghanistan). By the end of the summer, the regime consisted almost solely of Khalqis and Amin was becoming increasingly dominant.

Khalq now came out into the open and by the end of the year had produced a number of decrees and other measures that, taken together, were to tip the country into rebellion. On the economic side, the medicine prescribed was thoroughgoing land reform and the abolition of usury. The land reform decree was designed to bring about a far-reaching redistribution of land. It placed strict limits on land holdings, any surplus land being confiscated without compensation and distributed to landless peasants and other deserving cases. The usury decree cancelled most mortgages and indebtedness, and reduced payments on the remainder, future credit being the responsibility of the (virtually non-existent) Agricultural Development Bank. An accompanying enactment provided for the establishment of co-operatives to take the place of the traditional rural economic relationships. Along with these measures, a marriage decree was promulgated, which abolished *mehr*, bride price, set minimum ages for marriage and laid it down that freedom of choice must be allowed. The regime also tried to set in train a drive towards universal literacy, together with the introduction of universal education for both sexes, based on a Marxist curriculum and with Russian as the medium of instruction at the secondary level.

The problem about these measures was that they took no account at all of the complexities of Afghan society and the interlocking economic and social relationships on which it depended. If it was curious that Amanullah did not foresee the consequences of the reforms he proposed in the 1920s, it is almost inexplicable that most of the *Khalq* leaders, and not least Taraki, who had been brought up in rural society, were similarly blinkered. Ideology, however, was uppermost, and the actions of the *Khalq* leadership showed that they retained few connections with, and almost no understanding of, the 'workers and peasants' in whose name they were theoretically acting. They were also supremely confident that they would be able to destroy the rural power structures and re-educate the peasants. With the seemingly unconditional backing of the Soviet Union, how could they be thwarted?

When the various measures were first announced, nobody was much worried, remembering Daoud's inconclusive land reforms and the helplessness of the young zealots he had sent out to the provinces. This time, however, matters were different. The Khalqis dispatched to effect the reforms meant business and were backed by the provincial authorities and the police, with the army in the background. They were certainly right in believing that there was much inequality and exploitation in the existing system. Many mortgage contracts imposed wholly extortionate terms on the borrowers. What *Khalq* ignored, however, was that patronage and dependency were integral parts of the system. It was not just a question of land: tenants often relied on landowners for seed, fertiliser, credit and draught animals, while water rights were also crucial. Many rural inputs and services were provided communally rather than bought and sold. A further complication was that cadastral surveys were wholly incomplete and so there was very little reliable knowledge about who owned what. Often land had been registered in the name of a tribal or clan chief, while in practice its ownership was communally shared. The literacy and educational reforms, with their inclusion of women, their imposition on the elderly, the introduction of teachers from outside the community and the emphasis on Marxism and the Russian language, were also bitterly resented. So far as the marriage decree was concerned, whatever may be thought about the practice of buying and selling wives, bride price was part of a traditional marriage contract, by which the bride was given compensating security, and the reform struck at the heart of familial relationships[1].

By the spring of 1979, claims were being put forward in Kabul, accompanied by a wealth of statistics, that the reforms had been carried through with great success. The reality, however, was that the statistics were wholly bogus and that the country had instead been thoroughly unsettled and antagonised. The problems caused by the reforms were multifarious. With controversy and uncertainty about the ownership of land, customary inputs were withheld. State credit was badly organised and failed to replace the pre-existing private sources, which promptly dried up, and the co-operatives also failed to materialise. Nor did the state, almost needless to say, carry out the work, for example on irrigation systems, that had previously been undertaken communally. More often than not, no documentary records of mortgages existed. The speed with which the decrees were introduced also precluded accuracy and justice. The committees that were sent around the provinces to settle apportionments often did so in a totally arbitrary manner. Attempts were made to impose the reforms by force, sometimes to the extent of beatings, arrests and even assassinations. The result was widespread disruption and hardship, and possibly as much as a third of the land went out of cultivation. Moreover, it was not just the landowners who were embittered, but most rural Afghans believed that it was unjust and un-Islamic to accept property which had been expropriated from another. More often than not, rural communities were united in resistance to the reforms, rather than split by their acceptance. In essence, the *Khalq*'s aim was, in accordance with Marxist tenets, to shatter feudal and capitalist relationships, and establish the state as the single repository of patronage and authority. One view is that they were cynical enough to introduce the land reforms in the confident expectation that rural smallholdings would not be viable and that a transition to co-operatives would then be inevitable. However their own power and capacity were too weak, and those of the rural communities too strong, for their efforts to succeed. Unwilling to admit their own responsibility for the resistance that these reforms provoked, they tried to put the blame on 'foreign saboteurs'.

Further than this, the regime chose to replace the Afghan flag, with its green stripe representing Islam, with a solidly red flag which, apart from the symbols at its corner, was indistinguishable from the flags of other communist countries. Another step was the conclusion in December 1978 of a 'Treaty of Friendship' with the Soviet Union, which guaranteed the latter's support for what was clearly recognised by the Treaty to be a satellite state. Communist-style mass demonstrations were organised, while a personality cult of Taraki was introduced and pictures of the 'Great Teacher' became ubiquitous. The customary invocation of Allah was also omitted before official statements. Taken together, these measures could not have amounted to a more provocative flaunting of the alignment of the *Khalq* regime.

Even before it finished dealing with the Parchamis, the *Khalq* started to deploy a reign of terror against others whom it saw as its opponents. Large numbers of military officers, officials, clergy, former politicians and professional men were thrown into goal. Many more fled the country before they could be taken. In the countryside, religious and secular leaders were also targeted. The notorious prison at Pul-i-Charki, on the outskirts of Kabul, which had not been completed and was without sanitary facilities, was progressively filled with political prisoners, and executions were a daily occurrence. Moosa Shafiq was one of the early victims. In the autumn of 1978, Amnesty International reckoned[2] that there were some 4,000 political prisoners, and a year later they put the number of those held without trial since the Saur revolution at around 12,000. Little or no information was released about them, and their relatives usually had no idea where they were, nor even if they were alive or dead. In the summer of 1978, the regime arrested the whole of the Mujadidi family and early in 1979 killed its male members, some seventy in all. In June of that year all the Islamist militants whom Daoud had arrested in 1974 were murdered in a single night. Rural communities were also the victims of reprisals. The village of Kerala in Kunar Province, for example, was attacked and razed to the ground in April 1979, and more than a thousand of its inhabitants were killed.

The Soviet government was increasingly concerned at what was going on, but found that it possessed little leverage. As the purges took place in the Afghan government and armed forces, so Soviet advisors were drafted in to fill the gaps. Within a few months, there were perhaps as many as seven hundred with the armed forces and several thousand in the ministries and the ASGA. By the summer of 1979, there were probably between four and five thousand altogether. During 1978, a substantial quantity of Soviet weaponry was supplied, while a joint commission was established to regulate economic co-operation. The problem for the Russians was that despite all this military and economic assistance, and the presence of their military and civilian advisors, they were unable either to influence the core policies and activities of the *Khalq* regime, or to mitigate their consequences. The ousting of the Parchamis, the reign of terror, the crude imposition of Marxist dogma, the rural disaffection, all were beyond their reach, while there were also limits to what they could do to counter the growing inefficiency of a bureaucracy increasingly staffed by inexperienced PDPA zealots. Yet they could not just cut their losses and walk away. Apart from their sensitivity about their southern border, the one thing that was wholly unacceptable was counter-revolution. The onward march of Communism was irreversible and there was no way that a Communist regime, once in power, could be allowed to fail. Any such failure would be gravely damaging to Soviet prestige and would raise doubts about the USSR's ability to support other Communist regimes. No less than in Czechoslovakia in 1968, the Brezhnev Doctrine was held to apply. In Brezhnev's words[3],

> When external and internal forces hostile to socialism try to turn the development of a given socialist country in the direction of the restoration of the capitalist system .... this is .... a common problem, the concern of all socialist states.

Still blinkered by their Cold War preconceptions, the Russians also assumed that to the extent that their own influence might wane, that of the United States would replace it and an 'imperialist bridgehead' be created. This too was unacceptable.

From the summer of 1978 onwards, popular resistance to the *Khalq* regime built up. Starting in Nuristan, guerrilla warfare developed and desertions from the armed forces began. So far as the outside world was concerned, a watershed was the murder in February 1979 of Adolph Dubs, the American Ambassador, who had been abducted a few days previously by four members of an extreme left-wing party and held in a Kabul hotel. The Afghan government refused to talk to Dubs' captors and, with the active participation of Soviet advisors, stormed the room in which Dubs was held. The Americans were not consulted and their repeated pleas for restraint were ignored. The result was Dubs' death, as well as that of his captors[4]. American outrage was such that the bulk of its aid programmes were suspended, while other countries soon followed suit in cutting back their own programmes and withdrawing their aid personnel.

For *Khalq* and its Soviet patrons, the moment of truth came in March 1979, with a major uprising in the city of Herat, apparently triggered by protests against the inclusion of women in the government's literacy campaign. Virtually the whole of the garrison joined the revolt and the government lost control of the city for several days. Government officials and Soviet personnel were hunted down, and they and their families were tortured and brutally murdered. Possibly as many as a hundred Russians, women and children as well as men, lost their lives. Many were publicly hacked to death and their bodies paraded around impaled on pikes. The city was only retaken after being bombed by aircraft, possibly piloted by Russians, and subjected to an all out assault, supported by tanks and helicopters. Much of the city was pounded to rubble and one estimate has it that as many as twenty thousand Heratis died. Many soldiers defected permanently and formed a well-armed guerrilla front in the region, under the leadership of a former army officer, Ismail Khan. It was probably at this point that the Soviet government began to think in terms of a possible invasion. As for the Kabul regime, far from trying to conciliate its opponents, its response was to harden its line. Again, foreign interference was alleged, this time by Iran. Taraki, always a weak man, was by now little more than a figurehead, while

Amin tightened his grip on the government and assumed the post of Prime Minister. Later he took responsibility for military operations and instigated further purges. As resistance grew, so dependence on the Soviet Union and its advisors increased. More weapons, including MI–24 helicopter gunships, were brought in. Before long, however, unrest had spread to virtually all parts of the country and several of the major towns came under attack. An assault on Jalalabad in May 1979 was repulsed with heavy losses. In the north, Faizabad was besieged, as was Bamian in the Hazarajat. In June, a major demonstration in Kabul against the regime was dispersed by troops, leaving many killed and wounded. The Afghan army also became increasingly disaffected. In April, a major mutiny in Jalalabad was crushed, as was another in August, this time by an armoured unit in Kabul. In May, a complete motorised brigade defected while operating in Paktya, while in August, the unit defending Asmar in the Kunar Valley joined the resistance in attacking the provincial centre of Chaga Serai. However the attack disintegrated in a welter of mutual recrimination and many of the attackers departed for Pakistan to sell their weapons.

As the situation deteriorated during 1979, so the Soviet government's efforts to find a solution assumed increasing urgency. They started by sending a veteran diplomat, Vasily Safronchuk, to urge Taraki and his ministers to adopt a less confrontational attitude and broaden support for their regime by bringing non-Communists into the government. Largely, it seems, as a result of Amin's opposition, Safronchuk's mission failed. In April, a mission headed by General Yepishev, the Chief of GLAVPUR, the central political office of the Soviet armed forces, arrived to review the situation. It seems that he was greatly concerned by what he saw and recommended a significant strengthening of the Afghan army and air force. In August, he was followed by General Pavlovsky, the commander of the 1968 invasion of Czechoslovakia, accompanied by a sixty-man military team. Ostensibly, he was there to advise the Afghan government how to counter the growing insurgency, but in fact he was also surveying the ground for a possible invasion. The conclusion reached by the Soviet government seems to have been that the *Khalq* regime was in danger of total collapse and that the root cause of the problem was Amin's refusal to countenance any moderation of the regime's confrontational policies. The decision was taken to remove him from the scene; and the opportunity was taken to consult Taraki about this when the latter stopped off in Moscow in September on his way back from a non-aligned conference in Cuba.

Precisely what passed between Taraki and the Soviet leadership on this occasion is not known. One story is that the Russians produced

Babrak Karmal, whom they had been keeping in cold storage since his disappearance from Prague a year earlier, and that he and Taraki reached an agreement on a carve-up of posts in a new government. However that may be, it is reasonable to suppose that it was agreed that Amin should be disposed of, and that the broadening of the government and less militant line urged by Safronchuk should be adopted. Even less certain are the events that took place after Taraki's return, but the speculation is that Amin was tipped off about the Moscow agreement by Shah Wali, the Afghan Foreign Minister, who was with Taraki at the time. In an apparent effort to pre-empt any move against him, Amin promptly demanded the dismissal of four pro-Taraki ministers from the cabinet, but did not succeed in preventing a showdown. This occurred on 14 September, three days after Taraki's return, when Amin was summoned to a meeting at the Presidential Palace. He is said to have got in touch with Puzanov, the Soviet Ambassador, who gave him his personal assurance that there was no danger and urged him to come to an accommodation with Taraki. When Amin arrived at the Palace, however, he was ambushed and a gun battle broke out. Amin's bodyguard was killed, but Amin survived and promptly mobilised a force with which he invested the Palace. It remains uncertain whether Taraki was killed on the spot, or whether he was wounded and died later, or whether Amin captured him and subsequently had him killed. A circumstantial account[5] of his murder later appeared, which gives some credibility to the third alternative. For public consumption, it was announced on 16 September that he had asked to be relieved of his post for medical reasons and that Amin had taken over as General Secretary of the PDPA. The following day, Amin was declared President. On 10 October, it was announced that Taraki had 'died of his illness'. The Soviets were thus left with the worst of all possible worlds. They were still stuck with Amin, who was now completely in charge and who had good reason to believe that they had been implicated in the attempt on his life. Nevertheless, there could still be no question of an abandonment of Afghanistan, while, much as he may have feared it, Amin for his part was unable to dispense with Soviet support. Civilities were preserved in public, but in private there was total estrangement. Amin demanded, and eventually received, the withdrawal of Puzanov, while the Russians continued to search for means of getting rid of him.

During the remainder of 1979, the situation continued to deteriorate. Assassination squads began to appear in the capital and took a toll of leading Khalqis. In October, an infantry division mutinied on the outskirts of Kabul and was only subdued with difficulty. A campaign was launched the same month, with extensive

Soviet participation, to regain control of an area along the Pakistan frontier in Paktya Province. Many insurgents were killed, but there were also considerable Afghan and Russian casualties, and much equipment was lost. Moreover, when the government forces withdrew, the guerrillas simply returned to their former haunts. Little lasting impact was made and the insurgency continued to spread.

Meanwhile, the Russians considered their options. In October, General Pavlovsky returned to Moscow to report. The most straightforward option would have been another attempt to dispose of Amin, although now with the disadvantage that, without intervention from outside, it would not be easy to ensure that a more moderate successor would replace him. Nevertheless, there is some evidence[6] that one, or possibly two, such attempts were made in the course of December, but that they again failed. Amin may have been slightly wounded and his nephew, Asadullah Amin, whom he had appointed chief of his secret police (now renamed the KAM, the Workers' Intelligence Agency), may have been wounded more severely. Increasingly shocked at the revelation that the Russians were out to remove him from the scene, Amin tried to mend fences elsewhere. He soft-pedalled the Pushtoonistan issue and made increasingly desperate attempts to open a dialogue with the Pakistanis. Internally, he cut back on purges, proposed a new constitution, tried to conciliate the mullahs, offered an amnesty to refugees, released some prisoners and muted hostility to the USA. But his efforts cut little ice with his fellow Afghans and the Pakistanis were in no hurry to respond. There was a bitter reaction when he drew up in November a list, widely believed to have contained some 12,000 names, of people who had died in prison since the Saur revolution. In December, the better to defend himself, he removed his headquarters to Darulaman and took up residence in the palace originally built by Amanullah.

The evidence suggests that from September onwards, the Russians started to make the deployments necessary in order to be able to invade. It may be that they felt it advisable from the outset to commit sufficient numbers of troops to ensure the security of the major towns and supply routes. But it is also possible that they wished to avoid an all-out invasion and hoped to have to do no more than execute a *coup de main* in Kabul, topple Amin and replace him with Babrak Karmal. However, if there was, in this sense, a 'Plan A' and a 'Plan B', it seems that they reached the conclusion that an airborne assault on Kabul alone would not be enough and that a land invasion would also be necessary. By early December, the Soviet Politburo had taken the decision to invade and, despite public disavowals of a military presence in Afghanistan, they quietly positioned a battalion of infantry at Kabul airport and three battalions and an armoured unit at the air base at Bagram. Further units in the Turkestan and Central Asian Military Districts were brought up to strength through the recall of reservists and moved towards the Afghan frontier. By the middle of the month, the Americans had deduced from intelligence sources that Soviet troops were about to enter Afghanistan and were giving public briefings to that effect. Late on 24 December, units of the 105th Guards Airborne Division started to land at Kabul airport, employing a round-the-clock shuttle of AN–22 and AN–24 transport aircraft. By late on the 27th, they had built up a force strong enough to attack the city. Meanwhile, Soviet advisors had managed to disable some of the Afghan units in or near the capital by locking up their officers, removing tank batteries for 'maintenance' and replacing live ammunition with blanks for 'training exercises'. Late on the 27th, part of the Russian force took the central part of the city and the main ministries, while a Spetsnaz unit headed for Darulaman. Sometime in the night, in the face of strong resistance, the palace was assaulted and Amin was killed. The next morning, two Soviet motorised divisions crossed the Amu Darya and headed south, followed later by two more. Part of the force took the Soviet-built road over the Salang Pass, which had earlier been secured by units from Bagram, while the remainder crossed the frontier further west and headed for Herat, Farah and Kandahar. Within a few days, 50,000 troops and 1000 armoured vehicles were occupying the main population centres of the country. Within a few weeks, three further divisions were committed and total numbers grew to some 85,000.

A somewhat bizarre story exists about the events on the 27th[7]. It is that Amin and his family became unconscious after eating lunch prepared by their Russian cooks. The idea apparently was to remove him into Russian medical custody while the coup took place and then, confronting him with a *fait accompli*, give him the alternatives of exile or service under Karmal. However, he recovered consciousness before he could be moved, and the plan collapsed. A Soviet general, Victor Paputin, who appeared in Kabul at the end of November, is thought by some to have been the man responsible for this stratagem. He was reported to have died on 28 December, and speculation has it that he committed suicide over his failure to carry it through, which left the killing of Amin as the only remaining option. Another, again somewhat incredible, story is that until the very end, Amin did not believe that it was Soviet troops who were attacking him.

To retain the least shred of legitimacy for their invasion, the Soviet government would have had to show that they had responded to a genuine request from a duly constituted Afghan authority. Unfortunately for them, the best they could produce were explanations that were both implausible and mutually contradictory[8]. One

147

was that they had had a request from Karmal, who, they alleged, had earlier taken over the government and had broadcast on Radio Kabul on the night of the attack, announcing Amin's overthrow and his own appointment as president. This explanation, however, did not dispose of the objection that it was Amin, and not Karmal, who was in charge up to and including the 27th. Moreover, it soon became clear that although the broadcast was on the Radio Kabul frequency, it came not from Kabul, but from Termez in the Soviet Union. Karmal himself was not seen in Kabul before 1 January, having, it is said, been flown into Bagram and driven to the capital in a Soviet tank. A contradictory story was that it was Amin himself who requested Soviet military assistance. However, he was on record as having said on several occasions in 1979 that he had no need of Soviet troops. Also the invasion had already started by the dates initially given by the Russians for the requests – 26 December for that by Amin and 27 December for that by Karmal. Moreover, if they were responding to a request from Amin, why should they have killed him? Either way, they failed totally to conceal the truth, which was that they had unilaterally sent troops into an independent, non-aligned, Islamic country, killed its President and installed a puppet regime. Far from stabilising the situation, they were now even deeper in the mire.

Portrait of Alexander the Great on a silver tetradrachm of his general Lysimachus. c285 BC.

Graeco-Bactrian silver tetradrachm of Demetrius I. Heracles on reverse. 200-190 BC.

Indo-Greek silver tetradrachm of Menander I. Athena on reverse. 155-130 BC.

Kushan gold stater of Kanishka I. Mithras on reverse. 100-126 AD.

Gold dinar of Mahmud of Ghazni. 1011 AD.

Plate 1 Coinage

Plate 2 Medallion from Kapisa

Plate 3 Head of the Buddha from Hadda

Plate 4 The Great Buddha at Bamian

Plate 5 Nuristani Ancestor Figure

Plate 6 Shahr-i-Golgola, 'City of Sighs'

Plate 7 Ruins of a Sistan Fortress

Plate 8 The Gazargah, Herat

Plate 9 Minaret at Herat

درختهای بینا... عم هست که دا کرد حوض تمام سبزه زار

بانی عین باغ همین است در وقت زرد شدن نی نجها بسیار

Plate 10 Babur in his Garden

Plate 11 The Battle of Panipat

Plate 12 Amir Dost Mohammed

Plate 13 Shah Shuja

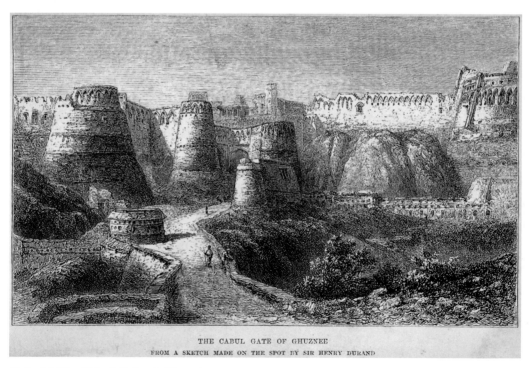

THE CABUL GATE OF GHUZNEE
FROM A SKETCH MADE ON THE SPOT BY SIR HENRY DURAND

Plate 14 The Kabul Gate at Ghazni

VIEW OF CABOOL, FROM THE EAST.

Plate 15 Kabul in 1842

BELOOCHEES PROFESSIONALLY EMPLOYED.

Plate 16 'Baloochees professionally employed'. Afghan tribesmen, as perceived by the British in the 1830s

"SAVE ME FROM MY FRIENDS!"

"IF AT THIS MOMENT IT HAS BEEN DECIDED TO INVADE THE AMEER'S TERRITORY, WE ARE ACTING IN PURSUANCE OF A POLICY WHICH IN ITS INTENTION HAS BEEN UNIFORMLY *FRIENDLY* TO AFGHANISTAN."—*Times*, Nov. 21.

Plate 17 Punch's Comment on Amir Sher Ali's predicament

Plate 18 Amir Abdur Rahman

Plate 19 Amir Habibullah during his visit to India

Plate 20 Amir Amanullah

Plate 21 Queen Soraya

Plate 22 The Bacha-i-Saqao (in white) and followers

Plate 23 The Musahiban Brothers. From left to right:
Mohammed Aziz, Shah Mahmud, Nadir Shah, Shah Wali,
Hashim Khan

Plate 24 King Zahir

Plate 25 President Daoud

Plate 26 President Nur Mohammed Taraki

Plate 27 President Babrak Karmal

Plate 28 President Hafizullah Amin

Plate 29 President Najibullah

Plate 30 Ahmed Shah Mahsood

Plate 31 Gulbuddin Hekmatyar

Plate 32 The Mujahidin

Plate 33 The Taliban at Charasyab

Plate 34 The Execution of Najibullah

Plate 35 The Taliban Destroy Cans of Beer

Plate 36 The Burqa

Plate 37 Harvesting the Poppy Crop

CHAPTER FIFTEEN

Occupation and Resistance

It is unlikely that the Soviet leadership foresaw the extent of the international opprobrium that their invasion of Afghanistan would attract. Equally, however, it is unlikely that, had they foreseen it, they would have acted differently. To the extent that they weighed the international consequences of their action, they were no doubt encouraged by the spectacle of the United States' preoccupation with Iran, where some fifty of its diplomats had been held hostage since early November. They saw the Carter administration as weak and, after the Vietnam experience, reluctant to become involved in the Third World. As seen from the Kremlin, moreover, there were few damaging sanctions that the Americans could apply, even if they were so minded. They might delay the ratification of the Salt II arms limitation treaty, but it seemed as if the US Senate would delay that anyway. As for the rest of the world, the Russians may have been prepared for criticism, but were equally prepared to shrug it off. They hoped to be able to mute it by finessing the transition from Amin to Karmal without it appearing that they were directly responsible, and they expected to be able to withdraw their 'limited military contingent' before many weeks were out. If there were an international outcry, therefore, they did not see it lasting long.

In trying to explain the reasons for the invasion, the Russians resorted to crude, unsubstantiated allegations. Amin, they alleged, was a 'US spy', and their action was taken in response to 'external aggression and interference'. It is true that Pakistan had by the end of 1979 given asylum to some 80,000 Afghan refugees and that, as we have seen, resistance groups had been formed and were mounting small-scale incursions into Afghanistan. There may have been a few training camps in the Frontier area and some arms may have already arrived from China. But there were also groups operating in Nuristan, Badakhshan, the Hazarajat and elsewhere which had no contact at all with the outside world. Overall, foreign involvement was at that stage minimal and the Russians' allegations were – and were seen to be – an attempt to construct an alibi and to divert attention from the roots of the problem, which were overwhelmingly bilateral or internal. Not surprisingly, the Russians were unable to provide credible evidence to substantiate their charges.

The Americans, for their part, denounced the invasion as a 'threat to peace' and President Carter promised that the USSR would not be allowed to carry through its action 'with impunity'. On 28 December, Carter exchanged messages with Brezhnev and subsequently characterised the latter's response as 'completely inadequate and completely misleading'. As a bitter war of words developed, the Carter administration (who, despite the evidence of Russian preparations to move in troops, had not done any contingency planning) cast around for measures to take. In addition to delaying the Salt II treaty, they put together several other sanctions, the most significant of which were the cancellation of a contract to supply the USSR with seventeen million tons of grain intended for cattle-feed, a ban on contracts involving high technology transfers and a curtailment of Russian fishing in American waters. On balance, these measures probably hurt the Americans more than they did the Russians. American farmers suffered and the United States' reputation as a reliable trading partner incurred lasting damage. Other countries, notably the Argentine, stepped in to replace the American grain at lower prices, while European and other companies proceeded to sell the technology which their American counterparts were now debarred from supplying. The United States also decided to boycott the 1980 Moscow Olympics, and attracted support to the extent that their universality was destroyed. Among others, three countries who had previously been major medal winners, the USA, West Germany and Japan, absented themselves. Nevertheless, significantly more countries participated than stayed away.

The Soviet intervention also triggered controversy about its motivation. The Carter administration, with its Cold War presuppositions uppermost, nailed its colours to the mast of the 'strategic' theory. According to this, the move was designed to put the USSR within striking distance of the Persian Gulf oil fields and warm water ports, and should therefore be seen as a further step in the progress of Russian expansionism that had earlier brought them to the Amu Darya. It was perhaps inevitable that President Zia of Pakistan should have exploited this theory for all it was worth. In response, President Carter enunciated the 'Carter Doctrine', a declaration that the United

States had vital interests in the Persian Gulf and that any 'assault' on that region would be repelled, if necessary by military action. To back this up, the administration set about establishing a 'rapid deployment force', capable of operating in the Gulf at short notice. Subsequent events in Afghanistan have meant that the 'strategic' theory has never been put to the test, and it is now of course of no more than academic interest. It is possible that the Russians had at the back of their minds the thought that if they could consolidate communism in Afghanistan, strategic advantages might follow. But there can be little doubt that it was their fears about the imminent collapse of a communist regime, and the consequent threat of chaos, hostility and contamination along their southern frontier, that were the predominant factors in their thinking.

The immediate focus of condemnation was the United Nations. On 14 January, after the USSR had vetoed a non-aligned resolution tabled in the Security Council, the General Assembly passed a resolution[1] condemning the invasion by the overwhelming majority of 104 to 18, with 18 abstentions. Virtually the only satisfaction the USSR could derive from the vote was that India, the high-priest of non-alignment, abstained, rather than join the majority of non-aligned countries voting in favour. Romania, on the other hand, was conspicuously absent. The vote held up, and was even improved upon, in General Assembly votes in subsequent years. By 1987, the voting was 123–19–11. In the Third World, a strong line was taken by the Islamic Conference and the Non-Aligned Movement. A meeting of the foreign ministers of the Islamic Conference, held in Pakistan early in 1980, roundly condemned the invasion, while at a Non-Aligned foreign ministers' meeting in Delhi shortly afterwards, a resolution[2] was passed calling for the withdrawal of foreign troops and respect for Afghanistan's 'independence, sovereignty, territorial integrity and non-aligned status'.

It would be no exaggeration to say that this single act of invasion did more damage to the Soviet Union's reputation than any other event since the revolution of October 1917. The collectivisations, purges and genocide of the 1920s and 1930s, in which perhaps fourteen million people had died, had passed mostly unnoticed by the world at large, as had the creation of 'gulags' and the forced migrations that had occurred both then and later. Attention had traditionally been centred on 'salt-water' colonialism, and the vast territories seized by the armies of the Tsars and retained by the Bolsheviks had escaped attention as areas of colonialist expansion. On the contrary, the USSR had succeeded in establishing solid anti-imperialist credentials. Nor had the non-aligned majority been much exercised by the earlier invasions of Hungary and Czechoslovakia, if only because these countries were European and 'part of the Soviet bloc'. Now, however, the Soviet Union's invasion of one of their number created shock-waves that threatened to undermine the concept of non-alignment itself. It was seen as a recrudescence of colonialism, from which the vast majority of the non-aligned had struggled to free themselves; and the victim was, moreover, a country that had, throughout its history, successfully maintained its independence in the face of colonialist pressures.

Condemnation of the invasion, therefore, was fiercely expressed and well-nigh universal. However it was tempered by the assumption that it was almost bound to be futile. Effective sanctions did not exist, and the Soviet Union showed no sign at all of bowing to the weight of world opinion. For this reason, many governments, particularly in Europe, took the view that the United States had overreacted and that Afghanistan was not important enough to risk damage to the wider international order. For similar reasons, there was little disposition to attempt a negotiated solution. On the initiative of Lord Carrington, the British Foreign Secretary, the European Union did put forward a peace plan by which Soviet withdrawal would have been balanced by an 'Austria-type' arrangement, supported by guarantees, both internal and external, of Afghan neutrality. The mechanism would have been the convening of two conferences, one of potential external guarantors, the other of the internal parties. The initiative predictably foundered of the rocks of the Soviet Union's insistence that it was not interested in a settlement, other than one that would guarantee the permanence of the Karmal regime. So far as the outside world was concerned, therefore, the Afghans stood virtually alone. It was accepted that little was likely to happen on the ground during the hard Afghan winter, but the general belief was that as soon as better weather came, the Russian forces would have little difficulty, if not in eliminating all armed opposition, then at least in reducing it to tolerable levels.

As after the Saur revolution, the immediate preoccupation of the new regime was to gain internal acceptance. Karmal started by promising a broadly based government, although in practice the new regime was broadly based only to the extent that it included just three ministers who were not members of the PDPA, together with a few Khalqis who were not closely associated with Amin. *Parcham* was predominant, and intended to remain so. Karmal also promised a 'New Phase' of the Saur Revolution, to include a fresh constitution with provisions for elections and a multi-party system, a review of the land reform programme, an amnesty for returning refugees and the release of political prisoners. The regime claimed that some 8000 prisoners had been released, but it seems that these were mainly

Parchamis and it was clear that a considerable number, perhaps as many as 12–15000, were still held. Meanwhile executions continued and new arrests were made, until before many months were out, Afghan jails were even fuller than they had been under Amin. On 11 January, there were harrowing scenes at Pul-i-Charki, when a crowd of Afghans who had gathered to receive members of their families who were to be released defied Soviet guards and invaded the prison when only 120 prisoners emerged. For many, this was the end of any hope of seeing their relatives alive.

Karmal also tried to placate religious opinion by 'guaranteeing' freedom of religion and by establishing new Islamic institutions to give direction to national affairs, and to appease opinion more generally by restoring the old black, red and green national flag. This move provoked strong *Khalq* opposition and it was noteworthy that at the April military parade celebrating the Saur revolution, many tanks continued to display the red flag. He also tried to broaden support by creating Soviet-style mass organisations and, at the end of 1980, he formed a National Patriotic Front, later to be the National Fatherland Front, in an effort to rally all shades of opinion. Behind the facade, however, the reality was that the new regime was firmly in the hands of its Soviet masters. Many more Russian 'advisers' were placed in the ministries and the KhAD (Government Intelligence Agency), which had replaced Amin's KAM, and it soon became evident that it was they who were taking all the key decisions. Safronchuk, still in the Soviet embassy, kept a firm grip on the country's external relations. The old rivalry between *Khalq* and *Parcham* also soon re-emerged and the two factions again became engaged in bitter in-fighting. Power struggles within the cabinet and the armed forces were to be a constant feature of the regime and gravely weakened its ability to win support. As disaffection continued to spread, trade, industry, agriculture and the educational system all began to collapse. Those parts of the country still under government control became almost wholly dependent on the Soviet Union for such basic necessities as food and fuel.

The Soviet invasion meanwhile transformed the position of the groups which had begun to organise themselves in Pakistan. From being small and largely unknown they expanded and formed the linkage between much of the internal resistance and the outside world. Other, mainly Shia, groups operated in the centre and east of Afghanistan, and drew support from Iran. These groups had already declared a *jihad* against the Kabul regime, and they now extended this to the infidel invaders. Correspondingly, their combatants came to be generally known as *mujahidin*. As the composition and alignments of these groups constantly fluctuated, there are dangers in being too

153

dogmatic in describing and classifying them. However in 1980 the Pakistanis proceeded to recognise seven main groups based in Peshawar, all with a Sunni religious ideology, four of them 'Islamist' and three 'traditionalist'. The difference between the two groups was broadly that the 'Islamists' were radical in outlook, regarding their struggle as primarily one for a state and society fashioned in accordance with Islamic principles, while the 'traditionalists' saw it primarily as a struggle for national liberation. Thus the latter were willing to see a return of King Zahir, but the former regarded a monarchy as un-Islamic. Of the Islamist groups, Hekmatyar's *Hezb-i-Islami* was the most radical and uncompromising. Hekmatyar himself was a Ghilzai Pushtoon from northern Afghanistan, and his commitment and powers of organisation made him a favourite not only with the Pakistani civilian and military establishments, but also with the CIA. Predominantly Pushtoon in composition, his *Hezb-i-Islami* was the best structured and disciplined of the *mujahidin* groups, was well supported within the refugee groups in Peshawar. It maintained its own schools and training camps, and operated mainly in Nangrahar Province and around Kunduz and Baghlan in the north. However of more concern to Hekmatyar than the resistance were his personal ambitions and his objective of an Islamic revolution, and his quest for domination resulted in more by way of conflict with other *mujahidin* groups than of effective opposition to the Soviet invaders and the Kabul regime. He also became heavily involved in drug manufacture and trafficking. The 1990 set-piece attack on Kabul by his *Lashkar-i-Isar* (Army of Sacrifice) resulted in a complete failure and he was eventually 'seen off' ignominiously by the Taliban. There was also a second *Hezb-i-Islami*, a breakaway from Hekmatyar's, led by a populist mullah by the name of Yunis Khalis. Although coming from the small Khugiani tribe, he attracted support among the *ulama* in the east of the country and more widely among the Ghilzai and around Kandahar. One of his most effective commanders was Abdul Haq, who managed to build up an effective guerrilla movement around and within Kabul, while another was Maulvi Jalaluddin, who operated in Paktya with Pakistani and CIA support.

The third of the 'Islamist' movements, Rabbani's *Jamiat-i-Islami*, was more moderate in its orientation than the two *Hezbs*. It was recruited primarily from among Tajiks and other non-Pushtoons, and its main strength lay in the north-east, although it also had an operational presence around Kandahar. Ahmed Shah Massoud became one of its commanders and, with his colleagues, was allowed more freedom of action by Rabbani than was normal among the resistance groups. This freedom was further enhanced by the distance between many of their areas of operation and the Pakistan frontier, although this often meant that they received less than their share of the weaponry on offer. Their relationship with Iran was, however, good. The leadership of the *Jamiat-i-Islami* combined men of Islamist credentials and commanders of ability, and it developed into the strongest and most effective of the *mujahidin* groups. Finally, of the 'Islamist' groups, the *Ittihad-i-Islami Bara-i Azadi Afghanistan* (Islamic Union for the Freedom of Afghanistan) was formed by Abdal-Rab al-Rasul Sayyaf, like Rabbani a former academic. Sayyaf, who was imprisoned under Daoud and the PDPA and was lucky to escape with his life, was largely supported by Saudi Arabia and was noteworthy for his practice of recruiting Arab volunteers. His group started as a coalition with other parties, but he managed to subvert it to his own ends and struck out independently. However it achieved relatively little in terms of military activity.

Of the 'traditionalist' groups, the *Harakat-i-Inqilab-i-Islami* (Islamic Revolution Movement) was led by a former MP, teacher and mullah, Maulvi Nabi Mohammedi. It was largely Pushtoon in composition, had a strong Sufi following and was active in Logar Province, south of Kabul, as well as in the Helmand Valley, but it came to be regarded as relatively corrupt and ineffective, and it too was involved in the drugs trade. Another of the 'traditionalist' parties, the *Mahaz-i-Melli-i-Islami* (National Islamic Front), was led by Sayyid Ahmad Gailani, who traced his descent from the Prophet and was the spiritual leader of the Qadiriyya Sufi sect. A wealthy businessman and former associate of King Zahir, Gailani was strongly nationalist, hostile to the Islamists and supportive of the King's return. His party's relationship with the Pakistanis was uncomfortable, it was shunned by the Arabs and failed to attract as much support from the Americans as its relatively moderate, pro-Western complexion might have suggested. It had a particularly strong following around Kandahar and among the Turkmen population in the north-west. Finally, of the Sunni parties, the *Jabha-i-Nejat-i-Melli* (National Liberation Front) was led by Sebghatullah Mujadidi, an orthodox Islamic teacher and virtually the only survivor of that family. A man with close links with the pre-revolution elite, Mujadidi derived his influence within the resistance largely on the basis of his personal position. He fled Afghanistan following Daoud's coup and spent some years in Denmark before arriving in Peshawar. The *Jabha* was mostly ineffective as a guerrilla force and it too had an uneasy relationship with the Pakistanis and the Arabs.

Just as Pakistan supported, with varying degrees of commitment, the Sunni parties with bases in Pakistan, so a number of Shia parties, mainly Hazara in complexion, were financed, trained and armed by Iran. Initially they formed the *Shura of the Hazarajat*, in effect an independent government under traditional leadership. However factionalism soon became rife and a number of competing Shia groups, of varying ideological commitment, were formed, of which the most forceful was the *Sazman-i-Nasr-i-Afghanistan* (Victory Organisation of Afghanistan), commonly known as NASR, which took a radical Islamic stance. As a result, the Hazarajat suffered more from civil war than from the effects of the Soviet invasion, and it was not until after the Soviet withdrawal that the Iranians managed to reunite them into the *Hezb-i-Wahdat* (Unity Party).

Other than their hostility to the Russians and the Kabul regime, the resistance groups had little in common, and their record was one of persistent factional dispute. From the beginning, they were as apt to fight each other as to co-operate. Neither their shared Muslim faith nor the concept of *jihad* were strong enough to outweigh their personal, tribal and ethnic antipathies, and all efforts to bring them together into a unified movement failed. In May 1980, a *jirga* was held in Peshawar to try to forge a united front, but this soon fell apart. There was talk from time to time of unity under the leadership of King Zahir, but this again came to nothing. While Gailani and Mujadidi, as well as, probably, a majority of the refugees, were in favour, Hekmatyar and the other Islamists were implacably opposed. Unity was in any case against the policy of the Pakistan government, who had no wish to see a strong, unified, well-armed Afghan organisation established on their soil. As arms from other countries began to flow in, the Pakistan authorities assumed the responsibility for issuing them to the individual groups, under the direction of the Directorate of Inter-Services Intelligence (ISI). This allowed them to keep the groups under control and ration deliveries at what they saw as a prudent level. It also provided opportunities for corruption, a typical arrangement being for a resistance group to sign for more arms than it had received, the balance being sold and the proceeds split between the group and the ISI. In addition to international aid, the production and sale of narcotics became a major source of income for both the *mujahidin* and the Afghan refugee community. Arms captured in Afghanistan were also not just used by the *mujahidin*; often they were sold in the bazaars in Pakistan and then repurchased with American, Saudi or other funds, with suppliers and middlemen taking a profit at each stage of the process. The reputation of the groups in Pakistan accordingly deteriorated over the years, as their infighting continued and they became increasingly involved in gun-running, drug dealing and corruption generally.

This lack of unity meant that, except very rarely, the *mujahidin* were unable to co-ordinate their activities inside Afghanistan or carry out an agreed strategy. However it at least had the corollary that the various groups between them represented a diversity that encompassed virtually the whole Afghan nation. Moreover it was not a decisive impediment to the conduct of the guerrilla war. Given the nature of the terrain in which they fought, their often local sympathies and lack of military sophistication, they could in any case normally only function as small, independent units. Military commanders also emerged inside Afghanistan who were able to fight effectively without much reference to the groups in Pakistan and were prepared to co-operate on the ground. The Pakistanis meanwhile established training camps through which a great many of the *mujahidin* passed before being committed to hostilities.

The strategy that the Russians had hoped to adopt was a simple one. It was to occupy centres of population and key sites, and provide firepower and logistic support for the Afghan army as the latter deployed into the countryside to deal with the resistance. At the same time, they would strengthen the Afghan army, so that, hopefully after a few months, it could be left to control the country itself. It was no part of the initial plan that the Red Army should itself become involved in hostilities and problems arose as soon as this became inescapable. It had been trained for conventional, large-scale, fast-moving operations against China or across the central European plain, and found the mountainous terrain of Afghanistan a totally unfamiliar proposition. It had brought in a disproportionate number of tanks and other heavy equipment, which were unable to deploy effectively in the narrow Afghan valleys. It was able to bring immense firepower to bear, both on the ground and from the air, but the resistance simply left the area under attack, only to return later and resume the harassment and ambushing of Russian units. An early example was an offensive mounted in March 1980 in the Kunar Valley, which relieved the beleaguered garrison at Chaga Serai, but made no lasting impact on the area.

The Afghan army, for its part, was, at least to begin with, largely ineffective. Purges, executions and desertions had reduced its officer corps to perhaps half its original number, while many of the rank and file also deserted, with their arms if possible, as soon as they were given the chance. Sometimes whole units mutinied or went over to the resistance. By the end of 1980 the Afghan army had probably shrunk from a force of around 90,000 men to one of around 30,000, and the reliability of the units that were left was often dubious. Forcible conscription was introduced, but made little impact on the problem. A further embarrassment for the Soviets was that the units they had initially brought in contained numbers of Tajik, Usbek, Kirghiz and Turkmen troops, partly because they were readily available in the region, but partly also in the hope of making a successful 'hearts and minds' impact on the Afghan population. They soon found, however, that these troops were sympathetic to, and fraternising with, the local people, and they were before long replaced with ethnic Russians.

If, therefore, the Soviet Union ever had any illusions about the acceptability of its puppet regime to the Afghan people and its own ability to withdraw its troops within a short time span, these were soon dispelled. Less than two weeks after the invasion, the London *Times* correspondent, Robert Fisk, reported[3] an ambush of a Russian convoy on the main road south of the Salang Pass, and he was also present at a further attack a few days later at Sarobi, on the road between Kabul and Jalalabad. In Kabul and other cities, a remarkable series of protests began during February, when, defying curfews, virtually the whole population gathered on their rooftops at nightfall and chanted the Muslim call to prayer, *Allah-o-Akbar* (God is Great). *Shab-namah* were circulated and processions and demonstrations held. On 22 February, at least 300 civilians were killed during a strike and demonstrations in Kabul, and calm was not restored until the end of the month. In late April and early May, students and school-children held a series of demonstrations and there were almost daily confrontations with the security forces. Numbers of students, including girl students, were killed, and more were wounded or arrested. Defections of soldiers, government officials, diplomats, pilots and even sports teams, multiplied. Across the country generally, the Russians soon found that their writ ran no further than the principal centres of population, strategic bases and main lines of communication. Even the latter were not safe and all movement had to be in convoys, which were frequently attacked. Most of the country, by some accounts as much as 90 per cent, was outside their control. As refugees fled in increasing numbers to Pakistan and Iran, so the groups based there received fresh inputs of fighting men. By May 1980, there were probably as many as 750,000 refugees in Pakistan and a further 100,000 in Iran. A year later, their numbers had grown to 1.7 million and 400,000 respectively. By 1984, the numbers had grown to 3.5 million and 1.5 million, more than one in three of the total population. Perhaps another 1.5 – 2 million became internal refugees and fled from the countryside to the relative safety of the towns. At the peak of their strength, the *mujahidin* may have been able to muster more than 150,000 combatants, although by no means all would have been in action at any one time.

Much of the reporting of the Afghan struggle was grossly exaggerated. It does not, for example, seem that the Russians ever used chemical weapons, despite American allegations, while *mujahidin* accounts of the fighting inevitably improved considerably in the telling. Nevertheless, even by the standards of this century's guerrilla wars, that waged in Afghanistan during the 1980s was exceptionally vicious. Partly, this was because, except at the outset when a few Western correspondents were in the country, it was conducted well out of the view of the international community. As has been noted, international conflicts are better reported when there is a tolerable hotel within reach. In Afghanistan, only the occasional correspondent managed over the years to make the long and dangerous march to the areas in which the *mujahidin* were fighting. Of the very few international organisation on the ground, *Medecins sans Frontières* did report[4] something of what was going on, but was concerned not to jeopardise its limited ability to help the victims of the war. Several of the hospitals it was manning in the interior were deliberately bombed by the Russians. In most guerrilla wars, the strategy of the occupying power has been to separate the guerrillas from the people of the countryside, so that they are deprived of food, shelter and information. The normal means of achieving this, particularly under the glare of publicity, has been to move the civilian population into 'protected villages', guarded by troops or militias, so keeping them apart from the insurgents. A hard war is then fought against the latter, while a 'hearts and minds' operation is aimed at those under protection, with the aim of winning their loyalty to the occupying power. In Afghanistan, the Russians did not begin to attempt this type of strategy. Instead, they simply did their best to depopulate the countryside by attacking civilians in the villages in which they lived. They sent armoured columns, supported by artillery, aircraft and helicopters, into areas where the *mujahidin* might be present. When the population fled into the hills to escape them, they employed a 'scorched earth' policy, destroying buildings, animals, crops and irrigation systems, and killed anyone who had been left behind. When they departed, they left booby traps behind them. Sometimes they simply carpet bombed villages and valleys.

Beginning in the summer of 1980, as they realised that they were in for a long haul, the Russians regrouped their forces and refined their strategy. They repatriated many of their tanks and heavy equipment, and made a greatly increased use of helicopters, both for ground attack and to transport troops. Command was devolved and tactics made more flexible. Major sweeps were preceded by air bombardment, and units were landed by helicopter in the rear of *mujahidin* groups to cut off their retreat while a frontal assault was made. In response to helicopter attacks, the *mujahidin* took to moving by night, and continued to disappear as attacks took place, returning after the Russian and Afghan forces had left. A particular focus was the Panjshir valley, where Massoud continued to campaign and which

159

was strategically placed near the road north from Kabul to the Salang Pass. During the years of Soviet occupation, Massoud acquired an international reputation as an outstanding guerrilla leader. His intelligence was good, his campaigning effective and his flair for public relations second to none. Over the years, except when he had negotiated a temporary truce, the Russians mounted a succession of major assaults into the valley, employing heavy air strikes as well as several thousand troops. Casualties on both sides were invariably high. Eventually the valley was cleared, both of the *mujahidin* and of civilians, and Massoud transferred his operations to the north of the Hindu Kush, where he co-ordinated resistance through the *Shura-i-Nawaz* (Council of the North). The Russians also tried, with limited success, to interdict the roads and trails leading into the country by strewing them with 'butterfly-bombs', anti-personnel mines dropped from aircraft or helicopters. These were often camouflaged as stones or children's toys, and were designed to maim rather than kill. Nothing was more disabling to a guerrilla group than to have to cope with a wounded comrade who, far from medical assistance, was likely to die in any case. The mines were also useful in destroying livestock.

Few nations in the world would have withstood this type of terror, but Afghanistan was an exception. The *mujahidin* continued to operate, despite high casualties, while the people went into exile if they could not stay where they were. In this they were following basic Islamic precepts, of *jihad* and *hijra*: it was as legitimate to uphold the faith by leaving an area controlled by *kafirs* as it was to fight them. Meanwhile a steady toll was taken of Soviet troops and equipment. The few outside observers who travelled in Afghanistan found the Afghan highways strewn with the wrecks of Soviet tanks and vehicles. Until late in the war, the *mujahidin* were rarely able to assault strongholds or fixed positions, and suffered heavy casualties before they learnt their lesson. While the towns were increasingly fortified, they were however able to penetrate them with small groups and were later able to bombard them with rockets. In Kabul, there were continuing assassinations and attacks on key targets, organised mainly by Khalis' *Hezb-i-Islami*. Fighting also broke out from time to time in Herat, Kandahar and other nominally government-held towns.

Faced with a continuing stalemate, the question arises why the Soviet Union did not escalate the war. The numbers of troops they employed varied between about 90,000 and 115,000, far too few to seal the frontiers and root out the *mujahidin*. The answer seems to be that they came to realise that even massive troop reinforcements would be unlikely to achieve a decisive victory, and could only hope that slow attrition would eventually win the day. In any case, problems of communications, maintenance and supply were such that it would have been an immense task to maintain higher force levels in this remote and difficult country. Additionally, there was the question of cost. Soviet expenditure on the war, although not accurately known, has been estimated at between $7 and $12 billion a year over the nine years of occupation. Given its other defence commitments and its general financial and economic constraints, it is doubtful if the Soviet government could have tolerated a much higher figure. To strengthen their communications, the Russians built a permanent road/rail bridge across the Amu Darya, and undertook a variety of other logistic improvements, designed to support the long haul. The Kabul regime also took measures to enlarge its para-military forces and part-time militias, while the KhAD was expanded, under the command of a Parchami doctor and activist, Mohammed Najibullah. Organised on the lines of the KGB, it became expert in infiltrating *mujahidin* groups and in suborning tribes and individuals, numbers of whom formed pro-government militias.

The *mujahidin*, meanwhile, acquired more and better arms, and gradually became more formidable opponents. Whereas, at the beginning, they were armed with obsolete weapons, notably the British .303 rifle and even flintlocks and hunting rifles, soon they were being equipped not only with arms brought across by deserters or captured in battle, but with weapons supplied by the outside world. Until 1986, the Americans were careful not to supply their own arms, but bought Soviet-made weapons from Egypt, Israel and elsewhere, and sent them in through Pakistan. Many were 'lost' en route, but enough got through to make a significant, and growing, difference. The Chinese also supplied arms, while other countries, notably Saudi Arabia and the Gulf states, contributed financially. The Pakistan government, for its part, found itself in an increasingly uneasy position as the war developed. President Zia came under intense verbal and diplomatic pressure from the Russians, and there were repeated violations of Pakistani airspace. The presence of so many refugees, with the accompanying pressures on land, employment and services, also created considerable difficulties, even though tempered by the principle of *melmastia*. In 1980, the Carter government offered $400 million worth of military and economic aid, but, in an astute move, Zia dismissed this amount as 'peanuts'. He had his reward in 1981, after President Reagan came to power, when he was offered, and accepted, a $3.2 billion deal.

On the Russian side, there were increasingly difficult problems of morale. From the beginning, it was a shock for the Red Army to find that, far from being in Afghanistan to help a fellow communist country resist external aggression, it was deployed against patriots who were defending their freedom against the Red Army itself. Quite apart from the battle casualties – by the end of 1983 some 6,000 dead and more than 10,000 wounded – standards of hygiene and medical care were so low that casualties from such complaints as heat stroke, hepatitis, typhus, dysentery, meningitis and malaria were appalling, and the Russians were hard put to it to keep their units up to strength. Drug and alcohol abuse also became serious problems. The Afghan army, on the other hand, gave a better account of itself as the war progressed. One factor was that, whereas the *mujahidin* had welcomed deserters in the early stages, they were later more inclined to kill any Afghan soldiers who might come across. This stiffened considerably the Afghan army's willingness to fight.

But for a lack of awareness in the Soviet Union of what was happening, it is doubtful if the government could have sustained the war as long as it did. By and large, a news blackout was maintained, the numbers of Soviet killed and wounded were kept secret and wounded soldiers were sent to remote locations for treatment. By 1984, however, increasing numbers of returned or demobilised 'Afghantsi' were bringing back accounts of the war, and the fact of considerable numbers of Soviet casualties could no longer be concealed. Gradually the nation began to realise that Afghanistan was presenting it with an intractable problem. At the end of 1984, an official admission appeared in *Izvestia* that 'serious casualties' were being incurred. None of this influenced the succession of old men, Brezhnev, Andropov and Chernenko, who between them held the reins of leadership in the early 1980s. In March 1985, however, a new direction was given to the war, when Chernenko was succeeded by Mikhail Gorbachev. The Soviet Union was now, for the first time, to have a realistic policy for dealing with what he was to describe[5] in February 1986 as a 'bleeding wound'.

CHAPTER SIXTEEN

Humiliation and Withdrawal

While Gorbachev has been given much credit for accepting the inevitable and ending the Soviet Union's disastrous involvement in Afghanistan, it is less often remembered that he started by giving the military a year in which to see whether they could get on top of the problem. He was probably clear from the outset that a withdrawal was inevitable, not just because the war could not be won, but also because its continuance would impede the wider international initiatives he saw as indispensable, notably East-West détente and a rapprochement with China. However, in Kremlin terms he was absurdly young, he had been a member of the Politburo for barely five years and his election as General Secretary of the CPSU had been strongly contested. He also had a full and pressing agenda for the reform and modernisation of the Soviet Union. It is unlikely, therefore, that he could have afforded at that stage to challenge the military and security establishments whose prestige was very much at stake in Afghanistan. A year later, with his personal position more firmly established, the task would be a great deal easier.

1985 was, accordingly, a year in which the fighting was particularly intense and casualties, both civilian and military, high. During it, the Soviet and Afghan forces made fresh efforts to prevent arms and supplies from reaching the *mujahidin* from Pakistan and Iran. In May and June they launched major assaults in the Kunar valley, apparently using napalm in the process, but ended by having to withdraw. They also mounted several drives into the Logar valley and there was fierce fighting in Paktya, with the *mujahidin* unable to take the fortress town of Khost, but the Russians unable to relieve it. Increased and more enterprising use was made of helicopters and spetsnaz units, and there were frequent violations of Pakistan air space and raids across the border. The outcome, however, was little different from that of previous years. Both the *mujahidin* and the Russian and Afghan forces took casualties, but the latter were still unable to interdict the *mujahidin* supply routes or dominate the countryside. In the Panjshir valley, they suffered serious setbacks, and convoys over the Salang continued to be ambushed. In June, Massoud's forces attacked and took a strongly held government post at Pechgur, capturing a senior Afghan army delegation in the process. The *mujahidin* also made successful attacks on the air bases at Bagram, Kandahar and Shindand, while the Russian/Afghan grip on the larger towns such as Herat, Kandahar and Ghazni was intermittent and insecure. Kabul itself continued to be infiltrated and bombarded by rockets.

There was also increasing international concern over human rights violations in Afghanistan. In March 1985, a report prepared for the UN Human Rights Commission[1] gave an account of 'serious and widespread' abuses. 'Foreign troops' had been found to be adopting a deliberate policy of bombing villages, massacring civilians and executing captured guerrillas, while some 50,000 political prisoners were being held by the Afghan government. A later report concluded that one hundred villages had been bombed over a period of nine months, with 10,000 – 12,000 civilian casualties. Torture had been 'routinely used' and booby traps disguised as toys scattered around the countryside. The *mujahidin* were judged to command the support of the 'vast majority' of the nation.

Against this background, there was now a shift in United States policy. Hitherto, the Americans had provided arms to the *mujahidin* judiciously and discreetly. President Reagan's aim seems to have been to keep the Russian wound bleeding, rather than be a party to a *mujahidin* victory. The Americans had considerable reservations over Zia-ul-Haq's dictatorship, with its clandestine nuclear programme, its tolerance of drug smuggling and policy of giving preference to the more extreme of the Afghan resistance groups. The corruption and divisions among these groups were also serious disincentives to a policy of all-out support, while the risk of Soviet reprisals had to be borne in mind, if Pakistan were seen to be playing too large a part in arming and supporting the resistance. To hand over sophisticated weapons, such as surface-to-air missiles, with a corresponding loss of control over their eventual destination, was also seen as unwise and even dangerous.

In 1984, however, the Americans gave their first overt financial assistance – $50 million – to the *mujahidin*, and they increased this substantially in 1985, with a tranche of $250 million, dispensed from the CIA budget. Considerable Saudi, Chinese and other aid also continued to arrive. In April 1985, President Reagan issued a 'directive'[2] to the US administration, ordering it to use 'all available means' to compel a Soviet withdrawal. In September, when an Afghan Airlines aircraft was brought down by a surface-to-air missile, it was claimed in Kabul that this was an American-made Stinger, but it is more likely that it was a SAM–7 of Russian origin, as it does not in fact seem that Stingers reached the *mujahidin* until the following year. When they did arrive, together with Blowpipe missiles from the UK, they started to make a significant difference. Russian and Afghan aircraft and helicopters became much more vulnerable, and losses began to mount. They were forced to curtail air support and fly higher, and air strikes became less accurate and effective.

While giving the military its final chance to bring the war to a conclusion, Gorbachev also applied pressure on the Afghan government to put its affairs in order and reconcile itself to the nation. In April 1985 Karmal held a *loya jirga* in Kabul, allegedly attended by some 1800 representatives from all the provinces. However the true numbers attending seem to have been a mere six hundred and it failed to carry conviction as a genuinely representative body. This was followed by elections in August 1985, but these were similarly dismissed as a sham, it being clear that conditions in most of the country were such that any credible electoral process was out of the question. A further, rather larger 'High Jirga of the Frontier Tribes' was held in September, but with little more success, while later in the year, the government was expanded and non-communists brought in. In 1986, yet more initiatives were launched. A 'National Reconciliation Commission' was set up early in the year to draft a new constitution, while several 'workers organisations' were founded. In Soviet judgement, however, these various attempts at reconciliation were simply not adequate. From the outset, they had had doubts about Karmal, and they now decided to dispose of him and replace him by Mohammed Najibullah. Although a Pushtoon, the latter was one of the founders of *Parcham* and had been imprisoned by King Zahir and by Daoud. In his student days he had been given the nickname of the 'Ox', reflecting partly his muscular physique and partly his somewhat stolid cast of mind. He had been sent as Ambassador to Iran at the same time as Karmal had been exiled to Prague, and had similarly taken refuge in the USSR, returning to Kabul shortly after Amin's coup. He had shown himself stoutly pro-Soviet and had established a reputation as a tough and effective chief of KhAD. For the whole of April, Karmal was in the Soviet Union, ostensibly for 'medical check-ups', but doubtless being pressured into accepting a demotion. In May, Najibullah took over as General Secretary of the PDPA and immediately diluted Karmal's authority by proclaiming a 'collective leadership', consisting of himself, Karmal as President and Sultan Ali Keshtmand, another veteran Parchami, as Prime Minister. In November, Karmal was finally eased out and exiled to the Soviet Union, and was replaced as President by a relative nonentity, Mohammed Chamkani. In practice, Najibullah was effectively in charge. There was talk of Karmal being an alcoholic or even suffering from cancer. But the reasons for his departure were clearly political: an altogether stronger and more decisive character was needed if the PDPA was to survive a Soviet departure. Support for him nevertheless lingered within the PDPA, even after Najibullah was elected President by a further *loya jirga* in November 1987. At this *jirga*, yet another a new constitution was promulgated, providing, in theory, for a multi-party democracy somewhat on the lines of that produced in 1964. Elections were held in April 1988, but were again limited to areas under government control. In practice, Najibullah exercised a tight control of executive power.

On the *mujahidin* side, fresh efforts were made in 1985 to establish unity. A 'United Military Command' was formed, but soon fell apart, as did an association of the seven main resistance groups in Peshawar, known as the 'Islamic Unity of Afghanistan'. A persistent disinclination on the part of all concerned to subordinate individual interests was compounded by KhAD efforts, which met with some success, in sowing dissension and organising assassinations of key individuals. A particular problem for the groups was the attitude of Gulbuddin Hekmatyar, who set his face against all attempts at compromise, while continuing to enjoy the backing of the Pakistan government. Efforts were also made in 1985 to unite the Shia groups supported by Iran, among whom in-fighting had been particularly intense.

In 1986 and 1987, bitter fighting continued, but the pattern of the war remained largely unchanged. The Russians and Afghans made increasing use of bribes and other pressures in order to gain tribal support, and mounted fierce attacks in areas where these failed. Helped by improved intelligence and tactics, they often had the better of the fighting during specific operations. In April 1986, for example, the *mujahidin* suffered heavy casualties during an all-out Soviet/Afghan offensive in Paktya, when the frontier base at Zhawar was captured. Scorched earth policies and the depopulation of the countryside also made it progressively more difficult for the *mujahidin* to sustain themselves. But their supply lines remained open, they still got the better of many encounters, and nothing could prevent their returning to areas in contention, once government forces had withdrawn. Fighting continued in and around Herat and Kandahar, and Kabul was again bombarded by rockets. Whereas it could be said that in 1983 and 1984 the tide was beginning to turn against the

166

mujahidin, they were now showing that they could survive and all indications were pointing to a continuing stalemate.

Since 1982, when Diego Cordovez of Ecuador was appointed the UN Secretary General's Personal Representative for Afghanistan, negotiations had been under way for a resolution of the Afghan issue. A succession of 'proximity talks' between the Afghan and Pakistani governments had taken place in Geneva, so called because the Pakistan government had refused to recognise the Afghan regime and so delegations from the two sides sat in separate rooms, with Cordovez and his staff shuttling between them. In close proximity, too, were representatives of the Soviet and US governments, whose support for, and guarantees of, a settlement would necessarily be crucial. The Iranian government refused to take part in the talks, but kept itself closely informed. The *mujahidin* were not invited and reserved their right to ignore any agreement reached. In between the Geneva sessions, Cordovez shuttled between Moscow, Kabul, Islamabad and Teheran, in efforts to find a basis for taking the process further. There were five main points, or 'instruments', on which agreement was needed, non-interference and non-intervention in Afghan internal affairs, international guarantees for the settlement reached, the return of refugees, the withdrawal of Soviet troops and the formation of a 'friendly transitional government'. Until 1985, very little agreement was reached on any of these points, but at the proximity talks held in June of that year, some agreement was reached on non-intervention; and at the end of the year the United States agreed in principle to act as a guarantor. But the talks remained deadlocked on the two major issues, the withdrawal of Soviet troops and continuing support for the Afghan government on the one hand and the *mujahidin* on the other. There was also much disquiet over the prospect that agreement might not be reached over the composition of a coalition Afghan government, to take over after a Soviet withdrawal. The Soviet government was nervous about the survivability of the Najibullah regime, the Pakistanis that in the absence of a coalition, the civil war would be likely to continue and the refugees remain on Pakistani soil.

In 1986, however, as the year given by Gorbachev to his military expired, the log-jam started to move. Already, in November 1985, at a summit meeting with President Reagan at Geneva, he had conveyed the impression that he was seriously looking for a way out. In July 1986, he announced, as a token of good faith, the withdrawal of 8,000 troops, which took place in October of that year. He described this as 'intended to give further impetus to political development' and undertook that all troops would be withdrawn as soon as a satisfactory settlement had been reached. While there was no little scepticism about the substance of the withdrawal, its significance as a gesture was real. At the end of the year, Gorbachev summoned Najibullah to Moscow and informed him that a withdrawal was now settled policy. Thereafter, the main problem was the negotiation of a timetable, the Afghan negotiators beginning by offering four years and the Pakistanis stipulating three to four months. By March of the following year, the Afghans were offering eighteen months, the Pakistanis insisting on no more than seven. The deadlock was to continue until February 1988, when Gorbachev broke it by announcing that all Soviet troops would be withdrawn over a ten month period starting on 15 May of that year, subject to the conclusion of an overall agreement by 15 March. The withdrawal would be 'front loaded', with half the troops being withdrawn by the end of the first three months. This was irrespective of agreement over the composition of a new coalition government in Kabul, which was a 'purely Afghan issue'. Gorbachev was apparently now prepared to gamble on the survival of a PDPA regime, while the Pakistanis, equally recognising the impossibility of organising a PDPA/*mujahidin* coalition, reluctantly agreed to let the point go. This left to be resolved the question of external assistance to the two sides. The Russians having rejected 'negative symmetry' – an undertaking to cease arming the two sides simultaneously, the Americans turned to 'positive symmetry', the concept that they should continue to arm the *mujahidin* so long as the Russians continued to arm the Afghan government. This was tacitly accepted, and the 'Geneva Accords'[3] were finally signed on 14 April 1988.

Promptly on 15 May, the first contingent, of some 12,000 men, left Jalalabad for the Soviet Union. As the withdrawal proceeded, the *mujahidin* were, as usual, at odds about how to respond. Some wished to take revenge by attacking the Russians as they were at their most exposed, others thought it better to allow them a trouble-free departure. To begin with, the latter view prevailed, although a degree of harassment did take place and there was a major incident at Kunduz, where *mujahidin* looted the town shortly after the Soviet troops had left it. In response, a combined Soviet/Afghan force retook the town, with overwhelming air support, and inflicted heavy casualties on the *mujahidin*. Elsewhere, government units abandoned garrisons as the Russians left, concentrating their forces in a relatively few key posts. In reaction to the Kunduz incident, and as the scale of harassment increased, the Soviet withdrawal slowed and stopped, and large supplies of weaponry were brought in to protect their retreat and bolster the government. Among the new weapons were MiG–27 aircraft and SCUD-B surface-to-surface missiles. Gorbachev also sent in the First Deputy Foreign Minister, Yuli Vorontsov, with a remit to negotiate with the *mujahidin* and try to find a basis for a trouble-free withdrawal and a coalition government. He talked to the resistance groups in Islamabad and to Rabbani in Saudi Arabia, as well as to the Shia organisations in Iran and even to King Zahir in Rome. However he failed to persuade the resistance groups to agree either to a cease-fire or to the formation of even an interim government. By the end of the year, the situation in Kabul began to look desperate, as the *mujahidin* repeatedly blocked the road north and supplies of food and fuel for the capital dwindled. In the course of January, a considerable military effort had to be made, with air support, to clear the road and keep it open. The withdrawal nevertheless restarted, and continued up to the target date of 15 February, when the final contingent of Soviet troops crossed the Amu Darya into the Soviet Union. The last man to cross was the Soviet Commander, General Gromov, who, as he departed, asserted to the assembled media that the Red Army had 'fulfilled its international duty to the end'. Commentators likened him to the captain of a sinking ship, the last to leave it as it went down.

The Geneva Accords got the Russians off the hook on which they had impaled themselves, but there was little in them for the Afghans. In the words of one diplomat[4], the withdrawal was the only substantive achievement, 'everything else is just window-dressing'. There was no cease-fire and no undertaking on cutting arms supplies. A final bid by the Soviet Foreign Minister, Edouard Shevernadze, who went to Pakistan a few days before the completion of the withdrawal to try to persuade the resistance groups to participate in a coalition government, met with no more success than previous efforts. Similarly, the 'non-interference' provisions in the Accords, which ran to thirteen detailed and specific articles, and which, if adhered to, would have obliged Pakistan to cease all support for the resistance groups and prevent their operating out of Pakistan, remained a dead letter.

In the nine years that the Soviet occupation lasted, some 15,000 Soviet soldiers and airmen were officially admitted to have died and a further 37,000 wounded[5]. The true numbers were possibly of the order of three times those figures[6]. The cost to the Soviet Union in terms of the expenditure of resources that were badly needed elsewhere was immense, as was the loss of international prestige and reputation to which the invasion gave rise. The Afghan fiasco was also one of the catalysts that led to the break-up of the Soviet Union in the late 1980s and early 1990s. However the cost to Afghanistan itself was relatively much greater. The final civilian death toll was over one million. The extent of the refugee exodus and the massive violations of human rights have already been alluded to, and perceptions of the latter were reinforced by a further UNCHR report[7] in 1986, which spoke of a 'situation approaching genocide'. Lidice- and My Lai-type atrocities were repeated many times over. The whole country also suffered extreme economic disruption. Many if its towns were extensively damaged, while the countryside was polluted by the millions of mines which were estimated to have been sown in it, most of them in unmarked minefields.

The withdrawal left many students of Soviet affairs in a state of shock. As one of them put it[8],

> The well-established axiom that 'the forces of socialism march only in one direction' had convinced nearly all of us who studied the Soviet Union that withdrawal simply wasn't possible – that it would amount to the kind of admission of error that no Soviet leader would make. It would also be an invitation to other countries involuntarily occupied by Soviet forces to begin to hope that perhaps their occupation was not permanent – another reason why withdrawal seemed impossible.

Perhaps understandably, Gorbachev says comparatively little in his *Memoirs*[9] about what he calls the 'hopeless military adventure' in Afghanistan, other than to remark that 'if one recalls how many lives this war cost us, how many young people were crippled for life, and the loss and sufferings of the Afghan people, one can understand the explosion of hope that came from the promise to end this conflict that had brought shame on our nation'. More outspoken was the Soviet dissident, Andrei Sakarov, at the first Congress of Peoples Deputies, held in Moscow in May 1988. In response to allegations that by condemning what had happened in Afghanistan, he had insulted the Soviet army, the nation and the war dead, he replied[10],

> ... the war in Afghanistan was in itself criminal, a criminal adventure taken on, undertaken by who knows who, and who knows bears the responsibility for this enormous crime of our Motherland. This crime cost the lives of about a million Afghans; a war of destruction was waged against an entire people. ... And that is what lies on us as a terrible sin, a terrible reproach. We must cleanse ourselves of this shame that lies on our leadership.

CHAPTER SEVENTEEN

Civil War

I t was widely predicted that the Najibullah regime would collapse in the face of *mujahidin* pressure within a few months, or even weeks, of the completion of the Soviet withdrawal. That it did not do so was due to two main factors, massive Soviet support and the failure of the resistance groups to combine and pursue an effective strategy for its removal.

The departing Soviet forces took with them little more than their vehicles and personal weapons, and the Afghan government acquired the large quantities of arms and equipment that were left behind. Soviet assistance also continued, in the form of financial aid and of military and other supplies, at a level that was reckoned to amount to some $3–$4 billion a year. Much of the financial aid was used by the Afghan Government to continue to buy the support, or at least the quiescence, of tribal and guerrilla leaders. A short while after the withdrawal, substantial deliveries of tanks, artillery, armoured personnel carriers and other weaponry arrived, with the result that the Afghan army probably had more armaments than it could profitably use. The Russians also supplied the government with a stock of SCUD-B missiles, with a range of up to 175 miles, which could be used against *mujahidin* bases and concentrations. These were not particularly accurate, but were a potent terror weapon, as they arrived without warning and could not be intercepted. While Najibullah's regime lacked the protection of Soviet air power, which had been indispensable in covering the withdrawal, its air force was still functional and possessed some two hundred aircraft of various types, as well as helicopters. The army had also to some extent been rebuilt, and numbered some 55,000 men, plus a Presidential Guard of some 10,000 and other units of paramilitary *sarandoy*, security police and assorted party and other militias. Divisions remained within the government, with *Parcham* still opposed to *Khalq*, and *Parcham* itself divided between supporters and opponents of Najibullah. However in the immediate aftermath of the Soviet withdrawal, Najibullah took decisive steps to strengthen his personal position, including the declaration of a state of emergency and the suspension of civil rights. Most of the non-PDPA members of the cabinet were ousted and a new *Parcham*-dominated Supreme Council set up. While the government remained widely unpopular, the more doctrinaire aspects of its policies were dropped and it was able to make much of the argument that the *jihad* was over and that Afghanistan's troubles should be resolved peacefully. For Afghan consumption, Najibullah sought to project himself as a practising Muslim and nationalist, while internationally he tried to present himself as a bulwark against Islamic extremism.

In Peshawar, meanwhile, the performance of the resistance groups was as unimpressive as ever. With the departure of the Russians and in the face of personal and ethnic rivalries, much of the motivation which had kept them together evaporated. A *shura* was called in February 1989 to elect an 'interim government'; but it was blatantly manipulated by the ISI and lavishly bribed with Saudi money, to the extent, it was said, of $26 million in all and $25,000 or more for each delegate. Few of the commanders or tribal leaders in Afghanistan attended, nor was a place found for the Shia groups based in Iran. Mujadidi was, by the narrowest of margins, elected President of an 'Afghan Interim Government' and a 'Cabinet' was formed, with Sayyaf as Prime Minister. However even the Pakistanis withheld recognition, while the American position was that they would only recognise the AIG when it could show that it held significant territory in Afghanistan and enjoyed broad popular support. The next move, therefore, again under the direction of the ISI, was to try to gain territory, but rather than achieve this piecemeal and build on the minor acquisitions, for example at Torkham in the Khyber Pass and at Spin Baldak, which had been made while the Russians were withdrawing, the decision was taken to stake everything on an attack on Jalalabad, which could then act as a credible seat of government. In March, a force of some 15,000 guerrillas attacked the town, but, contrary to all expectations, met stubborn resistance. Part of the problem, yet again, was that the *mujahidin* were not prepared to take prisoners, and this inevitably stiffened the defence. For a while, the town was cut off and had to be supplied by air, but after a few weeks the garrison was reinforced and was able to counterattack, with air support, while the attackers lost whatever cohesion and discipline they had possessed. By mid-May, the assault had patently failed, with

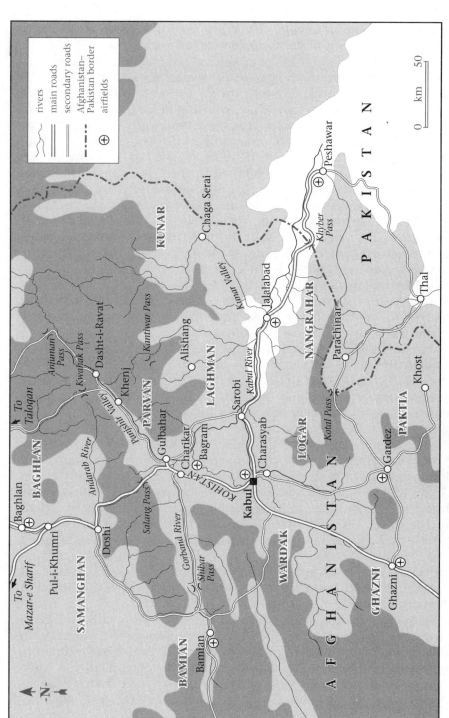

Map 8 The Battlefields in Central and Eastern Afghanistan

perhaps a thousand *mujahidin* killed and three times as many wounded, resulting in considerable loss of face for the ISI and the Peshawar groups, and a major boost for Najibullah and his government. The divisions in the *mujahidin* leadership and its inability to conduct a set piece battle were brutally exposed, while the government forces showed that they could give a good account of themselves without Soviet backing. As a result of the fiasco, the role of the ISI was curtailed by the Pakistan government, but the American response was to appoint a Special Envoy to the Peshawar groups and to resume supplies of arms, which had lapsed at the time of the Soviet departure in the expectation of a quick *mujahidin* victory. A further attempt to take Jalalabad was planned, but was forestalled in July by a sortie by the garrison which succeeded in driving the *mujahidin* out of the area. The latters' credibility was further weakened by a continuance of internal dissension. In July, thirty members of the *Jamiat-i-Islami*, including seven commanders, were ambushed and killed by members of Hekmatyar's *Hezb-i-Islami*, in the course of a 'turf war' over Panjshir. In response, Massoud captured, tried and hanged four of those responsible. The incident then developed into a major feud between the two groups.

In May 1989, encouraged by the successful defence of Jalalabad, Najibullah called a further *loya jirga* and again offered inducements to *mujahidin* commanders to declare a cease-fire in return for arms and subventions and a free hand in their areas. Gradually a pattern emerged, with the *mujahidin* in control of 'liberated' areas, the government still holding out in the main towns and scattered garrisons, and an increasing number of tribal leaders and military warlords colluding with the government or maintaining their independence of both parties. Prominent among them was General Abdul Rashid Dostum, who commanded a well-armed militia in the north of the country. During the year, Kabul came under persistent rocket attack, countered by firings of SCUD-B missiles on *mujahidin* positions. The route north was interrupted, as were flights bringing supplies into Kabul airport, and the population of the capital remained acutely short of food. In the north, Massoud put together a *shura* and a civil administration, with his headquarters at Taloqan in Takhar province.

Towards the end of the year, as the stalemate continued, crisis struck Najibullah. A number of army officers were arrested in December, allegedly for plotting a coup, while fresh dissension arose between the *Khalq* and *Parcham* factions in the government and army. The policies of reconciliation that Najibullah had been trying to pursue were opposed both by rival Parchamis and by the *Khalq* army leadership under General Shah Nawaz Tanai, the Defence Minister. In

March 1990, there was a showdown, when a trial of some of the arrested officers produced evidence of General Tanai's implication. The following day Tanai tried to launch a coup, but was pre-empted by Najibullah, who, with his KhAD experience, was no innocent in these matters. Within a few hours the coup was over and General Tanai fled by helicopter to Pakistan, where, in a bizarre development, he and Hekmatyar teamed up. There were suggestions that the alliance had been formed before the attempted coup, with the intention of forming a *Khalq/Hezb-i-Islami* government, composed principally of Ghilzai Pushtoons[1]. Either way, this alliance between a hard left communist and a hard right Islamist could only be accounted for by unprincipled ambition. It dealt a blow to the concept of *jihad* and it further estranged Hekmatyar from his *mujahidin* allies. A further setback for Najibullah occurred in Herat in April, when 3,000 *mujahidin* who were supposedly surrendering opened fire on the officials sent to receive them, killing the Governor of Herat and several others. It was fortunate for Najibullah that he had taken a late decision not to be present.

During the remainder of 1990, little advantage was gained by either side. In May, Najibullah lifted the state of emergency and called yet another *loya jirga,* at which a multi-party system was endorsed and a (theoretical) welcome given to private enterprise and foreign investment. The PDPA was reformed as the *Hezb-i-Watan* (Homeland Party), communism was further soft-pedalled, and Islam and nationalism again emphasised. While Najibullah achieved little by these gestures, he managed to make some further progress in buying the allegiance, or at least the neutrality, of local *mujahidin* leaders. Increasingly, as movement throughout the country became easier and parts of it began to recover from the effects of the Soviet invasion, so the local warlords received more external aid and developed their own economic activities, often drugs-related. Later in the year, having learnt nothing from the fiasco at Jalalabad, Hekmatyar launched his major attack on Kabul with the *Lashkar-i-Isar*, but was decisively repulsed.

Diplomatic efforts had meanwhile been under way to try to resolve the issues left open by the Geneva Accords. In July 1989, inconclusive talks were held in Stockholm between American and Soviet officials, while the Soviet Foreign Minister, Edouard Shevernadze and the United States Secretary of State, James Baker, later met for talks which continued at intervals throughout 1990. With the Cold War coming to an end, neither power had any continuing strategic interest in Afghanistan, although the Russians remained nervous about its joining Iran as a hotbed of Islamic extremism. Progress was gradually made, until there was some agreement on 'negative symmetry' and what in the jargon became known as the 'interim entity', a coalition government to be formed in Kabul prior to nation-wide elections. The main point still to be resolved was whether, as the Russians wished, Najibullah's regime should act as this 'entity', or whether, as the Americans insisted, he should stand down in the interests of establishing a level playing field. Well into 1991, however, American attention was diverted from Afghanistan by the invasion of Kuwait and the Gulf War, while the Russians were preoccupied first with the break-up of their hegemony in Eastern Europe and then by the strains developing in the Soviet Union itself. During the Gulf war, Hekmatyar and other Islamists sided with the Iraqis, while the traditionalist groups sent a small force of *mujahidin* to fight with the Saudis, a further indication of the rift between the two groupings. In Afghanistan itself, as it became progressively clearer that no winners were in sight, many of those concerned became more ready to talk to each other. Several of the *mujahidin* commanders in the north had begun to hold meetings, and these developed into more formal 'Field Commanders Conferences', in which Massoud's influence became predominant. Following the failure of Hekmatyar's offensive, Massoud went to Pakistan for consultations with the government and the resistance leaders, his first visit to that country for ten years. The outcome was that his forces began to receive more material support and an 'Islamabad Agreement' was reached, providing for closer cooperation between the Peshawar groups and the commanders in Afghanistan. Najibullah also travelled, and in November 1990 met *mujahidin* leaders and King Zahir's representatives in Geneva, while in February 1991 the Russians also started to talk to the *mujahidin*, initially in Pakistan. In May 1991, the Russians and Pakistanis began to confer, while King Zahir broke a long silence and put forward his own peace plan.

Encouraged by these various developments, as well as by the kudos the United Nations had gained as a result of the Gulf War, the Secretary General, Perez de Cuellar, set out in May 1991 what he described as an 'international consensus' for a peaceful settlement in Afghanistan. His remit came from a General Assembly Resolution[2] of November 1989, which required him to 'encourage and facilitate the early realisation of a comprehensive political settlement in Afghanistan'; and in March 1990 he had established an Office in Afghanistan and Pakistan (OSGAP), headed by a UN Under-Secretary, Benon Sevan. The Secretary-General's ideas were familiar enough, and included independence and self-determination, a cease-fire, a cessation of arms supplies and a 'transition mechanism' leading to 'free and fair' elections and a 'broad-based' government. The Kabul government promptly accepted the plan, as did Pakistan and Iran, but the AIG were unable to agree on it. In general, they had little confidence in the UN and were still rankling from their exclusion from the negotiations leading to the Geneva Accords. They were also suspicious about some of the points in the plan. For example, it referred to 'transitional arrangements acceptable to the vast majority of the Afghan people', without suggesting any test of acceptability; and it also talked about 'elections in accordance with Afghan traditions', another vagueness that gave rise to misgivings about what was intended. However the traditionalist groups decided to accept the plan, while the commanders in Afghanistan were not opposed. Hekmatyar and Sayyaf, however, turned it down flat.

For several months, no progress was made. In July, however, there was a meeting between the Pakistanis, the Iranians and the *mujahidin* in Islamabad, which identified some 'positive features' in the plan, and this was followed by a meeting in Teheran in August, chaired by the Iranian Foreign Minister, Ali Akbar Vellayati, at which the Iran-based *mujahidin* were also present. On the ground, meanwhile, the *mujahidin* had at last managed to achieve a success, with the capture in March of the town of Khost, although, far from setting it up as a resistance capital, they instead comprehensively looted it. However their efforts during the summer to take Gardez failed, despite their use of tanks for the first time. When, therefore, a more positive outlook emerged in Moscow following the failure of the attempted coup there on 19 August, pressure for a compromise grew. In September, the Americans and Russians were able to reach an agreement on a cut-off date, 1 January 1992, for the supply of weapons, while the Russians abandoned their insistence that Najibullah should be a member of an interim government. As negotiations continued into 1992, Russian and American military aid stopped, and the Russians ceased to supply Kabul with food and fuel. Pakistan also put an end to all its support for the *mujahidin*, although this was less damaging, as aid from Saudi Arabia and elsewhere continued. Meanwhile in the north, Dostum's Usbek militia joined forces with Massoud and took Mazar-i-Sharif. Together, these developments sounded the death knell both for the UN plan and for the Najibullah regime. They shifted the advantage decisively in favour of the *mujahidin*, who now believed victory to be within their grasp and saw no need for any UN settlement which might call for a role for Najibullah or his supporters in a transitional administration. With the Russians and the UN intensifying the pressure on him, Najibullah agreed on 18 March to step down, and intense and complicated bargaining developed over the transition arrangements. The agreement eventually brokered by Benon Sevan provided for the formation of a 'pre-transition council' of about fifteen 'politically neutral' politicians, to take over until a full interim government could be set up. On 10 April, the UN Secretary General, now Boutros Boutros Ghali, announced that at the end of the month, a truce would be called and this council would take over in Kabul. On 15 April, however, Najibullah tried to leave from Kabul airport and, when his way was blocked, disappeared from view (to the UN compound, as was later revealed). The circumstances surrounding his attempted departure remain obscure. One theory is that he was ousted by a combined *Hezb-i-Watan* and army coup, another is that Sevan had offered him a safe passage from the country, and yet another is that he simply threw in the towel. His disappearance was followed by the suicide of General Yakubi, the Head of KhAD. This left a power vacuum, which the *mujahidin* hastened to fill. Massoud, Dostum and their allies, who were joined by other local militias and defecting Afghan army units, advanced on Kabul from the north, while Hekmatyar's forces, similarly reinforced, advanced from the south. In the rest of the country, local government militias surrendered to, or made power-sharing arrangements with, the *mujahidin,* as the main towns and garrisons capitulated peacefully. On 25 April, Massoud and Hekmatyar halted on the outskirts of Kabul, while the resistance leaders in Peshawar, who had now repudiated the UN's interim council and had opted for their own Islamic Jihad Council, continued to argue about its composition. They eventually settled the issue, but before they could arrive in Kabul, Hekmatyar's troops started to infiltrate the city. Massoud immediately sent his own men in, and a battle for control ensued. Hekmatyar was better equipped, but Massoud, the more astute commander, quickly put into effect a plan which within two days left him in command of virtually all the city's key points. Hekmatyar's men resisted in the Ministry of the Interior and there was a further two days' fighting before they finally succumbed. Hekmatyar then withdrew to the south of the city, while Massoud was left in possession. On 28 April, thirty members of the IJC arrived, led by Sebghatullah Mujadidi, and formally received the surrender of the city from members of Najibullah's regime. Mujadidi proceeded to proclaim the 'Islamic Republic of Afghanistan', in which Massoud became Minister of Defence, Gailani Foreign Minister and Sayyaf Minister of the Interior. Hekmatyar was invited to be Prime Minister, but refused to take part so long as Massoud was also included. In fact he wanted the Presidency and was unwilling at that point to settle for anything less. Even at the moment of victory, the *mujahidin* remained stubbornly divided.

CHAPTER EIGHTEEN

Enter the Taliban

The first three years of *mujahidin* rule, if it could be called that, were characterised by a total inability to agree between themselves on any lasting political settlement and a readiness to fight each other at the slightest provocation, or indeed without any apparent provocation at all. As previously, underlying their persistent divisions were not only clashes of personal ambition, but also ethnic, tribal and religious antipathies. At the heart of the problem was Hekmatyar, who remained determined either that he himself should be preeminent in any administration which might be formed, or, for as long as this remained unattainable, that Kabul should prevented from becoming a secure base for a government run by those whom he saw as his opponents. It was, moreover, as unacceptable to the Pushtoons in general as it was to Hekmatyar in particular that Rabbani, Massoud and Dostum, two Tajiks and an Usbek, should play a leading role in guiding the country's destiny. Tensions also grew within the *Jamiat-i-Islami*, where Rabbani and his Badakshi adherents increasingly resented the growing power of Massoud, who, backed by an experienced fighting force with a core of loyal Panjsheri fighters, quickly became indispensable to their survival. The role played by external influences also exacerbated the *mujahidin's* internal divisions. Hekmatyar continued to be supported by the Pakistanis, while Sayyaf was supported by Saudi Arabia and the *Hezb-i-Wahdat* by the Iranians, each sponsor hoping that its client would be able to gain a predominant position in the country, or at least play an influential role in the eventual outcome.

The arrangements agreed by the *mujahidin* when they took power were that the fifty-one member Islamic Jihad Council, with Sebghatullah Mujadidi as its President and including thirty field commanders, ten mullahs and ten 'intellectuals', would rule for two months. It would then be replaced by an interim government, which would hold power for a four-month period, by the end of which time elections would be held and a permanent government formed. Within days, however, this impossibly optimistic scenario fell apart, as Mujadidi announced that he intended to retain the presidency for two years. Hekmatyar, for his part, demanded Dostum's withdrawal from Kabul and, when this was not conceded, started to bombard the city from his positions to the south, causing many civilian casualties. Negotiations were then held between Hekmatyar and Massoud, which ended in an agreement at the end of May that hostilities should cease, that Dostum and his militia should leave the capital, that Hekmatyar should join the government and that a Leadership Council should be formed under Rabbani, with a view to a general election being held within six months. However the agreement remained unfulfilled, as Dostum's forces failed to leave and Hekmatyar, in protest at this, refused to join the government. By way of a side-show, in early June the *Hezb-i-Wahdat* became embroiled in fighting in Kabul with Sayyaf's *Ittihad-i-Islami*, and there were many casualties before a cease-fire was called. On the issue of a settlement, the only undertaking that was honoured was that, despite his initial insistence on a two year appointment, Mujadidi grudgingly stood down at the end of June and was replaced as President by Rabbani. In July, as a compromise gesture, Hekmatyar sent one of his deputies, Abdul Sabour Fareed, to serve as Prime Minister, but Rabbani dismissed him from the government a few weeks later. By August, Hekmatyar was again shelling the capital, killing as many as 1,800 civilians in a single rocket attack, and in turn he was expelled from the Leadership Council. Fresh attempts were then made at the end of October to reach a general agreement. Rabbani's Presidency was extended until December, to provide time for the formation of a consultative assembly and a Council of Resolution and Settlement (*Shura-i-Ahl-i-Hal wa Aqd*). This met at the end of the year and reelected Rabbani for a further two-year term. Yet again, however, it was boycotted by Hekmatyar, as well as by the *Hezb-i-Wahdat*.

The winter of 1992/3 was a bitter one for the population of Kabul, as they struggled to survive in the face of Hekmatyar's continuing bombardment and the restrictions he imposed on supplies being brought in from Pakistan. The city itself, which had not been much damaged during the Soviet occupation, was now being progressively reduced to ruins. During the winter, the *Hezb-i-Wahdat* joined forces with Hekmatyar, compelling Massoud, who had meanwhile allied himself with the *Ittihad-i-Islami*, to fight on two fronts. Eventually, new peace talks, brokered by Pakistan, Saudi Arabia and Iran, culminated in a conference in Islamabad early in March and a peace agreement was signed. Hekmatyar would join the government as Prime Minister, the *mujahidin* groups would be merged to form a national army, to which they would surrender their heavy weapons, an assembly would be elected by the end of the year to draw up a constitution and elections would be held before June 1994. However neither Massoud nor Dostum attended the talks and Hekmatyar was prevented from entering Kabul to take up his post. Massoud and some 20,000 of his men kept control of the capital, where heavy fighting again broke out during May. Over the year following the *mujahidin* take-over, it was estimated that some 30,000 Kabulis had been killed and possibly 100,000 wounded, while many more had left the city for internal or external exile. Over most of the country, however, conditions were relatively peaceful, as local *mujahidin* commanders and other leaders, often supported by *shuras*, assumed control. In Herat, Ismail Khan, as a *Jamiat* commander, ran a reasonable administration, as did Dostum in Mazar-i-Sharif. The latter strengthened his links with the Central Asian Republics, while Ismail Khan obtained support from Iran, in recognition of the favourable climate he was creating for the return of refugees. In the eastern provinces, conditions varied under collective leaderships of greater or less cohesion. In Kandahar, however, various *mujahidin* leaders fought for supremacy and considerable anarchy prevailed.

During the summer and autumn of 1993, there was a lull in the fighting around Kabul, but it was resumed at the beginning of 1994, when, taking everyone by surprise, Dostum and Hekmatyar joined forces and subjected Kabul to a major attack. After heavy fighting, which caused a substantial exodus of the civilian population, Massoud was successful in repelling the combined onslaught, but a major food crisis persisted until Hekmatyar lifted his blockade of the capital in March. In May, Massoud managed to retake Kunduz, which had fallen to Dostum a few weeks earlier, and in June he also achieved a significant success in Kabul, when, after two days of bitter fighting, he drove the combined Dostum/Hekmatyar forces from their positions near the capital. Dostum retired to northern Afghanistan where he licked his wounds and remained on the sidelines for the next two years. During September, there was more fierce fighting in Kabul between government forces and Hekmatyar, who had now again allied himself with the *Hezb-i-Wahdat*. Meanwhile Rabbani was reconfirmed in office for an extra six months, while Hekmatyar was finally stripped of the Premiership. The same year, the United Nations again came into the picture, with the establishment of a fresh Mission to Afghanistan under the leadership of Mahmood Mestiri, a former

Tunisian Foreign Minister. Mestiri began work in March, and was supported in August by a Statement[1] issued by the Security Council. In October, he submitted peace proposals to the main *mujahidin* groups and these were accepted in November by the *Jamiat-i-Islami*. By January 1995, he was making optimistic noises about plans for a transfer of power to an interim council of all the parties involved. However he had by then been pre-empted by the appearance of a new actor on the stage. This was the Taliban, a movement that drew much of its strength from the general disillusion with the *mujahidin* parties and rejected all suggestions that it might work with them.

'Talib' means 'religious student', and the movement had as its core numbers of Afghan refugee students from *madrassas* (religious schools) in Baluchistan and the North West Frontier Province. The story related by the Taliban about their origin is that in July 1994, a guerrilla leader in the Kandahar region raped and killed three women. A mullah from the frontier area, Maulvi Mohamed Omar, who was asked by the local people to do something about the outrage, proceeded to recruit a group of religious students, who executed the commander and dispersed his militia. The group were then called upon to deal with other atrocities and started to gain a reputation. This induced them to decide that they should recruit comrades and launch a *jihad* against those who, in their eyes, had betrayed the country. They proceeded to clear the road from Quetta to Kandahar of the roadblocks which were being used to levy ransom on traffic, captured Spin Baldak and its well-stocked arsenal, and went to war.

While this story reads well, and some observers[2] have given credence to the idea that the Taliban movement originated more or less spontaneously, the truth has to be that its genesis was altogether more deliberate. In the first place, the Taliban have themselves said that groups of them were organised in a number of Afghan provinces from the late 1980s onwards, and that before acting themselves, they had waited to see if the *mujahidin* would succeed in uniting and running the country. Also, while a number of them had fought as *mujahidin* with the *Hezb-i-Islami (Khalis)* and Mohammedi's *Harakat-i-Inqilab*, others had operated as independent bands. Further than this, the road-clearing operation was not as unpremeditated as it made out to be. A prime mover in it was the Pakistani Interior Minister, General Naseerullah Babar, who seems to have decided that irrespective of any views that the Rabbani regime might have, he should take steps to open up an overland trade route to Central Asia which, following the Soviet departure, had become a major objective of Pakistan policy. In October 1994, Benazir Bhutto, the Pakistan Prime Minister, met Dostum and Ismail Khan in Turkmenistan and secured their cooperation, and a number of Ambassadors accredited to Pakistan were flown to Kandahar and Herat as part of an effort to attract foreign funding for the rehabilitation of the route. Babar also reconnoitered the route personally and at the end of the month, in a move to demonstrate that the venture was practicable, led a convoy of thirty trucks, guarded by Taliban fighters, across the border towards Kandahar. When their way was blocked, the Taliban proceeded to deal with the militia responsible and went on immediately to seize Kandahar, which, to their own surprise and that of everyone else, they took in a matter of days and with minimal casualties.

A Pakistani hand was therefore evident at the outset of the Taliban's emergence; and, despite their denials, their complicity in the Taliban's subsequent successes is also beyond any reasonable doubt. At the outset, at a time when the ISI were still backing Hekmatyar, the Taliban were sponsored by Babar's Interior Ministry, although it was not long before the ISI was brought on side and played its part in their development and support. A strong influence behind their emergence was the *Jamiat-i-Ulema-i-Islam* (JUI), led by Maulana Fazlur Rahman, which was itself responsible for running many *madrassas* and in 1993 became a coalition partner in the Pakistan government. The Taliban forces which proceeded to advance through Afghanistan during the winter of 1994/5 were equipped with tanks, APCs, artillery and even aircraft, and, however much equipment and supplies they may have acquired in Spin Baldak, Kandahar and elsewhere, they could not, despite energetic denials, have operated without training, ammunition, fuel and maintenance facilities provided by Pakistan. Also their numbers quickly grew, until within no more than some six months, they had mobilised possibly as many as 20,000 fighting men. Most of them were allowed to come across from Pakistan – many, indeed, were Pakistanis – and their basic training took place in camps not only in southern Afghanistan but also on the Pakistan side of the border. It is also inconceivable that a force composed mostly of former guerrillas and student amateurs could have operated with the degree of skill and organisation which the Taliban showed almost from the outset of their operations. While there were undoubtedly former members of the Afghan armed forces among their numbers, the speed and sophistication with which their offensives were conducted, and the quality of such elements as their communications, air support and artillery bombardments, lead to the inescapable conclusion that they must have owed much to a Pakistani military presence, or at least professional support.

If only on account of the costs involved, however, the Pakistanis could not have acted alone. The Taliban had to fight hard for many of their successes, but not infrequently they simply bribed local tribal leaders and warlords to surrender without a fight. The taking of

Kandahar, for example, is said to have cost some $1.5 million in subventions to local leaders. From an early stage, the Taliban were able to raise money from tolls on transport, and the drugs trade was also to become a major source of revenue. But it is inconceivable that they could both have delivered bribes and acquired the provisions, fuel and other supplies they needed for a period of sustained warfare without considerable outside subventions. There can therefore be little doubt that Pakistan acted as a conduit for substantial financial assistance from Saudi Arabia.

There is also the question of the American role. While their active involvement seems to be unproven[3], it is noteworthy that initially, the United States government were not just muted about, but were even dismissive of, the social and judicial excesses which were from an early stage the hallmark of the Taliban's rule over the areas they controlled. American officials, including the Under-Secretary of State, Robin Rachel, had early meetings with Taliban leaders and went on record in remarkably favourable terms. One factor influencing the Americans seems to have been early indications on the part of the Taliban that they were not prepared to tolerate the opium trade. Much more cogent, however, was the fact that an American oil company, UNOCAL, was in the market to build an oil pipeline from Turkmenistan through to Pakistan, and its lobbying in Washington was clearly not without effect.

Before long, however, it all turned sour. Far from outlawing the drugs trade, the Taliban came to profit immensely from it; their human rights abuses were being increasingly castigated, in America as elsewhere; they were showing themselves incapable of suppressing all opposition in Afghanistan, and hence of producing the conditions of peace and stability that were required for the construction of a pipeline; and they were found to be tolerant of 'Muslim terrorism'. Not for the first time where Afghanistan was concerned, the vagaries and inconsistencies of American policy worked against their own best interests in the region.

From the outset, there is no doubt that the Taliban struck a chord with the war-weary populace. Having captured Kandahar, they brought the endemic criminality and factionalism there to a speedy end. Local leaders were shot or imprisoned, guns were impounded, roadblocks were demolished, the city was cleaned up and life improved. On the other hand, they soon showed signs of a determination to impose the strictest interpretations of Islamic law and custom. Criminals began to have their hands or feet amputated, women were forbidden to work, girls were excluded from schools, the wearing of the *burqa* was enforced, games, music and television were banned, punctilious attendance at the mosque was enforced. A *shura* was formed in the city under the leadership of Mohammed Omar, and this has since formed the effective government of the country. From Kandahar, the Taliban's advances were rapid and within a short while they were registering impressive successes. One force struck towards Herat and by early 1995 was within a short distance of the air base at Shindand. Another took Ghazni during January and the following month was close to Kabul, where it captured Hekmatyar's head-quarters and put him to flight. A few days later the Taliban were at the gates of the capital.

Within Kabul, meanwhile, Rabbani was refusing to stand down in accordance with the peace plan drawn up by Mestiri. At the outset, he and Massoud tried to adopt a non-confrontational attitude towards the Taliban, but it rapidly became clear that this was going to lead nowhere, and any prospect of an accommodation disappeared as soon as the Taliban became embroiled in the highly volatile situation which prevailed in and around the capital. During March, Massoud launched an all out attack on the *Hezb-i-Wahdat*, now deprived of Hekmatyar's support, and the *Hezb* turned to the Taliban for help. What then happened is unclear, and both the Taliban and the *Hezb* proceeded to accuse each other of treachery. When the dust cleared, however, the Taliban were found to have succeeded in supplanting the *Hezb*, whose leader, Abdul Ali Waziri, was killed in mysterious circumstances while in Taliban captivity. With both Hekmatyar and the *Hezb* out of contention, it was now a straight fight between the government forces and the Taliban, and, after some ferocious engagements, the Taliban were beaten back to Charasyab and beyond. In retaliation they started to bombard the capital, proving themselves no less contemptuous of civilian life than Hekmatyar had been. By March, however, they had been forced to retreat out of artillery and rocket range, and Kabul enjoyed a respite until September.

The main focus of the conflict then shifted to southern Afghanistan, where Ismail Khan's forces had succeeded in stabilising the front line at Shindand. In the course of August they counter-attacked, retook Delaram and Girishk, and were soon within striking distance of Kandahar. In the process, however, they became considerably overstretched and the Taliban, by now massively reinforced with fresh men and equipment, were able to deliver an overwhelming response. After a major battle, they retook Girishk, went on to capture the air base at Shindand and by early September were advancing on Herat. Ismail Khan fled to Iran, his forces melted away and the Taliban had little difficulty in taking the city, where they established their own local government and again imposed strict Islamic practices. The ban they placed on female education and employment caused particular hardship and resentment, as some

20,000 girls had been at school in the city and many women had been employed, in particular as teachers and in the health services.

Dismayed at this major setback, the government in Kabul publicly accused the Pakistanis of involvement, and a large mob sacked and burnt the Pakistan Embassy. One member of its staff was killed and the remainder, including the Ambassador, were beaten up. The focus of military activity then shifted back to the capital. Despite attempts by Mestiri to arrange a cease-fire, the Taliban launched a major attack during October and fierce fighting raged in the hills to the south of the city, which again came under indiscriminate artillery and rocket fire, and was bombed by Taliban aircraft. However the offensive petered out, leaving the Taliban once more resorting to almost daily rocket attacks. In the background, Mestiri shuttled to and fro in an effort to broker a settlement, but his efforts failed in the face of a refusal by Rabbani to stand down in favour of an interim council and by the Taliban's insistence that power could only be handed over to themselves. By the end of the year, after yet more fighting, a stalemate was reached around Kabul, while civilian casualties inexorably mounted and correspondents took to comparing the city with Dresden after the 1945 bombing. Deaths since the *mujahidin* take-over were now estimated to be of the order of 100,000, and many more had left the capital as refugees. With the road into the city from Jalalabad blocked by the Taliban, with no electricity and very little food and fuel, the plight of the inhabitants became acute. At the end of January, the UN launched an emergency air lift of 1,000 tonnes of food to relieve the besieged capital.

The stalemate around Kabul lasted until the early summer of 1996, when Hekmatyar, as opportunistic as ever, formed an alliance with his inveterate enemy, Rabbani, brought a small number of his men into Kabul and accepted the post of Prime Minister. In doing so, he abandoned Dostum and the three *mujahidin* groups with whom he had previously been allied. To mark his arrival in Kabul, the Taliban launched its biggest rocket and artillery barrage yet, causing many casualties in the city. In a bizarre development during April, the Afghan Supreme Court decreed that the Taliban's appointment of Mohamed Omar as *Amir ul-Mominin* (Commander of the Faithful – the title previously assumed by Dost Mohammed) was un-Islamic, on the grounds that no-one could assume this title whose vision was defective (Omar had lost an eye while fighting as a *mujahid*). Meanwhile Mestiri resigned, having achieved nothing whatsoever during his two years of effort, and was succeeded in July by a German diplomat, Norbert Holl.

Again thwarted before Kabul, where fighting continued through-out the summer, the Taliban turned their attention in August to eastern Afghanistan and were soon advancing through Paktya province, capturing many *Hezb-i-Islami* fighters and driving the remainder before them. Before long they had scored yet another major success with the capture of Jalalabad, cutting the main supply route between Kabul and Pakistan. They then took control of Kunar and Laghman provinces and advanced towards Sarobi, where they routed what remained of Hekmatyar's forces. The general expectation that they would now take Kabul was fulfilled towards the end of September, when there was a sudden collapse of government confidence, their forces withdrew to the north and the way was clear for the Taliban to enter the city. Almost their first action was to force their way into the UN compound, where Najibullah had been living in asylum for the previous four years. They shot him and his brother, and strung their bodies up at a cross-roads near the presidential palace. Flushed with success, they then advanced through Kabul to the north, pursuing the retreating government forces through Kohistan as far as the Salang Pass. By that point, however, they had again overreached themselves: Dostum re-emerged from the north, and he and Massoud forced them back to within a few miles of the capital.

Over many years, the outside world had studiously ignored Afghanistan, whose status as a pawn in the Cold War had receded into history. Each year, UN appeals for humanitarian relief had been massively under-subscribed – as they still are – and very little effort had been made to put weight behind Mestiri's ineffectual efforts at mediation. Until September 1996, when the UN Under Secretary for Political Affairs, Marrack Goulding, paid a three-day visit, no senior UN official had bothered to set foot in the country. There had been some desultory discussions of an arms embargo, but these had got nowhere. Now, however, the international media descended and filed a mass of reports, concentrating mainly on the consequences for human rights in the capital and elsewhere of the Taliban success[4]. While they were able say little about the Taliban leadership, who continued to maintain a very low profile, they had a field day describing the Taliban's various impositions, which ranged from the horrific to the merely bizarre – the stoning to death of a couple caught in adultery; the botched public execution of a murderer by the husband of the murdered woman; the banning from employment of thousands of widows, most of them the sole breadwinners for their families; the wholesale closure of girls' schools and colleges; the sacking of civil servants who had cut their beards; a woman beaten for showing her arm; windows painted black so that the women inside could not be seen; TVs, kite-flying, football, music, cage-birds and women's white socks banned – this and more zealously enforced by a Religious Police Force, under the direction of a Department for the Propagation of Virtue and the Suppression of Vice. Kabul was ruled by a six-man *shura*, but the overall direction of affairs rested with the Kandahar *shura* headed by Mohammed Omar, which remained in that city.

For several months, stalemate prevailed north of Kabul, with Dostum and Massoud unable to retake the city and the Taliban unable to make fresh headway northwards. Peace talks were held in Islamabad under UN auspices, with the support of the King, who offered to play a role in any settlement, but the Taliban held aloof and the talks failed even to bring about a cease-fire. The Taliban then resumed their advance and by the end of February 1997 had retaken Bagram and Charikar, and were close to the Shibar Pass, now the main gateway to the north following the blocking of the Salang Pass by Dostum's forces. There, in the depths of the winter, they were stalled by the *Hezb-i-Wahdat*, but with the coming of spring they again pressed on. In the north west, their forces advancing from Herat had similarly been engaged in heavy fighting, but in May they occupied Shibarghan and most of Faryab Province. They were then, in typical style, joined by one of Dostum's subordinates, General Abdul Malik, who switched sides under the influence, it is said, of a substantial bribe, or, according to other accounts, a blood feud between Dostum's family and his own. Dostum fled to Tashkent and thence to Ankara, and by the end of May the Taliban had taken the principal northern city, Mazar-i-Sharif.

At that point, the general supposition was that the Taliban had won the war and were in effect the masters of the whole of Afghanistan. The Pakistanis formally recognised the Taliban government and their Ambassador marked the event by going to Mazar in person. However the Taliban yet again overreached themselves: they excluded Malik from a share of power and proceeded to impose on Mazar, traditionally one of the most liberal of Afghan cities, their strict interpretations of Islamic law. Even more injudiciously, they tried to disarm the local *Hezb-i-Wahdat*. Malik again switched sides and attacked the Taliban from the rear, and a fierce battle ensued in the city, during which the *Hezb* slaughtered large numbers of Taliban fighters. By the end of the battle, the Taliban had been driven out of the city with heavy losses, only three days after their original occupation. In the process, their military commander, Abdul Razzaq, and their Foreign Minister, Mohammed Ghous, were taken prisoner. Within a short while, they were also forced to abandon Pul-i-Khumri, while Massoud engaged them in renewed fighting in the Kohistan Valley, took the air base at Bagram during July, and again launched rocket attacks on Kabul. Later in the year, the Taliban once more tried to take Mazar-i-Sharif, but were again driven back. Mass graves, containing some 2000 bodies, were later found near Shibarghan, reputed to be those of Taliban fighters who had been captured during the debacle in May and subsequently executed.

As of late 1997, therefore, the situation on the ground had reverted more or less to what it had been after the Taliban's capture of Kabul. The same autumn, at the urging of the UN Secretary-General, Kofi Annan, a Group of Concerned Countries, more generally known as the 'Six plus Two', was set up, consisting of Afghanistan's six neighbouring countries, plus America and Russia. This met at intervals, but made no headway towards a settlement, partly because, far from promoting this, several of the six continued to support and arm their warring clients. In April 1998, following an American initiative, peace talks were held in Islamabad, but they came to nothing and the fighting resumed. The Taliban were now masters of some two thirds of the country, while the remainder was held by the so-called Northern Alliance, which had been formed the previous summer. This was headed by Rabbani, who is, to the Taliban's fury, still recognised internationally as Head of State. He and Massoud controlled three provinces in the north east, while Dostum, who managed to return and oust Malik in September 1997, controlled several central-north provinces. Also part of the Alliance was the *Hezb-i-Wahdat*, now led by Usted Karim Khalili, who controlled the Hazarajat. The Taliban, however, had by no means shot their bolt. Yet again reinforced by a stream of recruits from the *madrassas*, and with renewed Pakistani and Saudi support, they retook Faryab province in July 1998 and headed towards Shiberghan. By early August Dostum had fled and they had again occupied Mazar-i-Sharif. They then went on to seize Taloqan, 120 miles to the east, with its air base through which Massoud had been receiving supplies from Central Asia. Reports soon began to circulate of Taliban atrocities in Mazar-i-Sharif, including mass executions of possibly as many as 6,000 Hazaras, and it seems that this time, the Taliban were determined that their gains would be permanent. In September, they occupied Bamian, but Massoud managed to retake Taloqan and also made advances in Kapisa province north of Kabul. Fighting continued over the winter, until, in March 1999, further peace talks were held in Ashkhabad, the capital of Turkmenistan. At first there was some optimism about the outcome, as they ended in agreement that the two sides should try to form a broad-based government and would hold further talks. When, however, these took place the following month, they quickly collapsed, and Mohammed Omar declared that the Taliban would 'not share power with those who have destroyed the country or have looted the state's territory'. In April, the *Hezb-i-Wahdat* retook Bamian, but it was once more captured by the Taliban the following month. In late July, the Taliban launched a major offensive north of Kabul but this was followed within a few days by an equally fierce counter-offensive by Massoud, who drove the Taliban out of the ground they had gained. In

October, Lakhdar Brahmini, who had earlier been appointed over Holl's head as the UN Secretary-General's Personal Representative, announced that he was suspending his efforts to broker a settlement, and would only resume them if the parties concerned proved themselves 'serious about finding a peaceful solution'.

The year 2000 saw a continuance of the previous pattern, of inconclusive peace negotiations accompanied by fierce fighting. Early in the year, King Zahir proposed the holding of a *loya jirga* in Rome, but this was rejected by the Taliban. With the assistance of yet another UN Representative, Francesc Vendrill, talks were held in Jedda in March, and again in May, under the auspices of the Organisation of Islamic Unity, but these again came to nothing. In March, heavy fighting erupted north of Kabul, and in August a large scale Taliban offensive in the north-east led once more to their capture of the key town of Taloqan. Efforts by Massoud to retake the town had not succeeded by the end of the year.

Further efforts to bring about a peace settlement continued late in the year when, at a meeting in Ashkhabad, Vendrill persuaded both parties to sign undertakings that they would not abandon negotiations until all avenues to an agreement had been exhausted. Further talks on this basis are due to be held in Ashkhabad early in 2001, but it remains to be seen whether they will be held, or, if held, whether they will lead anywhere. Although the greater part of the country is now relatively peaceful, Afghanistan can only recover from two decades or more of warfare if a comprehensive peace settlement is reached. Such are the enmities, however, that this still seems unlikely, at least for so long as the warring parties receive assistance from outside the country. The key to peace lies with Afghanistan's neighbours, who continue to support and supply the combatants, and seem still to prefer that matters should be settled on the battlefield.

CHAPTER NINETEEN

Afghanistan and the Wider World

After nearly twenty years of communist revolution, Soviet occupation and civil war, Afghanistan faces an unenviable future. At the most fundamental level, it has severe environmental problems. There is widespread soil degradation, deforestation and desertification. Much of the country is overgrazed and the few forests that remain are being rapidly felled for fuel and construction material. Such commerce and industry as it possessed during the 1970s has mostly disappeared, its infrastructure has been devastated and less than two-thirds of its agricultural land is cultivated. Kabul is a mass of ruins, while Kandahar has been extensively damaged, as have been parts of Herat. In 2000, the country was hit by the worst drought for over a generation and large numbers of the population were struggling to survive. With cereal production cut by nearly half, the country has no hope of being able to feed its people without outside assistance.

In human terms, Afghanistan is one of the poorest and most miserable countries in the world. In addition to the million or more who died during the Soviet occupation, tens of thousands have lost their lives since. Life expectancy[1], at about forty-six years, is among the lowest in the world, while at least one in six – some say as many as one in three – Afghan children will die before their fifth birthday. TB is rampant and malaria is spreading. Outside the main cities, there are virtually no medical services, while levels of education remain abysmally low. The educational system has for the most part broken down or has been deliberately destroyed, Kabul University has been closed for long periods and has been extensively damaged, a third of the staff have been dismissed, women have been excluded from it by the Taliban and it now exists in little more than name. Over one hundred thousand 'intellectuals' are said to have left the country during the past two decades, most of whom have settled in America and Europe and are most unlikely ever to return. The nation's artistic heritage, including the priceless treasures from Kapisa and many other sites, has been comprehensively looted or destroyed[2].

There is also an acute problem of landmines. While there may be some exaggeration in estimates that as many as ten million may have been sown in over four thousand minefields across the country during the Soviet occupation and the subsequent civil war, there is little doubt that it is the most densely mined country in the world. While some progress has been made in surveying and marking mined areas, many remain unmarked and unrecorded. United Nations figures[3], as of March 1999, were that while 166 square kilometers of land had been cleared over the previous ten years, more than 700 square kilometers were still contaminated by mines or unexploded ordinance. The UN admit that at the current rate of progress, it will take up to a further decade to clear the remaining high priority areas and that the whole task will not be complete for 'many, many years'. Meanwhile, nearly 500,000 Afghans, up to half of them women and children, have been killed or wounded by mines. Amputees are a common sight and their numbers continue to grow. Other effects have been to restrict movement, deter the return of refugees, disrupt the economy and make farming extremely dangerous.

Of rather more concern to the outside world is Afghanistan's position as one of the two main global producers of opium (the other being Burma). UN estimates[4] are that over 2000 tons of dried opium were produced during 1995, between 2200 and 2300 tons in 1996, and as much as 2800 tons in 1997. In 1998, due to bad weather, the total dropped to 2100 tons, but more land came under poppy cultivation and in 1999, stimulated by high prices, production more than doubled, to some 4600 tons. This has meant that Afghanistan has in recent years been responsible for around three-quarters of total global production, with a street value of some $80 billion. By contrast, less than 200 tons were produced in 1978, before the Soviet invasion. Most of it has come from areas in Helmand and Nangrahar provinces under the control of the Taliban. With most of the local transport in the hands of Pushtoons, there has been no difficulty in moving the opium to the frontier areas of Pakistan, where numerous small laboratories have refined it into heroin. Much of it has then been shipped out via Karachi, while routes also exist through Iran to Turkey and from northern Afghanistan through the Central Asian Republics to Russia. Some is said to have been transported from Kandahar to the Gulf states in aircraft belonging to the Afghan national airline, Ariana. A major participant in the trade has been the PKK, the Kurdistan Workers Party, a Marxist, separatist organisation established in the Kurdish areas of Turkey, which runs its own processing laboratories and trafficking arrangements. Some of the product has been seized en route, or consumed in Pakistan, Iran and Central Asia, where there are serious, and growing, problems of drug addiction. The bulk, however, has ended up as heroin on the streets of Europe or even the United States.

The attitude formally adopted by the Taliban[5] has been that the production and shipment of illicit drugs throughout its territory is 'illegal and prohibited', as is the consumption of narcotics and alcohol. It has maintained that it has made 'serious attempts to curtail and eliminate poppy production in areas under its control'. In 1999, Mohammed Omar issued an edict calling for poppy cultivation to be cut by a third, and in July 2000 he followed this up by announcing a total ban. At the same time, however, he called for international assistance and insisted that the Taliban had 'only limited means' to enforce their decision. For as long as there existed a lucrative world market, and for as long as the economic circumstances of Afghan farmers were such that they 'give drug dealers the opportunity to exploit their poverty', the problem would continue to be 'difficult and costly for all concerned'.

What, if anything, has been the effect of these pronouncements is unclear. The expected decline in Afghanistan's opium production in 2000 is likely to have been due more to the widespread drought than to any official intervention. It is also very unlikely that there will be any significant international assistance. In 1997, the United Nations International Drug Control Programme signed an informal, $16.4 million, four year agreement[6] with the Taliban to eliminate opium cultivation in exchange for assistance to help restore conventional agriculture, but this seems to have achieved very little, partly through incompetence and lack of funding, and it now seems likely that it will be wound up. The bottom line is that opium has become an economic necessity for very many farmers and that the traditional *zakat*, a 10% or even 20% tax on agricultural production paid to the village mullahs, goes into the Taliban's coffers, as do levies on transportation. With opium selling at up to $60 a kilo, current estimates are that the Taliban derive something between $60 and $300 million a year from drug production[7]. But for this source of revenue, it is most unlikely that they could have continued to fund the costs of their campaign against the Northern Alliance. For quarter of a million impoverished farmers in the Taleban-held areas of Afghanistan, opium is far and away the most worthwhile of crops, even if their share of the eventual returns is less than 1%. At the same time, the profits for the middlemen and those who connive in the trade, reportedly including the Taliban leadership, are, as elsewhere, immense, and nobody is much concerned for the effects on the *kafirs* who use it at the end of the line.

On a different aspect of Afghanistan's external relationships, that of the refugees, there is a mixed story to tell. Between 1979 and 1990, the number of refugees who fled to Pakistan and Iran amounted in total to over six million. The United Nations High Commissioner for Refugees and the World Food Programme have between them spent immense amounts of money in sustaining what has been described as the biggest emergency operation in history, while further large sums have been spent by governments and humanitarian aid agencies. Despite the pressures exerted by the refugees on land and infrastructure, a remarkable feature of the exodus was the readiness of Iran and Pakistan to accept it with what has rightly been described by the UNHCR as an 'unrivalled generosity of spirit'. In Iran, the great majority of refugees were allowed to mix with the local population, while in Pakistan the refugee 'villages' were never closed societies. In both countries, the refugees were able to work and set up businesses, despite the disadvantages this caused for the local population, although since September 1995, when the supply of rations finally ceased, many have faced a major struggle to survive through intermittent daily labouring.

Even before the Russians finally left, a trickle of refugees started to return to their homes, and in 1992, when the communist regime fell, optimism was such that over 1½ million refugees returned from Pakistan and Iran within the space of some eight months. Subsequently, even during the civil war, refugees continued to return, and the degree of stability and security created by the Taliban in the areas they controlled had contributed by the beginning of 1999 to the return of over four million in all. A significant factor in the return was the measures adopted by the UNHCR, who provided for the transportation and escorting of refugees back to their home villages, as well as for grants in the form of cash and food, and practical assistance in resettlement. Nevertheless a sizable refugee problem still exists, exacerbated the exodus of perhaps 400,000 people from Kabul as a result of the fighting there, and of half as many again from the battlefields north of the city. In the west of the country too, where there is widespread distrust of the Pushtoon-based Taliban, repatriation came to a halt in 1995 and a fresh exodus began. A problem also exists in that many refugees are reluctant to return to a country in which their daughters will be deprived even of such education as they are receiving in exile. Recent estimates[8] are there are still about 2½ million refugees in Pakistan and Iran. What has to be said, however, is that the whole unhappy saga has been characterised not only by the resilience of the Afghan people, but by the overall efficacy, in the most trying circumstances, of international assistance programmes. Above all, it has demonstrated the strength of the obligation of hospitality which is an integral part of the ethos both of Pushtoon society and of Islam as a whole. Remarkably, most of the returned refugees have been able to recover their land and property, although they continue to suffer from an acute lack of health and education facilities. More recently, however, Pakistan has closed its frontier to Afghans trying to escape the drought and hardships from which they are currently suffering, and international financial assistance is drying up.

In terms of their foreign relations, the Taliban have consistently taken the line[9] that their version of Islam is for internal consumption only and that they have no intention of trying to export it. However few have been convinced and it is possibly not without significance that Mohamed Omar's title, *Amir ul-Muminin*, is an honorific with global connotations. Certainly their run of successes has aroused concern, and even alarm, within Russia and the Central Asian Republics. When Kabul fell in the autumn of 1996, representatives of Russia and several of the Republics held an emergency meeting to review the situation and concluded that it represented a 'direct threat to their national interests and security'[10]. Afghanistan had become, in the words of Talbak Nazarov, the Tajikistan Foreign Minister[11], a 'dangerous source of military, political, criminal and economic turbulence'. Subsequently, with the capture of Mazar-i-Sharif and the extension of Taliban control in northern Afghanistan, further meetings have been held and declarations made of a readiness to take any 'necessary measures', should the borders of any of the Commonwealth of Independent States (CIS) be violated.

The concerns expressed both publicly and at these meetings stem partly from the ethnic and religious congruity that exists between the Central Asian Republics and Afghanistan, with some six million Usbeks, Tajiks, Turkmen and others living on the Afghan side of the border. Many of them are refugees, or the descendants of refugees, from Soviet rule, while others have in recent years moved across from Tajikistan as a result of the conflict there. While, following the suppression of the *basmachi* movement in the 1920s, some relaxation of tension and a growth in social and economic contacts took place under Soviet rule, the latter's invasion of Afghanistan contributed to a growth of anti-Soviet feeling on both sides of the border, and attempts were made by the Afghan *mujahidin* to cause trouble for the Soviets on their home ground. When, in 1991, the Central Asian Republics became independent, they were very conscious of their inherent weaknesses, both political, military and economic, and their Moscow-backed governments have since remained nervous that the religious-based opposition movements which have been – and still are – active within their borders might receive support from the south. Tajikistan in particular was, between 1992 and 1997, the victim of what was in effect civil war, with a radical Muslim movement, the Islamic Renaissance Party, maintaining a 'government in exile' in northern Afghanistan and receiving arms, ammunition and subversive literature smuggled in by Afghan *mujahidin* groups. Limited cross-border attacks by opposition forces and Afghan *mujahidin* took place in 1993, which prompted the Russians to send in 20,000 troops to support the Tajikistan government, and these have remained ever since. The appearance on their borders of an militant Islamic militia, even if largely of a different ethnic complexion, has accordingly given rise to acute fears within the Republics of renewed subversion or even invasion, or at the very least the possibility of having to cope with the arrival of numbers of refugees. The Russians for their part, smarting from their experiences in Chechnia, seem also to have been genuinely fearful of a spread of Islamic extremism and concerned for the security of the large Russian-speaking minority in Central Asia. They are also angered by the realisation that the Taliban are giving training and assistance to the Chechnyan rebels. Both the Russians and the Republics have therefore provided continuing assistance to the Northern Alliance, without which it would be unlikely to survive for any length of time. The one state which did not go along with the general concern was Turkmenistan, which ostentatiously stayed away from the regional conferences. With their sights set on the establishment of a gas and oil pipeline through Afghanistan to Pakistan as the only conceivable cure for their ailing economy, they had taken care to maintain good relations with Ismail Khan and they renewed these with the Taliban after the latter had taken Herat.

The Iranians have also been concerned at the Taliban's successes, particularly as they were accompanied by the defeat and massacre of fellow Shias and the murder of nine of their own 'diplomats' in the course of the Taliban's capture of Mazar-i-Sharif in August 1998. Following these murders, tension between Iran and Afghanistan rapidly rose, as some 70,000 Iranian Revolutionary Guards were moved to the frontier and large scale exercises were held. However, the danger of being sucked into an unwinnable war in Afghanistan has been clear to the Iranians and, although relations have remained tense, both sides have been careful to avoid hostilities. Tension between Iran and Afghanistan has deep historical roots, and it would be surprising if it were now to disappear. Apart from the religious divide and the ancient legacy of invasion and counter-invasion, the problem of the Helmand waters has been a long-standing bone of contention. The cultural affinities between the two countries have also been more of a hindrance than an aid to a closer relationship, as the Afghans have tended to see them in terms of 'cultural imperialism' and have sought to protect their own Dari and Pushtu linguistic and literary heritage. The Iranians for their part remain frustrated at their inability to secure the safe return home of the refugees on their soil, they fear acts of terrorism in their eastern provinces and they are wary of the growth of Saudi influence in a neighbouring country.

So far as Afghanistan's remaining neighbour, Pakistan, is concerned, there seem to have been two main factors behind their continuing interventions in Afghanistan following the Soviet withdrawal. Both in supporting Hekmatyar and subsequently the Taliban, there can be little doubt that they have been anxious that a well-disposed, Pushtoon-dominated government should be installed in Kabul. They have been concerned that the long-standing Pushtoonistan issue should be settled for once and for all, and for that they need an Afghan government which will see eye to eye with them on the issue. Having helped to establish the government, however, the Pakistanis must be feeling that they have released the genie from the bottle. The Taliban probably have closer links with the Pushtoon tribes on both sides of the border than any previous Afghan government, they are well connected with the *Jamiat-i-Ulema-i-Islam* and other radical political/religious groups, and their links with the powerful Pakistani 'transport mafia' are also close. Not only is there the risk that, with a robust, self-confident and independently minded Pushtoon regime established in Kabul, pressures may emerge for a revival of the Pushtoonistan issue, but there is also every incentive for extreme Islamic movements within Pakistan to draw encouragement from the Taliban's success and try to radicalise a country which is already faced with considerable political, social and economic problems.

The other strand of Pakistan's policy is geopolitically more far-reaching. It is to establish an economic bloc extending as far as Central Asia, with a friendly Afghanistan acting as a conduit for the flow of oil and gas, as well as for trade more generally, between themselves and the Central Asian Republics. Not only did the Soviet withdrawal appear to make this a viable policy, but the potential which Turkmenistan and, to a lesser extent, Usbekistan and Kazakstan possess as major producers of oil and gas has become increasingly apparent. With Iran still subject to American sanctions, and with Russia limiting its take-off of gas from Central Asia and reluctant to pay full market prices, the Afghanistan option has obvious advantages. The opening of a trade route would also bolster Pakistan's hard-pressed economy and give the country greater strategic weight in its confrontations with India. The potential of such a route is demonstrated by the considerable illicit trade in consumer goods which has developed from the Persian Gulf through Herat to Pakistan and Central Asia. Taxes on this trade form a useful supplement to the Taliban's earnings from drugs trafficking.

So far, the continuing conflict in Afghanistan has prevented the Pakitanis' ambitions from being realised. The American oil company, UNOCAL, was at one time negotiating[12], in alliance with the Saudi corporation Delta Oil, for the construction of gas and oil pipelines from Turkmenistan through Afghanistan to Pakistan, while an Argentinean company, Bridas, also showed interest. In 1998, however, UNOCAL pulled out, following American missile strikes on supposed terrorist bases in Afghanistan, and it has since not been clear what the prospects for a pipeline are. Certainly the peace and stability needed for such a substantial project is still far from being achieved, although Pakistan, Afghanistan and Turkmenistan have been in continuing talks and have reiterated their determination to persist with it.

Also of international concern is Afghanistan's continuing contribution to the problem of terrorism. According to the US State Department's report, *Patterns of Global Terrorism, 1999*, the epicentre of global terrorism has shifted from the Middle East to South Asia, with a major threat emanating from Afghanistan. There are historical reasons for this, for which the United States must itself take some of the blame. During the Soviet occupation, Pakistan, with Saudi support, encouraged Islamic militants from the Middle East and elsewhere in the world to come and fight with the *mujahidin*. In 1986, in conformity with Ronald Reagan's Presidential Directive, the CIA lent its support to this activity, and it has been estimated that as many as 35,000 'Arab-Afghans' received military training in Pakistan and fought with the resistance. In the enthusiasm for making life as difficult as possible for the Soviet Union, little thought was given to the longer term consequences, and the likelihood that these militants, now trained, experienced and self-confident, might later turn to subversion in their own countries, or even against the United States itself, was, if it was considered at all, dismissed as of secondary importance. It came as a considerable shock to the United States when it was realised that the bombing of the World Trade Centre in 1993 was the work of terrorists with an Afghan background.

More recently, American and international concern has been focussed on one particular member of this Arab-Afghan fraternity, the Saudi-born plutocrat Osama bin Laden, who himself fought with the *mujahidin* and in the late 1980s was responsible for running a base for the militants in Peshawar. Having left and operated in the Sudan for some years, he returned to Afghanistan in 1996 and was allowed by the Taliban to resume his training activities and plan terrorist operations. He established the headquarters of his organisation, *Al Qaida*, in the former *mujahidin* bases outside Khost, not far from the border with Pakistan. On 7 August, 1998, the American Embassies in Kenya and Tanzania were bombed by terrorists, killing over 250 people and wounding more than five thousand others. The conclusion reached by the United States Government was that those responsible belonged to Osama bin Laden's group, and, in retaliation, the Americans launched some 75 Tomahawk cruise missiles against his bases, but failed to kill him and achieved only limited success in neutralising them. Anti-US demonstrations took place in both Afghanistan and Pakistan, feelings in both countries ran high, and bin Laden swore vengeance.

Although clearly uncomfortable at bin Laden's activities and the American retaliation, the Taliban leadership took the line that there was no evidence that he was responsible for the terrorist activities in question and that while they would ensure that he would not carry out political or military activity from Afghan soil, the rules of Islamic hospitality ruled out their expelling him, and still less responding to demands that he be handed over for trial. They adhered to this decision despite a problem with Saudi Arabia, which wanted bin Laden handed over for trial there. Late in September 1998, the Saudis withdrew their diplomatic presence in Kabul, and there have to be doubts over their continuing financial and other support for the Taliban. In October 1999, the issue came to a head, with a demand by the UN Security Council for bin Laden's extradition for trial. When, after a month's grace, the Taliban leadership refused to hand him over, the Security Council applied economic sanctions on Afghanistan, freezing the country's financial assets abroad and preventing Ariana from flying outside the country.

Predictably, the sanctions failed to bring about the slightest concession from the Taliban, and further sanctions were accordingly applied by the Security Council at the end of 2000. Uniquely, these call for a one-sided arms embargo, on the Taliban but not on their opponents, in addition to preventing the Taliban leadership from travelling abroad and enforcing closure of their overseas missions. The sanctions were promptly denounced by Kofi Annan, who predicted that they would facilitate neither the peace efforts nor the UN's humanitarian work in Afghanistan. It is unlikely in the extreme that they will bring about any softening of the Taliban's position, but are likely to cause serious difficulties for Pakistan. Any restriction on the supply of arms would be a recipe for internal unrest, particularly among the growing Islamic movement there, while any continuance would be likely to jeopardise the supply of the international aid and economic support that Pakistan so badly needs.

Quite apart from the effect of the sanctions, the position of the UN and other humanitarian agencies working in Afghanistan has become highly uncomfortable. Ever since they began to work in the Afghan countryside, they found themselves having to tread extremely carefully, particularly when anything relating to work with women was in question. When the Taliban took over in Kandahar, the agencies' situation there was not much changed, but in Herat, considerable difficulties emerged. Both UNICEF and Save the Children came to the conclusion that in face of the gender policies introduced by the Taliban, they could no longer work there. Subsequently, when Kabul was captured, the agencies' predicament became even more acute. On the one hand, they were almost wholly responsible for the maintenance of primary and public health care, as well as for relief more generally in the capital. Nevertheless they found that despite their best efforts, hunger and malnutrition were rife, women were being deprived of healthcare, girls were being barred from education and restrictions on the employment of women were hampering their work. Because so many teachers were women, boys' schools also had to close. In October 1966, issue was joined by the United Nations, the European Commission and the USA, all of whom stressed their concern at human rights violations in Afghanistan, in particular discrimination against women. However these various pronouncements had little or no effect on the Taliban, who dismissed them – certainly wrongly – as contrary to the precepts of the Koran and *sharia*, and as reflecting Western, rather than international, values. They also professed astonishment at the concern expressed by the agencies over female employment, when the women in question were a tiny minority of the total female population. Women in need, they protested, were protected by charity and the extended family system. In September 1997, relations reached a low point when the European Commissioner, Emma Bonino, was briefly arrested after she and a party of journalists had visited a hospital, defying in the process two of the Taliban's injunctions, against contacts with women and the taking of photographs. Later, in July 1998, the aid agencies were ordered by the authorities to concentrate in a derelict compound on the outskirts of Kabul, and, following their refusal, were expelled from the city. Following the American missile attack, they withdrew their expatriate staff, and have done so again with each fresh application of sanctions. They have, however, found it possible to return and humanitarian aid has continued, although gravely restricted by shortages of funding and the problems of working in the environment the Taliban have created.

Bound up with the other problems inherent in Afghanistan's relationship with the rest of the world is the question of international recognition. Afghanistan's United Nations seat continues to be held by the Rabbani alliance, although, if normal criteria were employed, of being in administrative control of the greater part of the country, there would be no doubt that the Taliban would be internationally recognised as the legitimate government. They have shown interest in recognition and have held discussions with United States and other representatives. However as long as the United States and others remain concerned by the Taliban's human rights record, its harbouring of Osama bin Laden and its failure to cut drug production, general international recognition is unlikely in the extreme.

CHAPTER TWENTY

The Taliban and the Future

For as long as hostilities continue and there is no political settlement between the Taliban and their opponents, any forecast of the future course of events in Afghanistan is bound to be highly speculative. A difficulty also exists in that few observers have attempted a serious analysis of the Taliban regime and hence formed a judgment of the way it is likely to develop. Part of the problem is that the Taliban leadership in general and Mohammed Omar in particular are mostly inaccessible, conduct their affairs in an atmosphere of exceptional secrecy, and leave few clues as to their real intentions and ambitions. Partly too, the obscurity is due to the focussing of international attention on the more superficial and sensational aspects of the Taliban's rule, the fanaticism of its adherents, its tolerance of drugs production and trading, its role in international terrorism and its human rights abuses. It is also partly the consequence of a tendency to apply labels to radical movements in the Muslim world and to assume that to categorise them as 'extremist' or 'fundamentalist' is a sufficient aid to understanding. One academic has even coined[1] the term 'neo-fundamentalist' to describe the Taliban – again an unhelpful concept unless it is carefully defined. Such categorisations stem from the commonly held view of contemporary Islam that it is an essentially militant – even fanatical – religion, the primary concern of which is to reject, as often as not by violent means, a vigorous and increasingly pervasive Western culture and way of life. On this reading, the Taliban are merely another of the many 'extremist' movements which have emerged throughout Islam. While others, having no immediate hope of achieving legitimacy, have resorted to terrorism, the Taliban are different only in that, while abetting terrorism elsewhere, they themselves are, exceptionally, in a

202

position to impose their beliefs on a country which they now largely control.

The true complexion both of contemporary Islam and of the Taliban is a good deal more complicated than such simplistic views might suggest. As is likely to happen in an era of rapid change, a spectrum of attitudes is developing within the Islamic world. Some Muslims, mainly the richer and more cosmopolitan, have been corrupted by their contacts with the West and have allowed their beliefs and practices to atrophy. At the other extreme, there are those who have been concerned to safeguard Islam in its most uncompromising form, to bar Western influences and to take a militant stand both against unbelievers and against Muslims who, as they see it, have betrayed the faith. In turning to violence, many of this persuasion have caused much death and destruction. The general trend, however, is in sharp contrast to what is happening at the extremes. Across the Muslim world, there is an explosion of new ideas, stirred up by an unprecedented spread of education and a proliferation of communications by means of radio, television, video, satellite and computer. In the past four decades or so, even in a country like Iran, schools and universities have multiplied, literature on religious and social issues is in wide circulation and television is becoming ubiquitous. Some regimes try to censor and regulate the media, but they increasingly lack the means to do so effectively. The result is what has been described as an 'immense spiritual and intellectual ferment'[2]. To an ever greater extent, there is knowledge of what is going on in the world and a basis for serious consideration of religious and social issues. Extremes of wealth and poverty are being increasingly seen not just as the product of divine will, but as socially and morally unacceptable. Some Muslims possess a degree of admiration of the dynamism of the West and, while remaining committed to their faith, would like – as did Tarzi and Amanullah – to incorporate some of what they see as the West's better aspects into a society which they realise is in many ways backward and obscurantist. The outcome of all this has often been anything but negative: rather an unthinking observance of ritual and acceptance of religious authority is being replaced by conscious reflection on the implications of received religious belief for the individual and society. While it is true that this has often given rise to more vigorous and conservative interpretations of Islam, among the results are also an increasing willingness to examine the concepts of tolerance, social responsibility, openness and democracy.

To understand where precisely the Taliban stand in this maelstrom, it is necessary to look more narrowly at the particular society in which they were nurtured and the effect on that society of many of the developments described in previous chapters of this book. Their main religious roots go back to the establishment, in 1867, of a School of Islamic Studies at Deoband[3] in northern India. Over many years, the influence among Afghans of the once great *madrassas* at Bokhara, Samarkand and Tashkent declined in relation to that of the Indian *madrassas*, of which Deoband became the most prominent, reaching its apogee in the late 19th and early 20th centuries under the leadership of an inspirational *maulvi*, Mahmud al-Hassan. From the early years of the 20th century, a succession of Afghan *ulama* were trained at this school and its offshoots, which were strongly anti-British in outlook and highly orthodox in their religious teaching, while Deobandi scholars were in the habit of visiting Afghanistan. Under Deobandi influence, *madrassas* were set up in the frontier areas, and their numbers increased dramatically after the Soviet invasion, when Fazlur Rahman's JUI and the various *mujahidin* parties took a hand in their establishment. The education they offered was narrowly circumscribed, often consisting of little more than the Koran, the elements of Islamic law and the sayings of the Prophet Mohammed. Nevertheless, many young Afghans, including numbers of orphans, were attracted to these *madrassas*, which recruited actively and were seen as an attractive alternative to the boredom and dreariness of refugee life. A good deal of Saudi money also went into them, and with the money came Saudi influence, itself based on the harsh, puritanical tenets of a tribally based Wahhabism. Both the *ulama* who form the Taliban's leadership and the movement's rank and file are to a great extent the product of these *madrassas*, most of them even more obscurantist than the original Deobandi model.

Over the years, Deoband and these other *madrassas* became progressively divorced from the mainstream of Afghan education. Traditionally, education had been undertaken in an exclusively religious context, and legal and educational matters, as well as questions of morals and customs, were regulated by men who had had a religious training. As, however, from the turn of the 20th century, secular schooling gradually took root in Afghanistan, and more particularly as graduates from the Law Faculty of Kabul University, as well as from al-Ahzar University and other Middle Eastern institutions, began to compete for establishment posts, so the role of Deoband and other *madrassas* was marginalised. With no expectation of a career in public service, their students resented their lack of opportunity and felt increasingly alienated from a society which was developing in ways of which they fundamentally disapproved.

A second determinant is that most members of the Taliban are tribal Pushtoons who, even if they have spent much of their lives as refugees or *mujahidin*, retain an ethnic orientation and are imbued with the mores of Pushtoon society. Conversely, they know little of Afghanistan more generally, let alone of the wider world. Most are Durrani Pushtoons from the south-eastern provinces of Afghanistan, and only a minority come from other areas of the country. While there is no doubt that contradictions exist between the tribal code and some aspects of the religious orthodoxy embodied in *sharia* law, they also have much in common and, so far at least, they seem not to have given rise to any serious friction within the Taliban. This is no doubt due in part to the Pushtoon custom, where there has been potential for friction, of accepting the mullahs and *ulama* as legitimate arbiters between the two. The Taliban thus embody both religious traditionalism and a Pushtoon tribal ethos, a combination which has given the movement an exceptionally vigorous dynamic and has enabled it to prevail not only against the secular tendencies in Afghan society, but also against the adherents of an Islamist ideology, which calls for a Muslim internationalism and the radical restructuring of government and society in the context of the contemporary world, rather than a return to traditional values. It is not merely the ethnic or tribal divide that separates the Taliban from such 'Islamists' as Rabbani, Hekmatyar and Massoud, but also the fact that the latter were educated in 'modern', rather than 'traditional', educational institutions.

In political and social terms, the consequences of the Taliban's ascendancy can be seen in two main areas, arising respectively from their views of the nature of governance and from their social tenets, in particular those affecting the position of women. So far as governance is concerned, the Taliban have taken the position in their public statements[4] that after they captured Kabul in September 1996, they simply abolished all the laws and regulations promulgated by the communist regime and reintroduced the system of law that was in place in the reign of Zahir Shah. Apart from the provisions relating to the monarchy, the 1964 constitution was once again put into effect. Except during the communist era, the country had always been ruled with reference to the teachings of the *sharia*, and they had done no more than restore the fundamental legal code on which, as an Islamic state, Afghanistan had always based its political, economic and judicial systems. The Taliban also claim to support the principle of representative, non-discriminatory government based on the teachings of the *sharia*, and insist that 'when circumstances change and an appropriate environment more conducive to political dialogue is created, the Islamic State will take further steps towards solidifying its representational foundations'. In the meantime, a 'caretaker administration' had been chosen by the *ulama* of the country, representing 'all the groups which had struggled for the freedom of Afghanistan'.

The Taliban's assertion that they have merely reintroduced the 1964 constitution is clearly disingenuous, since that constitution contained distinct elements of secularism and liberalism, and, for example, gave men and women equality before the law. It would be more correct to say that the Taliban are reverting to the era following the overthrow of Amanullah, when first under the Bacha-i-Saqao and then under Nadir Shah and Zahir Shah, the final authority in legal and social affairs was conceded to the *ulama*. The Taliban's model is thus closer to Nadir Shah's constitution of 1931 than to Zahir Shah's of 1964, and closer still to the state of affairs existing under the Bacha. So far as the restoration of representative institutions is concerned, there has been up to now no sign of any intention to modify the pattern of oligarchic rule exercised by the Kandahar *shura*. On the contrary, in October 1997 a step was taken in what would appear to be the opposite direction, with a change in the name of the country to the Islamic Emirate of Afghanistan, with Mohammed Omar formally becoming Head of State. So far as can be discerned, decisions appear to be taken increasingly by Mohammed Omar personally, and the role of the Kandahar *shura* is becoming less influential. In general, the governmental structure is decrepit and in many areas it barely exists, and its style would not have seemed unfamiliar to Dost Mohammed. It is said that its Treasury consists of no more than a tin trunk in Mohammed Omar's house outside Kandahar.

On the position of women, the Taliban's contention is that the communist regime 'exploited women for the purpose of advancing their political and social agendas'. Their own aim, by contrast, was to revive the Afghan family and household, for that purpose paying the women salaries in their homes, so that they could care for their families and children. They were determined to provide educational and employment opportunities for women 'as soon as the social and financial circumstances under which the Islamic State operates allow such a step to be taken. ... Unfortunately, however, the conditions for the implementation of a sound, effective and Islamic programme for the women of Afghanistan are non-existent'. Most school buildings had been wrecked, qualified teachers had left the country and school books were full of communist propaganda. The limited resources at the disposal of the state were being used to finance a war which had been 'imposed on Afghanistan', while the task of providing security for schools and public buildings had been made extremely difficult. As regards the *hejab*, the head to toe veiling of women, this was undertaken simply in order to 'protect the honour, dignity and personal safety of Afghan women', in contrast to the position in the

West, where women 'are used only for sedating men's lust and are prey to an animal way of life'.

Again, many of the Taliban's assertions have to be regarded as disingenuous. Except in some cases where they have forced women to cease work, they are not paying women 'in their own homes', nor does it seem that they have any intention of abolishing 'gender apartheid' by reopening girls' schools or allowing women to return to work. It is true that particularly outside the cities, a very limited access to schools and health facilities has been permitted, and foreign agencies[5] have been able to assist. In practice the Taliban have sometimes chosen not to contest a local community's wish to maintain a girls' school or employ women health workers. As a matter of general policy, however, there seems to be little disposition on the part of the Taliban to make any compromises. In this overall context, it has to be realised that while their ignorance of the outside world is profound, their puritanical outlook stems, in part at least, from their revulsion at the corruption and immorality they see as emanating from the West, and that that it has to be conceded that there is some foundation for their view. In the particular case of Afghanistan, part of the revulsion derives from the memory of the streams of hippies and 'overlanders' who passed through the country in the 1960s and 1970s in search of their individual nirvanas in Goa, Kathmandu and elsewhere. True to their obligations of hospitality, the Afghans treated these people with remarkable forbearance and generosity, and they were not much exercised by their drug culture, if only because a similar culture was often to be found in Afghan villages. At the same time, Afghans were deeply shocked at the visitors' nihilism and irresponsibility, as well as at the loose morals which many of the women in particular displayed. If this was how Westerners behaved, Afghanistan wanted none of it.

In more than one sense, the Afghan wheel has come full circle. Having first been the victim of Anglo-Russian rivalry in Asia and then the arena for a proxy war between the Soviet Union and the West, yet again the country has purged itself of foreign occupation. However it is in Afghanistan's internal relationships that the turn of the wheel has been most evident. Throughout their history, the Afghans, and in particular the Pushtoons, have repeatedly seen themselves as having to defend the local and tribal autonomy that they prize so much against a succession of Afghan potentates. The rift first emerged under Dost Mohammed, whose British subventions enabled him to muster an army and establish an ascendancy over the tribes, and it developed more brutally and notoriously under Abdur Rahman. In this century, the stand-off assumed new dimensions as the army became more effective and as, from small beginnings in the reign of Habibullah, an educated elite, centred mostly in Kabul, gradually accumulated power. Under foreign influence, and bolstered in the 1950s onwards by external assistance, this elite acquired a degree of wealth and sophistication, and with it a desire, alien to tribal society, for political, economic and social development. This gave rise to a series of confrontations, first with Amanullah and then with Daoud, and later between the modernists and traditionalists in the parliament established by Zahir Shah. Many of the elite, particularly among disaffected youth and the officer corps, adopted anti-monarchist and anti-establishment attitudes, which, thanks to the influence that the Soviet Union was able to bring to bear, found their most effective expression not as a social-democratic movement, but as one that was avowedly communist. Eventually the tribes rebelled, as this increasingly despotic elite attacked their religious and secular structures and tried to impose on them what they saw as a profoundly alien way of life. What has since occurred has been the triumph of traditional society, which has now found its expression in a ruthlessly puritanical movement which has reached a position of predominance in reaction to the widespread conflict and misrule for which the victorious *mujahidin* parties were responsible.

Within the greater part of Afghanistan, therefore, the upper hand is now held by Pushtoons whose roots lie in religious conservatism and their long-standing tribal culture. Given the country's ethnic and cultural diversity, as well as all the internal conflict, which has included ethnic massacres and forced displacements perpetrated by all sides, there is little prospect of the resurgence of a sense of national unity. Indeed, one of the saddest aspects of the Afghan scene has been that, on top of the loss of the country's earlier traditions of tolerance towards non-Muslims, there is now, as a result of years of internecine strife, a much intensified hostility amongst themselves. An eventual rift between the tribes and the Taliban can by no means be ruled out, particularly given the grim condition into which the country has been allowed to deteriorate and that the latter's policies of forced conscription are a significant cause of discontent. However the present signs are that the Pushtoons have a government which they are prepared to tolerate and that the minorities are, for the time being at least, largely cowed. It is, indeed, perhaps just possible that a new, more stable, style of government is emerging in Afghanistan, based, among the Pushtoons at least, on a consensual, rather than a confrontational, relationship. It is noteworthy that the regime has so far allowed the tribes a considerable measure of autonomy, and has, for example, encouraged them to run their affairs through the traditional system of *jirgas*. The restrictions imposed on women also reflect not only the *ulama*'s interpretation of Islamic law and practice, but also the code of honour prevalent in tribal society, where contact between men and women outside marriage and the family has always been forbidden.

Notwithstanding their inexperience of government, the Taliban have so far shown themselves to be firmly united by their religious, ethnic and cultural ties, and there are, despite rumours, few signs of internal dissent. The leadership are men of strong convictions, and it is unlikely that they could in any case afford to appear to let down their young zealots, who have been ready to invite martyrdom for their cause. It is always possible that splits may develop, perhaps between the ultra-conservative and those, if there are such, with a less rigid outlook, or between the younger and older sections of the movement. The concentration of power in the hands of Mohammed Omar and an unrepresentative Kandahari clique could also at some point become a source of unrest. But so long as the movement stays together, it seems unlikely, given its military and territorial ascendancy, that it can be dislodged from power. While no regime can, in the longer term, remain impervious to influences both within and outside its borders, the Taliban's hallmark has so far been a total refusal to compromise, not merely with the outside world, but also with the *mujahidin* parties and the other elements, ethnic, political, religious or intellectual, which exist within Afghan society. Its rejection of liberal political and social concepts, including notably the electoral process and the emancipation of women, seems firmly rooted, and there appears little reason to suppose that for the foreseeable future, it will undergo any significant change. The 'immense spiritual and intellectual ferment', currently so apparent in other parts of the Muslim world, is, for the time being at least, firmly stifled in Afghanistan.

CHAPTER TWENTY-ONE

Epilogue

On 11 September 2001, Afghanistan suddenly found itself in the eye of a global storm. Any doubts that may have initially been entertained that the attacks on the World Trade Centre and the Pentagon were the work of Osama bin Laden and his al Qaida organisation were effectively dispelled when he publicly threatened further outrages. In the belief that he was based in Afghanistan and protected there by the Taliban government, the country quickly became the focus of an American-led campaign, conducted largely from the air, to bring about his capture or destruction, and his locally-based organisation with him. In the process, Afghans have been undergoing yet more of the suffering, privation and displacement that they have had to endure over the past two decades or more, from the time when their society was first disrupted by the PDPA coup and the Soviet invasion.

Until 11 September, the attention paid to Afghanistan since the imposition of the more stringent UN sanctions at the beginning of the year had been, at best, desultory. Fighting had continued between the Taliban and the Northern Alliance, but with little advantage to either side. There were periodic contacts between the US administration and the Taliban, but the latter persisted in their refusal to extradite bin Laden, except possibly to another Muslim country. Their reasons were straightforward: he was a fellow Muslim; he had fought alongside them against the Russians; and to have surrendered him would have violated the Pushtoon code of hospitality. Also his followers, experienced, motivated and well trained, were providing a useful stiffening in the fighting against the Alliance. Indeed it is credible that the Taliban may simply not have possessed the muscle to enforce his departure, even if they had wished to do so. In any event, they played it long, declaring themselves unconvinced by the evidence produced by the Americans of his complicity in the bombings of the US Embassies in Kenya and Tanzania.

Also during 2001, there was a brief flurry of interest when the Taliban blew up the two Bamian Buddhas, allegedly at the urging of foreign zealots, on the grounds that images of the human form were offensive to Islam. The fact that the faces and arms of the Buddhas had already been chiselled off by an earlier generation of Muslim iconoclasts was not, apparently, sufficient to allay their prejudices. Meanwhile, further evidence of the Taliban's inhumanity surfaced as a result of the efforts of a courageous young woman, Saira Shah, who travelled into Afghanistan with a hidden camera and, alongside other coverage of oppressive activities, produced a grim sequence showing the public execution of a woman in a Kabul sports stadium. Less obviously, and barely noticed by other than a few UN agencies and aid organisations, a catastrophe of major proportions was building up in the country following three years of drought, and the forecast was made that in the absence of sufficient aid, deaths from starvation over the coming winter might well run into millions. Reports indeed suggested that, already by November, starvation was spreading in the centre of the country, particularly in and around Bamian. The astonishing failure of American and Western intelligence agencies to anticipate the 11 September attacks was symptomatic of a gross lack of focus on a nation which not only harboured a patent threat to global security but was itself the victim of a singularly repressive government and a fast growing humanitarian crisis.

The initial objectives of the international coalition formed to deal with bin Laden were to destroy his training camps and facilities, no doubt in the hope of causing al Qaida casualties, and also to target the Taliban, presumably in the hope of destroying their morale and effecting their disintegration or submission. Neither objective was quickly realised. bin Laden and his followers had long since dispersed to prepared hideouts, as well as to villages and residential areas where they were almost impossible to distinguish from the local populace. To rely solely on bombing them was, as one distinguished academic remarked, like 'using a blow torch to eradicate cancer'. Moreover, it increased the suffering being endured by the Afghans, both directly and as a result of the disruption of food convoys from Pakistan. As pictures appeared of hits on civilian targets – a village or a Red Cross warehouse – so it also increasingly alienated the Muslim world. It was significant that, although supportive of the international coalition, President Musharraf of Pakistan was insistent that the bombing be as short in duration as possible.

Nor were the initial air strikes sufficient to cause the collapse of the Taliban as a fighting force and as a government, and it is likely that they too had dispersed to safe locations, except where they had to man a front line. However, at the beginning of November, the strategy changed, any inhibitions about directly supporting the Northern Alliance were discarded and heavy bombing was carried out against Taliban positions facing the Alliance in the Shamali Plain, north of Kabul, and around Mazar-i-Sharif. Within a few days, the Alliance were able to take Mazar, and this success was followed by the fall of other northern towns, notably Taloqan, Herat and, after a short siege, Kunduz. A major offensive also quickly ensued towards Kabul, and was successful in bringing about the fall of the city on 13 November. Just as in 1995 the Alliance had abandoned Kabul to the Taliban without opposition, so this time the Taliban similarly left without a fight. What became evident was the success of the coalition's strategy, in contrast to that of the Russians in the 1980s. The Russian intention was that the Afghan army would do the fighting against the *mujahidin* while they provided support with aircraft and heavy weapons, but this failed when the Afghan Army proved a broken reed and left the Russians with no option but to fight themselves. This time, the Alliance proved an effective fighting force, with fresh equipment provided by Russia and with American air power providing the critical edge to their operations. With Jelalabad falling to anti-Taliban militias, the Taliban were left with little more than their heartland in and around Kandahar, and when this was attacked by tribal militias, again supported by American air power, it was not long before it surrendered and the Taliban laid down their arms. The whole campaign had taken no more than two months.

The occupation of Kabul by the Northern Alliance, far more quickly than had been expected, left a dangerous political vacuum. Little progress had been made towards the formation of a national government, although Lakhdar Brahimi, once again the UN Secretary General's Personal Representative, had outlined a possible agenda, consisting of the formation of a provisional council which would in turn form a transitional government, approved by a *loya jirga*. This would be charged with ensuring security in the country, backed by a multinational force, and lead to a 'lasting political solution', hopefully within two years. On 27 November, talks on this agenda began in Germany between representatives of the various Afghan groups, and, after some days of wrangling, agreement was reached on a transitional government, under the leadership of a Pushtoon, Hamid Karzai. However, formidable political obstacles remain to be over-come. The prospects for unity and leadership have been worsened by the murders of two of the country's most able and respected military commanders, Ahmed Shah Massoud and Abdul Haq, while other former *mujahidin* leaders, notably Gulbuddin Hekmatyar, have re-emerged and, together with a host of warlords and tribal leaders, are, on past form, much more likely to stir up animosities than be positive influences towards national unity. The sad fact is that personal and ethnic antipathies across the nation, which prevented the formation of any stable government in the period before the Taliban took over, are now at a pitch where effective co-operation will be desperately hard to establish. Nor would the traditional recourse to bribery and corruption be any safeguard against subsequent treachery and double-dealing. However, a welcome note has been struck by the Northern Alliance who, despite possession of the capital and recognition as the legitimate government of Afghanistan, have been prepared to participate in a government of national unity. They no doubt realise that if they were to try to go it alone, they would meet strong opposition from Pakistan government, and that there would in any case be no peace, since they would face implacable hostility among the Pushtoon tribes.

Afghanistan now presents, in its most acute form, the problem of the 'failed state'. With so many of the world's nations having become independent during the past half century, there has been an understandable resistance to the idea that national sovereignty – often hard won – is not necessarily inviolate, and that the international community may have the right to intervene not merely when a state presents a threat to peace, but also when it is grossly oppressive towards its own people, or has disintegrated to the extent that it can no longer provide for their basic rights and needs. Gradually, however, precedents have been established; and there have been instances in which the international community has been able to intervene in situations of chaos, to prevent the oppression of minorities and to bring to justice national leaders whom it has seemed right to indict on charges of violations of human rights. The irony is that in Afghanistan, where a fiercely independent people have been more determined than almost any other to resist outside interference, the outcome has been that they have suffered from a regime with a human rights record which was by any standards appalling, which was too bigoted and incompetent to provide for even the basic needs of its citizens, and which had been facing a humanitarian crisis with which it had no prospect whatever of being able to cope. At the same time, it had been harbouring international terrorists for whose activities there could be no possible justification, it had been a major player in the international drugs trade, and it had been a threat to the peace and stability of its neighbours. In this context, there remain particularly serious concerns about the effect of the Afghan imbroglio on Pakistan, where there is a large Pushtoon minority, where there has been significant support for the Taliban and for an anti-Western *jihad*, and where the possession by an extremist regime of the country's nuclear arsenal and facilities would be a disastrous development.

If there is to be a tolerable outcome, there will somehow have to be a settlement of all these issues, no doubt brokered by the United Nations. This will have to accommodate the requirement of the international community that there be an end to the threat that Afghanistan poses in the areas of regional stability, drugs and terrorism on the one hand, and the Afghans' ingrained intolerance of any interference in their affairs on the other. Such an accommodation may not be achievable. If it is to be, it can only be through a realisation throughout Afghanistan that international assistance is indispensable if they are to be relieved of the suffering they have undergone for so long. After years of neglect, a major international effort to deal with the country's problems is an absolute necessity, on political, as well as humanitarian, grounds.

It would be outside the scope of this book to discuss the wider issues of the defeat of global terrorism, the attitude of the Muslim world more generally and the relationship between that world and the West, critical as these issues now are. One point, however, needs to be made. The bin Laden brand of terrorism is the product of a twisted mind and a subculture of religious fanaticism. But this fanaticism would not find a 'sea in which to swim' but for a growing resentment, verging on despair, among the 'wretched of the earth' at a world order under which a minority, mainly in Europe and North America, live in unprecedented affluence, while the great majority, not only in the Muslim world but more widely, are compelled to lead lives of abject poverty. It is unlikely to be a coincidence that Afghanistan, which is probably more wretched than any other country on earth, has also been the seat of a global terrorist threat.

The Durrani Dynasty

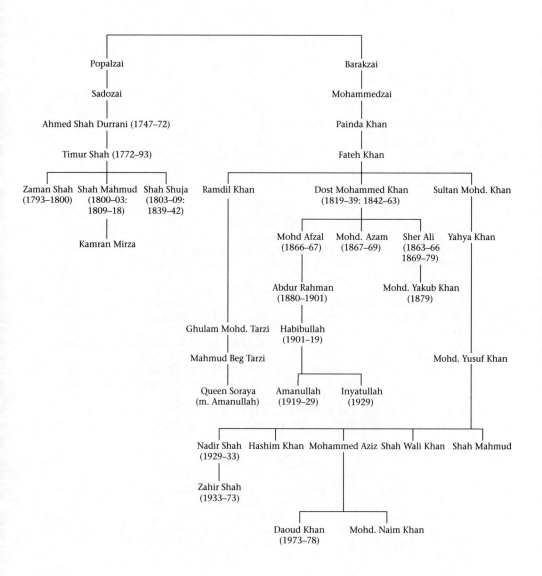

Popalzai				Barakzai	

Sadozai — Mohammedzai

Ahmed Shah Durrani (1747–72) — Painda Khan

Timur Shah (1772–93) — Fateh Khan

Zaman Shah (1793–1800) — Shah Mahmud (1800–03: 1809–18) — Shah Shuja (1803–09: 1839–42) — Ramdil Khan — Dost Mohammed Khan (1819–39: 1842–63) — Sultan Mohd. Khan

Kamran Mirza

Mohd Afzal (1866–67) — Mohd. Azam (1867–69) — Sher Ali (1863–66 1869–79) — Yahya Khan

Abdur Rahman (1880–1901) — Mohd. Yakub Khan (1879)

Ghulam Mohd. Tarzi — Habibullah (1901–19)

Mahmud Beg Tarzi — Mohd. Yusuf Khan

Queen Soraya (m. Amanullah) — Amanullah (1919–29) — Inyatullah (1929)

Nadir Shah (1929–33) — Hashim Khan — Mohammed Aziz — Shah Wali Khan — Shah Mahmud

Zahir Shah (1933–73)

Daoud Khan (1973–78) — Mohd. Naim Khan

215

Notes

Abbreviations (see bibliography, Part II):

BL British Library, St. Pancras, London
OIOC British Library, Oriental and India Office Collection
NAI National Archives of India, New Delhi
PRO Public Records Office, Kew, Surrey, UK.

INTRODUCTION

1 July 1998 estimate. *CIA World Factbook: Afghanistan, 1998.*
2 *Mémoires sur les Contrées Occidentales par Hiouen-Thsang,* tr. Stanislas Julien (Paris, 1857), Vol. II, p. 313.
3 *Memoirs of Zehir-ed-din Mohammed Baber, Emperor of Hindustan.* Tr. J. Leyden and W. Erskine (London, 1826). E.g. p. 140, 'The Afghans who live between Kabul and Lemghan are robbers and plunderers, even in peaceful times'.
4 E.g. D. H. Gordon, *The Pre-historic Background of Indian Culture* (Bombay, 1958), p. 94.
5 Herodotus, *The Histories.* Tr E. V. Rieu (Penguin, 1954). E.g. Book 3, p. 217. Olaf Caroe reviews the evidence from Herodotus at length in *The Pathans* (Macmillan, 1965), Ch. 11.
6 E.g. Y. V. Gangkovsky, *The People of Pakistan* (Moscow, 1971), p. 126.
7 Raja Anwar, *The Tragedy of Afghanistan* (Verso, 1988), pp. 126–7.

CHAPTER ONE

1 On lapis lazuli, see *Multiple Layers in the Aegean Bronze Age World-System,* presented by P. N. Kardulias at the 94th Annual Meeting of the American Anthropological Association, Washington, D. C., 1995. Also Emily Vermeule, *Greece in the Bronze Age,* Univ. of Chicago Press, 1964. On the Oluburun wreck, see *The Times,* 28 October, 1996 and 21 November, 1996.

2 Ai Khanum means, literally, 'Moon Lady'. It was in fact initially discovered by King Zahir, who, while on a hunting trip, noticed a Corinthian capital and base on the site. Developed from a pre-existing Persian city, it was probably called Alexandria Oxiana, but was founded not by Alexander himself, but a few years after his death. (See Peter Levi, *The Light Garden of the Angel King* (Collins, (1972) p. 203ff.).
3 Julien, *op. cit.* (1857), Vol. I, p. 37.
4 Li Chih-Ch'ang, *The Travels of an Alchemist*. Tr. Arthur Waley (Routledge, 1931).
5 *Voyages d'Ibn Batutah* (Société Asiatique, Paris, 1914), Vol. III, pp. 59, 88–89.
6 Robert Byron, *The Road to Oxiana* (Penguin, 1992), pp. 244–5.
7 Leyden and Erskine, *op. cit.* (1826), pp. 137–38.

CHAPTER TWO

1 George Forster, *A Journey from Bengal to England through the Northern Part of India, Kashmire, Afghanistan and Persia, and into Russia by the Caspian Sea* (2 Vols. London, 1808).
2 Sir John Kaye, *History of the War in Afghanistan* (London, 1851), Vol. I, p. 106.
3 Mountstuart Elphinstone, *An account of the Kingdom of Caubul and its dependencies in Persia, Tartary and India* (London, 1815). Olaf Caroe says of Elphinstone, 'No people could have wished for a foreign interpreter more penetrating in his combination of analysis with understanding, discernment and humanity'.

CHAPTER THREE

1 Kaye, *op. cit.* (1851) Vol. I, pp. 106–7.
2 Kaye, *op. cit.* (1851) Vol. I, p. 110.
3 Josiah Harlen, *A Memoir of India and Afghanistan* (Philadelphia, 1842), pp. 126–127.
4 General Sir Peter Lumsden, *Lumsden of the Guides. A Sketch of the Life of Lt. Col. Sir Harry Lumsden.* (London, 1899), p. 137.
5 Charles Masson, *Narrative of Various Journeys in Balochistan, Afghanistan and the Panjab* (Karachi, 1842). Vol. III. pp. 21, 23–25, 86–87).
6 Moreover, both in the months leading up to the First Afghan War and in its early stages, Auckland was engaged in an extensive tour of Northern India, and was, by his own admission, unable to form a clear view of events on the frontier. (Auckland to Secret Committee, 16 November 1838. OIOC L/P&S/5/44 No. 26). A fascinating account of this tour is given in *Up the Country* by the Hon Emily Eden, the Earl of Auckland's sister. (Reprinted by Curzon Press, Richmond, Surrey, 1978).
7 Secret Committee to Auckland, 25 June, 1836. OIOC L/P&S/5/586 Vol. 13 p. 88.
8 Dost Mohammed to Auckland, 31 May, 1836. BL. Parliamentary Papers. Vol. 40 (1839). India Papers 5.
9 Auckland to Dost Mohammed, 22 August, 1836. BL. Parl. Pps. Vol. 40 (1839). India Papers 5.
10 Alexander Burnes, *Travels into Bokhara*. 3 Vols (John Murray, 1834).

11 Burnes, *op. cit.* (1834) Vol. II, pp. 342–5.

12 Masson, *op. cit.* (1842). Vol. III, p. 479.

13 McNeill to Burnes, 13 March 1837. Kaye, *op. cit.* (1851) Vol. I, p. 293.

14 Macnaghten to Burnes, 15 May 1837. BL. Parliamentary Papers. Vol. 25 (1859), (Afghanistan), p. 13.

15 Masson, *op. cit.* (1842) Vol. III, p. 451.

16 Masson, *op. cit.* (1842) Vol. III, p. 432.

17 Masson, *op. cit.* (1842) Vol. III, pp. 405–6.

18 Macnaghten to Burnes, 11 September 1837. BL. Parl. Pps. Vol. 25 (1859), p. 28.

19 Burnes to Macnaghten, 23 December 1837. BL. Parl. Pps. Vol. 25 (1859) p. 89.

20 Burnes to Macnaghten, 26 January 1838. BL. Parl. Pps. Vol. 25 (1859) p. 120.

21 Burnes to Macnaghten, 26 January 1838. BL Parl. Pps. Vol. 25 (1859) p. 120.

22 Macnaghten to Burnes, 20 January 1838. BL. Parl. Pps. Vol. 25 (1859) p. 111.

23 Burnes to Macnaghten, 13 March 1838. BL. Parl. Pps. Vol. 25 (1859) p. 174.

24 McNeill to Auckland, 13 March 1837. Quoted in Kaye (1851) Vol. III, p. 193.

25 Burnes to Macnaghten, 2 June 1838. Parl. Pps. Vol. 25 (1859) p. 241.

CHAPTER FOUR

1 Tripartite Treaty. BL. Parl. Pps. Vol. 40 (1839). India Papers I.

2 Sir Henry Willock to Palmerston, 1 December 1838. BL. Broughton Papers, 36469, fo.202.

3 Auckland to Hobhouse, 15 November 1838. BL. Broughton Papers 36473 fo.338.

4 Kaye, *op. cit.* (1851) Vol. I, pp. 368–9.

5 Simla, 1 October 1838. Parl. Pps. Vol. 40 (1839), India Papers I.

6 E.g. Wellington to Hill, December 1838. PRO 30/12/26/1, and Elphinstone, quoted by Kaye, *op. cit.* (1851) Vol. I, p. 363.

7 BL. Parl. Pps. Vol. 40 (1839). India Papers Vols. I – VII. There has been a good deal of controversy about these papers. A problem has been that, no doubt due to the pressure of time under which they were prepared, some of the omissions are inconsistent, while the reasons for others are obscure. The common ground is that a main objective was to play down the Russian angle. Some (for example, G. J. Alder, *The 'Garbled' Blue Books of 1839 – Myth or Reality?* Historical Journal XV 2 (1972) pp. 229–259) have maintained that there was little more to it than this. However Burnes was incensed at the doctoring of the papers, which he denounced as 'pure trickery and a fraud', as a result of which the impression had, he believed, been given that he had been an advocate of Auckland's policy. Also, for example, the key despatch of instructions of 25 June, 1836 was excluded, as was McNeill's advice, in a despatch dated 23 February, 1838, that the retreat from Herat rendered 'all interference uncalled for'. Whatever the truth of the matter, it must be unique that expurgated papers put before Parliament should have been republished in their pristine version twenty years later (BL. Parl. Pps Vol. 25 (1859).

8 Secret Committee to Auckland, 24 October 1938. OIOC L/P&S/5/586/ pp. 42–54 Vol. I.
9 Kaye, *op. cit.* (1851) Vol. I, p. 467.
10 Emily Eden to Minto, 17 September, 1838. *Miss Eden's Letters* ed. V. Dickinson (Macmillan, 1919).
11 Macnaghten to Auckland, 25 April, 1839, quoted by Kaye, *op. cit.* (1851) Vol. I, p. 423.
12 Aukland, minute dated 20 August, 1839. Kaye, *op. cit.* (1851) Vol. I, p. 465.
13 Brigadier Skelton, quoted by Kaye, *op. cit.* (1851) Vol. II, p. 47.
14 Macnaghten to Auckland, 12 September, 1840. Kaye, *op. cit.* (1851) Vol. I, p. 551.
15 Nacnaghten to Robertson, 20 August, 1841. Kaye, *op. cit.* (1851) Vol. I, p. 603.
16 British Legation Diary. The author has been unable to trace the passage, but recollects reading it during his time in the Embassy in 1967–70.

CHAPTER FIVE

1 Ellenborough to General Sir Jasper Nicholls, 15 March, 1842. Kaye, *op. cit.* (1851) Vol. II, p. 458.
2 Wellington to Ellenborough, BL. Wellesley Papers 37415 fos.154ff. Also Peel to Ellenborough, 6 July, 1842. BL. Peel Papers 40471 f.193. Lady Sale (*A Journal of the Disasters in Afghanistan* (London, 1851)) probably caught the popular mood when she wrote:

> Let us first show the Afghans that we can both conquer them and revenge the foul murder of our troops; but do not let us dishonour the British name by sneaking out of the country, like whipped pariah dogs ... I have been a soldier's wife too long to sit down tamely whilst our honour is tarnished in the sight and opinion of savages.

3 L. Dupree, *Afghanistan* (Princeton, 1973), p. 400.
4 Masson, *op cit.* (1842) Vol. II, p. 244.
5 A. Fletcher, *Afghanistan, Highway of Conquest* (Cornell, 1965), p. 118.
6 C. U. Aitchison, *A Collection of Treaties, Engagements and Sanads Relating to India and Neighbouring Countries* (Calcutta 1929–33) Vol. XIII No. IV (Afghanistan).
7 Aitchison, *op. cit.* (1929–33) Vol. XIII No. V (Afghanistan)
8 Field Marshal Lord Roberts, *Forty-One Years in India* (London, Richard Bentley, 1897) Vol. I. p. 31.
9 Mayo to Argyll, 1 July 1869, Secret No. 23. BL. Parl Pps. Vol. 75 (1873), pp. 93–98.
10 BL. Parl. Pps. Vol. 75 (1873). Correspondence with Russia respecting Central Asia. 1. 1–16.
11 For a lengthy exposition of the 'forward policy', see Sir H. Rawlinson, *England and Russia in the East* (London, 1875). In *The Afghan Question, 1841 to 1878* (Strahan & Co., London, 1879), the Duke of Argyll sets out a sober and well argued defence of the 'stationary policy', and presents a quite damning account of the events leading up to the decision to invade Afghanistan.
12 Argyll, *op. cit.* (1879), pp. 85–6.

13 Northwood to Argyll, 1 July, 1869. OIOC L/P&S/5/263.
14 Disraeli to Queen Victoria, 22 July, 1877. *The Life of Disraeli, Earl of Beaconsfield*. W. F. Moneypenny and G. E. Buckle (London, 1913–20) Vol. VI, p. 155.
15 Salisbury to Northbrook, 22 January, 1875. OIOC L/P&S/18/A19 p. 57.
16 Northbrook to Salisbury, 7 June 1875. OIOC L/P&S/18/A19 p. 58.
17 H. M. Commissioner, Peshawar to Amir Sher Ali, 5 May 1876. OIOC L/P&S/18/A19 p. 68.
18 Amir Sher Ali to H. M. Commissioner, Peshawar, 22 May 1876. OIOC L/P&S/18/A19 p. 68.
19 H. M. Commissioner, Peshawar to Amir Sher Ali, 8 July 1876. OIOC L/P&S/18/A19 p. 69.
20 Sher Ali to H. M. Commissioner, Peshawar, 3 September, 1876. OIOC L/P&S/18/A19 p. 70.
21 Cranbrook to Lytton, 13 September, 1878. IOL Lytton Papers. MSS EurE 218/516/3 No. 52.
22 Disraeli to Queen Victoria. Moneypenny and Ruckle, *op. cit.* Vol. VI, pp. 386–8.
23 Cranbrook to Lytton. 24 October, 1878. OIOC L/P&S/7/19 p. 484.

CHAPTER SIX

1 Aitchison, *op. cit.* (1929–33) Vol. XI, pp. 344ff.
2 BL. Parl. Pps. Vol. 56 (1879), pp. 691–2.
3 Roberts, *op. cit.* Vol. II, p. 235.
4 Roberts, *op. cit.* Vol. II, p. 239.
5 BL. Lytton Pps. 518/4, pp. 732–3.
6 BL. Lytton Pps. 518/6, p. 1077.
7 Lytton to Cranbrook, 23 October, 1879. BL. Parl. Pps. Vol. 53 (1880), pp. 539–40.
8 Lytton to Cranbrook, 14 March, 1880. BL. Parl. Pps. Vol. 70 (1881), p. 47. For the records of the negotiations with Abdur Rahman, see PRO FO 65 (Russia) 1104, 1173: *Papers Printed for the Use of the Cabinet Relative to the Recognition of Sirdar Abdur Rahman Khan as Amir of Kabul.*
9 Ripon to Hartington, 14 June 1880. Ripon Pps, Vol. 43610. Letter No. 4.
10 Hartington to Ripon, Despatch No. 23. 21 May, 1880. OIOC L/P&S/7/325

CHAPTER SEVEN

1 Lepel Griffin to G.O.I., 3 August 1880. OIOC L/P&S/7/26 p. 473.
2 Abdur Rahman, *The Life of Abdur Rahman*, ed. M. S. M. K. Munshi. (London, 1900) Vol. II, pp. 174, 182.
3 Munshi, *op. cit.* (1900) Vol. II, p. 223.
4 Secret Minute No. 208. 14 September 1880. OIOC L/P&S/7/26 pp. 1117–1182 and Secret Minute No. 211, 21 September 1880. OIOC L/P&S/7/26 pp. 1217–1220.
5 BL. Parliamentary Debates Vol. 259. House of Lords, Cols. 227–413, 4 March 1881: House of Commons, Cols. 1831–1916 and 1938–2036, 24 and 25 March 1881.
6 Sir Thomas Gordon, *A Varied Life* (London, 1906).

7 Munshi, *op. cit.* (1900) Vol. II, pp. 2, 18.
8 Munshi, *op. cit.* (1900) Vol. II p. 251.
9 Frank A. Martin, Under the Absolute Amir (New York, 1897), gives horrific examples of some of these practices.
10 Munshi, *op. cit.* (1900) Vol. II, pp. 176–7.
11 Munshi, *op. cit.* (1900) Vol. II, p. 159.
12 Argyll, *op. cit.*. (1879) p. 143.
13 Interviews between the British Ambassador at St. Petersburg, Sir Edward Thornton, and M. de Giers, 14 March, 1885 and 28 March, 1885. BL. Parl. Pps., Vol. 77 (1885–1886).
14 Munshi, *op. cit.* (1900) Vol. II, p. 135.
15 India Treaties XIII No. 12 (Afghanistan), pp. 255–258

CHAPTER EIGHT

1 Tarzi's seminal role in Afghanistan's Twentieth Century history has only recently been acknowledged, Gregorian (*op. cit.* (1969)) being virtually the first historian to give him due recognition. He was for long treated as a 'non-person' by the Musahibans.
2 *British Documents on the Origins of the War, 1898–1914.* Ed. G. P. Gooch and H. Temperley (London, 1926–38), Vol. I pp. 306–7.
3 The exchanges leading up to the conclusion of the Dane-Habibullah Treaty are covered in detail in D. P. Singhal's *India and Afghanistan 1876–1907. A Study in Diplomatic Relations* (Univ of Queensland Press, Australia, 1963).
4 21 March, 1905. Aitchison, *op. cit.* (1929–33) Vol. XIII, No. XXI (Afghanistan).
5 Anglo-Russian Convention, St.. Petersburg, 1907. *British and Foreign State Papers*, HMSO. Vol. IV pp. 618–20.
6 Interview, 25 January, 1916. NAI, For. Sec. War, Nos. 1–212, June 1916, No. 118.
7 Habibullah to Chelmsford, 2 February, 1919. NAI For. Sec. F Nos. 705–816, No. 705, Notes.

CHAPTER NINE

1 Amanullah to Chelmsford, 3 March, 1919. British Government, White Paper; *Papers Regarding Hostilities with Afghanistan, 1919.* BL. Cmd.324 No. 2 (London, 1919), p. 3.
2 Chelmsford to Amanullah. 15 April, 1919. BL. Cmd.324 No. 2 (London, 1919), p. 5.
3 British Agent to GOI, 14 April, 1919. NAI . For. Sec. F, Nos. 705–806, Oct., 1920, No. 720.
4 Chelmsford to Montagu, 4 May, 1919. BL. Cmd.324 No. 2 (London, 1919), p. 7.
5 Telegram from Chief Commissioner, NWFP, 3 May 1919. BL. Cmd.324 No. 2 (London, 1919), p. 6.
6 Telegram P 698-S, May 21, 1919. NAI. For. Sec. Nos. 1–200B, August, 1919, No. 20.
7 Chelmsford to Montagu. 6 May, 1919. BL. Cmd.324 No. 2 (London, 1919), p. 8.

8 *The Third Afghan War, 1919.* Official Account. Government of India, 1926, p. 132.
9 One of the RAF pilots was 'Bomber' Harris, the Head of Bomber Command in the Second World War, whose belief in the value of strategic bombing was fired by this pioneering example.
10 Amanullah to Chelmsford, 24 May, 1919. Cmd.324 No. 2 (London, 1919), p. 25.
11 Chelmsford to Montagu. 1 June 1919. Cmd.324 No. 2 (London, 1919), p. 25.
12 Treaty of Rawalpindi, 8 August 1919. Aitchison, *op. cit.* (1929–33) Vol. XIII, No. XXIII (Afghanistan). L. W. Adamec, *Afghanistan*, 1900–1923 (Univ. Of California, 1967), pp. 136–166, deals in detail with the problems attendant on the negotiation of the Dobbs treaty.
13 Chelmsford to London, 2 October, 1919.
14 Adamec, (*op. cit.* 1967) pp. 163–4.
15 L. B. Poullada, *Reform and Rebellion in Afghanistan, 1919–1929* (Cornell, 1973), pp. 251–6. and Notes, p. 252, gives a series of examples of Humphreys' animus against Amanullah.
16 Text of letter is in *Dokumenty vneshnei politiki SSSR* (Moscow 1958–60) Vol. II, pp. 174–5.
17 Aitchison, *op. cit.* (1929–33) Vol. XIII, App VII (Afghanistan).
18 Text in Poullada, *op. cit.* (1973), Appx. A.
19 A report on Amanullah's visit to London is given in P. Sykes, *History of Afghanistan* (London, 1940), p. 304, and in R. Wild, *Amanullah: Ex-King of Afghanistan* (London, 1932). It was also noted that Queen Soraya's attractiveness was in marked contrast to a certain lack of it among the consorts of Amanullah's hosts.
20 A full account of this *jirga* is given in Wild, *op. cit.* (1932). Fraser-Tytler describes the delegates as looking like 'caricatures of non-conformist clergy'.
21 Poullada, *op. cit.* (1973), p. 83.
22 Sir F. Humphrys' telegrams No. 183 of 26 November, 1928 (PRO FO402, Pt. IX No. 46), and No. 212 of 13 December, 1928 (PRO FO402, Pt. IX, No. 57).
23 At this point, in the first airborne evacuation in history, the Royal Air Force flew out the entire European community in Kabul, a considerable feat across mountain ranges in the depths of the winter. There were no casualties, apart from one German lady, who walked into a propeller. Both the propellor and her head were broken, but she survived. (Royal Air Force, East India. *Report on the Air Operations in Afghanistan between December 12th 1928 and 2nd February 1929.* London, 1929)
24 e.g. *Daily Herald*, 5 and 7 January, 1929, *Daily News*, 4 February, 1929.
25 This, according to the British Legation, was the major cause of Amanullah's downfall. Sir F. Humphrys' despatch No. 11 of 25 June, 1929, para.3 (PRO FO402, Pt. XI).

CHAPTER TEN

1 Sir R. Maconochie's despatch No. 153 of 29 November, 1933 (PRO FO402, Pt. XVI).
2 Sir R. Maconochie's despatch No. 1 of 7 January, 1931 (PRO FO402 Pt. XIV).

3 31 October, 1931. H. M. Davis ed. *Constitutions, Electoral Laws, Treaties of states in the Near East* (Durham, N. C., 1953).

4 Text in Adamec, *op. cit.* (1967), Appdx. I p. 188.

5 Sir W. Kerr Fraser-Tytler, *Afghanistan* (London, 1953), pp. 236ff.

6 Sir R. Maconochie's despatches No. 50 of 24 April, 1931 (PRO FO402, Pt.XIV) and No. 48 of 31 March, 1932 (PRO FO402, Pt. XV).

7 Elphinstone, *op. cit.* (1815), discusses the question of Jewish descent at some length. His conclusion was that 'I fear we must class the descent of the Afghans from the Jews with that of the Romans and the British from the Trojans, and that of the Irish from the Milesians or the Bramins'.

8 Poullada, *op. cit.* (1973), p. 244. The text of the Treaty is in Aitchison, *op. cit.* (1933) Vol. XIII No. XXIV (Afghanistan).

9 Dupree, *op. cit.* (1973), p. 502. 'Show me a nomad who wants to settle down and I will show you a man who is psychologically ill'.

CHAPTER ELEVEN

1 H. S. Bradsher, *Afghanistan and the Soviet Union* (Durham, Duke Univ. Press., 1983), pp. 19–22.

2 *Khruschev Remembers* (Boston, 1971), pp. 560–62.

3 IMF. Report of Mission to Afghanistan, November, 1962.

CHAPTER TWELVE

1 1 October, 1964. The English text was published in 1964 by Franklin Book Programmes, Kabul. A full summary is in Dupree, *op. cit.* (1973), pp. 563–90.

2 Dupree, *op. cit.* (1973), p. 573.

3 For a discussion of Taraki's 'royalties' see Bradsher. *op. cit.* (1983), pp. 37–38. Taraki had given up his translation work in 1963 and could hardly have supported himself, as he was supposed to have done, on the writings themselves.

4 Kuldip Nayar, Report on Afghanistan (New Delhi, 1981), p. 107n.

5 The poem used, in honour of Lenin, the word 'daroud', normally reserved for use in praise of the Prophet.

CHAPTER THIRTEEN

1 Despatch No. 1014/63 of 3 May, 1963 (PRO FO 371/170194).

2 Republic of Afghanistan, Statements, Messages and Press Interviews, No. 1, p. 2, 1963.

3 An English version of the 1977 Constitution was carried in the *Kabul Times*, 5–16 March, 1977.

4 Afghan suspicions about Soviet exploitation of their natural gas output persisted over the years. Not only were the prices paid consistently much lower than world prices, but all monitoring of the quantity supplied took place in the Soviet Union.

5 An account of this confrontation is given by Dr Abdul Samad Ghaus, the Afghan Deputy Foreign Minister at the time, in *The Fall of Afghanistan: An Insider's Account* (Pergamon – Brassey, London, 1988), p. 179.

6 Seen personally by the author south of Kushka in the course of 1969.
7 Dr. Nodari Simoniya, Institute of Oriental Studies, Moscow. Interview in *Monthly Review*, September 1987.
8 Kuldip Nayar, *op. cit.* (1981), p. 151.
9 *Kabul Times*, 15 May, 1979.
10 A detailed account of the coup is given in Louis Dupree's *Red Flag over the Hindu Kush, Part 2: The Accidental Coup, or Taraki in Blunderland*. American Universities Field Staff Reports, Asia 45 (1979).
11 Louis Dupree, *op. cit.* (1979).

CHAPTER FOURTEEN

1 The Afghan practice over marriage settlements is the contrary to that prevailing in India and Pakistan, where the bride's family is expected to provide a substantial dowry. Female children thus constitute a financial liability and female infanticide is by no means unknown, as is 'bride-burning', the murder of a bride who has not brought with her what is regarded as a sufficient dowry. By contrast, the author's language tutor in Kabul, who had two daughters, reckoned that one of them would be worth a Volkswagen, and the other, presumably a less attractive match, a refrigerator. An Afghan groom has often had to spend years acquiring the means to purchase a wife, who is consequently valued not just as an economic asset and the source of children, but as one for whom a considerable financial burden has been incurred. From the time of Abdur Rahman, Afghan governments have tried to set limits on *mehr*, bride price, but have been uniformly unsuccessful in the face of the social pressures.
2 Amnesty International *1978 Annual Report*. London, 1978.
3 *Pravda*, 13 November, 1968.
4 This, the most straightforward explanation of Dubs affair, is probably the correct one, although several variations have become current. One was that the abduction was initiated by the Parcham, in an effort to discredit the Khalq. The Russians went so far as to allege that it was the outcome of a CIA plot, designed to achieve the same end.
5 A purported full report of Taraki's murder on 8 October was issued by the Karmal regime in January 1980. *Tass*, 5, 14 and 18 January, 1980. See also Nayar, *op. cit.* (1981), pp. 38–9.
6 *Afghanistan, Soviet Occupation*. Foreign and Commonwealth Office, London, 1980.
7 A full account of these supposed events is given in Raja Anwar, *op. cit.* (1988), pp. 187–190. Anwar was imprisoned in Pul-i-Charki with members of Amin's immediate family. See also Nayar, *op. cit.* (1981), pp. 7–13.
8 A full analysis of the confused Soviet explanations of their action is given by Bradsher, *op. cit.* (1983), pp. 179–188.

CHAPTER FIFTEEN

1 General Assembly Resolution No. ES 6/2,14 January, 1980
2 Non-Aligned Conference Final Declaration, Delhi, 13 February 1980.
3 *The Times*, 30 January 1980.

4 e.g. Dr Claude Malhuret, Executive Director of Medecins sans Frontières, speaking at the Russian Research Centre, Harvard University, 17 October, 1983. *Foreign Affairs* 62 (1983) 2: pp. 426–35.

5 Speech to the 27th Congress of the CPSU, 25 February, 1986. 'Counter-revolution and imperialism have turned Afghanistan into a bleeding wound'.

CHAPTER SIXTEEN

1 Report by Felix Ermacora, adopted by UNCHR Resolution of 13 March, 1985.

2 National Security Directive No. 166, April, 1985.

3 The full text of the Geneva Accords can be found in the Appendix to *Political Order in Post-Communist Afghanistan*, by William Maley and Fazil Haq Saikal (International Peace Academy: Occasional Paper Series, 1992).

4 *The Times*, 16 April, 1988.

5 By contrast, French casualties in Indo-China in the post-war years amounted to 50,000 killed and 100,000 wounded, while American casualties in Vietnam were 45,000 killed and 300,000 wounded. The Americans spent some $20 billion p.a. on Vietnam for the better part of a decade.

6 Jason Elliot, *An Unexpected Light* (Picador, 1999), p. 30.

7 Report by Felix Ermacora. 26 February, 1986.

8 Robert G. Kaiser, *Why Gorbachev Happened*. (New York, Simon and Shuster, 1995), pp. 202–03.

9 Mikhail Gorbachev, *Memoirs*. (London, Doubleday, 1966), p. 138 and p. 249.

10 R. G. Kaiser, *op. cit.* (1995), pp. 284–85.

CHAPTER SEVENTEEN

1 Another suggestion has been that the plot had been the general responsibility of the *mujahidin*, but was taken over, in their own interests, by Tanai and Hekmatyar. Another theory is that it represented no more than Khalq/Parcham factionalism. Yet another is that it was hatched by the KGB, for what reason is unclear.

2 General Assembly Resolution No. A/RES/44/15, 1 November, 1989.

CHAPTER EIGHTEEN

1 Security Council Statement No. S/PRST/1994/33, 11 August, 1994.

2 E.g. Nancy Dewolf, writing in the *Wall Street Journal*, 22 February 1995. In *Afghanistan, Mullah, Marx and Mujahid* (Westview Press, Boulder, Colorado, 1998), Magnus and Naby also retail this story about the genesis of the Taliban, but equally ignore the evidence of their prior existence and their support by Pakistan.

3 Speaking to the BBC in the course of 1996, the Prime Minister of Pakistan, Benazir Bhutto, is reported to have admitted that the Taliban received training in that country, with financial assistance from the USA. Alexander Cockburn, *The Nation*, 27 January 1997, Vol. 264, No. 3, p. 10.

4 Detailed and comprehensive reports of the Taliban's alleged human rights abuses were first published in Amnesty International's *Country Report, November, 1997* (London, 1997) and the US Department of State's *Country Report on Human Rights Practices for 1997* (Bureau of Democracy, Human Rights and Labour, 30 January, 1998). These reports have been updated in subsequent years and can be seen on *www.amnesty.org*. And *www.state.gov/www/global/human rights*.

CHAPTER NINETEEN

1 1998 estimates. *CIA World Factbook : Afghanistan, 1998.*
2 *The Times*, 22 October, 1996. See also *Museum under Siege* by Nancy Dupree, *Archaeology* Vol. 49 No. 2 (March/April 1996), pp. 42–52.
3 Statement by Mine Action Programme for Afghanistan (MAPA), Islamabad, 1 March 1999.
4 United Nations ECOSOC document E/CN.7/2000/5 of 22 December 1999.
5 Taliban Website: *www.taliban.com/tabsera.htm*
6 *The Times*, 13 April 1998
7 *The Times*, ibid.
8 UNHCR Country Profile: Afghanistan, March 1999
9 Taliban Website: *www.taliban.com/taliban.htm.*
10 *Inside Central Asia*, no. 141 (30 September–6 October 1996).
11 Speech to the Asia Society, New York, 30 September 1998.
12 *The Times*, 9 May 1997.

CHAPTER TWENTY

1 Olivier Roy, in *Fundamentalism Reborn?*, William Mabey ed. (New York, University Press, 1998).
2 Dale F. Eikelman, *Inside the Islamic Reformation*. The Wilson Quarterly, Winter 1998. Vol. 22. No. I. P80.
3 For an assessment of Deoband and its role in Afghanistan and the Indian subcontinent, see S. A. A. Rivzi's books:

   A History of Sufism in India. New Delhi. 2 Vols, 1978 and 1983.
   History of the Dar al-Ulum Deoband. Deoband, 1980.

   See also *the Essential Field Guide to Afghanistan and the Frontline Region*. Crosslines, May 1998: *www.alertnet.org.*
4 Again, the Taliban's own Website, *www.taliban.com*, provides most of the sources for their assertions reported in this chapter.
5 For example, the Swedish Committee for Afghanistan. See their website at *www.sak.a.se*

Bibliography

Afghanistan has, for more than a century and a half, inspired a large and varied literature, ranging from archaeology, anthropology, ethnology and religion, through international relations and political and military history, to travel, biography and fiction. Thus the bibliography attached to Vartan Gregorian's magisterial *The Emergence of Modern Afghanistan: Politics of Reform and Modernisation 1880–1946* (Stanford, Stanford Univ. Press, 1969) runs to all of 66 pages of closely printed text, even though it excludes several of these categories. This means that if a bibliography is to be anything more than a lengthy and uncritical nominal roll, mainly of books which are out of print and only obtainable from specialist libraries, rigorous selectivity is required. What follows is an unashamedly personal selection, which aims to include the classics and works of importance, while, hopefully, avoiding idiosyncrasy.

A. GENERAL

At the top of any list has to be Mountstuart Elphinstone's *An Account of the Kingdom of Caubul and its Dependencies in Persia, Tartary and India* (London, 1815), a comprehensive study which has stood the test of time and still contains relevant insights. A much later, but important, general work is Louis Dupree's *Afghanistan* (Princeton, Princeton Univ. Press 1973), which covers not only the history of the country, but also its archaeology, ethnology, economics and culture.

B. ARCHAEOLOGY

The best, well illustrated, general introduction is *The Archaeology of Afghanistan from the Earliest Time to the Timuid Period*, by F. R. Allchin and N. Hammond (London, Academic Press, 1978). *The Art of Afghanistan* by Jeannine Auboyer (Paul Hamlyn,1968) illustrates many of the sites and objects found. The Gandhara legacy is the subject of Sir John Marshall's *The Buddhist Art of Gandhara* (Cambridge,1960).

C. HISTORY

1. General

In addition to Gregorian, general histories include Sir Percy Sykes' *History of Afghanistan* (London, Macmillan, 1940), Sir W. Kerr Fraser-Tytler's, *Afghanistan. A Study of Political Developments in Central and Southern Asia* (London, Oxford Univ. Press, 1953) and Fletcher's *Afghanistan, Highway of Conquest* (Ithaca, New York, 1965). A religious and ideological perspective is given in Asta Olesen's *Islam and Politics in Afghanistan* (Richmond, Surrey, Curzon Press, 1995).

2. Early History

The Greek period is covered in W. W. Tarn's The *Greeks in Bactria and India* (Cambridge, 1951). Michael Wood's *In the Footsteps of Alexander the Great* (BBC Books, 1997) is a vivid and generously illustrated account of a journey undertaken along the route of Alexander's conquests. The standard works on the Ghaznavids are C. E. Bosworth's *The Ghaznavids: Their Empire in Afghanistan and Eastern Iran, 994–1040* (Edinburgh, 1963) and *The Later Ghaznavids: Splendour and Decay* (Edinburgh, 1977). Tim Severin, *In Search of Genghis Khan* (London, Hutchinson, 1991), has combined a Mongolian travelogue with a fascinating account of Genghis Khan's career. The authoritative work on Ahmed Shah Durrani is *Ahmad Shah Durrani: Founder of Modern Afghanistan* by Ganda Singh (Bombay, 1959).

3. Dost Mohammed and the First Afghan War

Required reading on Dost Mohammed and Afghanistan during his reign is Christine Noelle's *State and Tribe in Nineteenth Century Afghanistan* (Richmond, Surrey, Curzon Press, 1997), while a contemporary account is contained in Mohan Lal's *Life of the Amir Dost Mohammed* (Karachi, Oxford Univ. Press, 1978 repr.). Easily the most attractive book on the First Afghan War is Lady Sale's *A Journal of the Disasters in Afghanistan, 1841–2* ed. Patrick Macrory (London, Longmans, 1969). The wife of Brigadier 'Fighting Bob' Sale, she was left behind in Kabul, survived the retreat and was taken hostage. Her narrative of events and scathing commentary make compelling reading. Among the histories are Sir John Kaye's *History of the War in Afghanistan* (3 Vols., London, 1851) and J. A. Norris' *The First Afghan War 1838–42* (Cambridge Univ. Press, 1967). Another eye-witness account is that of Lt. Vincent Eyre, *The Military Operations at Cabul* (London, John Murray, 1843), while Patrick Macrory has written an eminently readable account of the retreat from Kabul in *Signal Catastrophe, the Story of the Disastrous Retreat from Kabul, 1842* (London, Hodder, 1966).

4. Sher Ali and Anglo-Russian Rivalry

There is little specific coverage of Afghan internal affairs until the reign of Abdur Rahman, but the 'Great Game' has over the years attracted a huge literature, much of it written contemporaneously by such characters as 'An

Old Indian', an 'Indian Army Officer' and 'Anon'. However the non-specialist
cannot do better than read Peter Hopkirk's enthralling *The Great Game*
(London, John Murray,1990), which also suggests further reading. The Second
Afghan War is well covered in Col. H. B. Hanna's *The Second Afghan War,
1878–79–80* (3 Vols. London, 1899–1910), while Field Marshal Lord Roberts
Forty-One Tears in India (London, Macmillan, 1897) gives a first-hand account.
The First and Second Afghan Wars are covered together by Archibald Forbes in
The Afghan Wars, 1839–42 and 1878–80 (London, 1906).

5. Amir Abdur Rahman

Essential reading for Abdur Rahman's reign is M. H. Kakar's *Government and
Society in Afghanistan. The Reign of Amir 'Abd al-Rahman* (Austin, Univ. of Texas
Press, 1979). Abdur Rahman's own autobiography, *The Life of Abdur Rahman:
Amir of Afghanistan*, ed. Mir Munshi Sultan Mohammed Khan (London, 1900)
although possibly not wholly authentic, is a key source. First-hand accounts
of life at Kabul during Abdur Rahman's reign are contained in Frank A.
Martin's *Under the Absolute Amir* (London and New York, 1907) and John A
Gray's *At the Court of the Amir. A Narrative* (London, 1895).

6. Habibullah, Amanullah and the Third Afghan War

Afghanistan's external relations under Habibullah and Amanullah are
covered in Ludwic W. Adamec's *Afghanistan 1900–1923: A Diplomatic History*
(Berkeley, Calif., 1967), while internal affairs under Amanullah are the subject
of Leon B. Poullada's *Reform and Rebellion in Afghanistan, 1919–1929* (Cornell
Univ. Press, 1973). The whole ground is covered in Rhea T. Stewart's *Fire in
Afghanistan, 1914–1929: Faith, Hope and the British Empire* (New York,
Doubleday, 1973), while a first-hand account is given in *Amanullah – Ex-
King of Afghanistan* by Roland Wild (London, 1932). An account of the events
leading up to the Third Afghan War is given in the British Government's
White Paper, *Papers Regarding Hostilities with Afghanistan, 1919* (Cmd.324 No.
2, London, 1919), and an account of the war itself in *The Third Afghan War:
Official Account* (GHQ India, New Delhi, 1926). G. N. Molesworth has added to
the latter in *Afghanistan 1919. An Account of Operations in the Third Afghan War*
(New York, 1962).

7. Democracy, the Saur Revolution and Soviet Invasion

Although covered by the general historical works, there is little specific
material on the period between the Bacha-i-Saqao and Daoud's coup, other
than *Afghanistan in the 1970s*, Louis Dupree and Linette Albert eds. (New York,
Praeger, 1974). Henry S. Bradsher deals with the developments leading up to
the Soviet Invasion in *Afghanistan and the Soviet Invasion* (Durham, Duke Univ.
Press 1983), as does Anthony Hyman in *Afghanistan under Soviet Domination,
1964–91* (London, Macmillan, 1992) and Anthony Arnold in his two books,
Afghanistan's Two-Party Communism: Parcham and Khalq and *The Soviet
Invasion in Perspective* (Stanford, Hoover Institution Press, 1983 and 1985).
Raja Anwar's *The Tragedy of Afghanistan: A First Hand Account* (London: Verso,

1988) fully lives up to its title, as do M. H. Kakar's *Afghanistan: The Soviet Invasion and the Afghan Response, 1979–1982* (Berkeley, Calif.1995), Olivier Roy's *Islam and Resistance in Afghanistan* (New York, Cambridge Univ. Press, 1990) and Anthony Arnold's *The Fateful Pebble: Afghanistan's Role in the Fall of the Soviet Union* (Presidio Press, Calif., 1993). Mark Urban's *War in Afghanistan* (New York, St. Martin's Press, 1990) also covers the ground well. Among the handful of individual accounts by journalists who managed to visit the Afghan resistance, those by Sandy Gall, *Behind Russian Lines: An Afghan Journal* (London, Sidgwick and Jackson, 1983), Peregrine Hodson, *Under a Sickle Moon, A Journey Through Afghanistan* (London, Hutchinson, 1986), and Radek Sikorski, *Dust of the Saints* (St. Paul, Paragon House, 1989), stand out. A Soviet perspective is given in *The Hidden War: A Russian Journalist's Account of the Soviet War in Afghanistan*, by Artyom Borovik (New York, Atlantic Monthly Press). The events leading up to the Soviet withdrawal are covered in *Out of Afghanistan: the Inside Story of the Soviet Withdrawal* by Selig S. Harrison and Diego Cordovez (New York: Oxford University Press, 1995).

8. The Civil War and the Taliban

The post-war scene is examined in B. R. Rubin's *The Fragmentation of Afghanistan: State Formation and Collapse in the International System* (Yale Univ. Press, 1995), Olivier Roy's *Afghanistan: From Holy War to Civil War* (Darwin Press, 1995), William Maley (ed)'s *Fundamentalism Reborn? Afghanistan and the Taliban* (New York Univ. Press, 1998) and Peter Marsden's *The Taliban: War, Religion and the New Order in Afghanistan* (London, Zed Books, 1998). An account of the Taliban, based on extensive first-hand experience, is contained in Ahmed *Rashid's Taliban. Islam, Oil and the New Great Game in Central Asia* (London, I. B. Tauris, 2000). The regional implications are also examined in the same author's *The Resurgence of Central Asia: Islam or Nationalism?* (London, Zed Books, 1994).

C. ETHNOLOGY

Olaf Caroe: *The Pathans: 550 BC–AD 1957* (Oxford, 1958), draws on a wealth of first-hand experience and personal dealings with the Pushtoons. More general works are H. W. Bellew's *Afghanistan of the Afghans* (London, 1879), *The Races of Afghanistan* (Calcutta and London, 1880) and *An Enquiry into the Ethnography of Afghanistan* (London, 1981). A unique picture of the Nuristanis before their forcible conversion to Islam is contained in Sir George Robertson's *Kafirs of the Hindu Kush* (London, 1900). The Hazaras are the subject of S. A. Mousavi's *The Hazaras of Afghanistan* (New York, St. Martin's Press, 1997).

D. TRAVEL

Of the many nineteenth century travellers who passed through Afghanistan, Charles Masson (*Narrative of Various Journeys in Balochistan, Afghanistan and the Panjab, including a Residence in those Countries 1826–1838* (3 Vols., London 1842)) is probably the most knowledgeable and rewarding. An interesting study of Masson is contained in Sir Gordon Whitteridge's *Charles Masson of Afghanistan: Explorer, Archaeologist, Numismatist and Intelligence Agent* (London, Aria and Phillips, 1986). Other worthwhile nineteenth century travelogues are Alexander Burnes' *Travels into Bokhara. Together with a Narrative of a Voyage on the Indus* (3 Vols. London, 1834), Lt. John Wood's *A Journey to the Source of the River Oxus* (London, John Murray, 1841) and Arthur Conolly's *Journey to the North of India. Overland from England, through Russia, Persia and Afghanistan* (London, Richard Bentley, 1834).

Of more recent travellers, Robert Byron has written what is generally reckoned to be the classic account of a journey to Afghanistan, in *The Road to Oxiana* (London, Macmillan, 1937). Other attractive travel books have included Arnold Toynbee's *Between Oxus and Jumna* (Oxford, Univ. Press, 1961), Freya Stark's *The Minaret of Djam* (London, John Murray, 1970) and Eric Newby's *A Short Walk in the Hindu Kush* (London, Secker and Warburg, 1958). Jason Elliot's *An Unexpected Light: Travels in Afghanistan* (London, Picador, 1999) gives an account both of life with the *mujahidin* and of the period between the Taliban's capture of Herat and the fall of Kabul. The author's own firm favourite, however, is Peter Levi's *The Light Garden of the Angel King* (London, Collins, 1972). In it, Levi has composed descriptions of the countryside and the people that convey in writing (warts and all) what the Michauds (see below) have portrayed in photographs, a vivid impression of the country before it was overtaken by the tragedies of recent decades.

E. BIOGRAPHY

Two eminently useful books are Ludwic W. Adamec'c *A Biographal Dictionary of Contemporary Afghanistan* (Graz, ADEVA, 1987) and *Historical and Political Who's Who of Afghanistan* (Graz, ADEVA, 1975). A few biographies are mentioned above or in the Notes, but for the author, the outstanding work is the Emperor Babur's autobiography: *Memoirs of Zehir-ed-din Mohammed Baber, Emperor of Hindustan*. Tr. J. Leyden and W. Erskine (London, 1826).

F. PICTORIAL

As suggested above, anyone who wishes to see what Afghanistan and its people looked like before the Soviet invasion, three books by Sabrina and Roland Michaud provide the most skilful and sensitive of insights. They are;

Caravans to Tartary (London, Thames and Hudson, 1879)
Afghanistan (London, Thames and Hudson, 1980)
Horsemen of Afghanistan (London, Thames and Hudson, 1988)

G. FICTION

Although set wholly in British India, Rudyard Kipling's *Kim* (London, Macmillan, 1900) is *the* classic of the Great Game. A fascinating commentary on it is *Quest for Kim: In Search of Kipling's Great Game*, by Peter Hopkirk (Oxford, 1997). Two novels by George MacDonald Fraser, *Flashman*, and *Flashman at the Charge* (London, HarperCollins, 1999 repr.), typify the Pushtoons as vicious savages, but have a well-researched Afghan background.

The same, however, cannot be said of James A. Michener's *Caravans* (New York, Random House, 1989 repr.), which gives a wholly sentimentalised picture of Afghan *kuchi* life.

H. OFFICIAL RECORDS

British official records are, understandably, a major source of information about Afghanistan, in particular for the nineteenth century and the first half of the twentieth. The British Library, in its Oriental and India Office Collections (OIOC) and Parliamentary Records Section, holds a variety of these archives, of which the most important are the series of Political and Secret Correspondence between the pre-Partition Government of India and the Government in London. They include:

- Correspondence to and from India between 1756 and 1874 (L/P&S/ 4–6).
- Correspondence between 1875 and 1911 (L/P&S/7).
- Correspondence between 1912 and 1930 (L/P&S/11).
- Correspondence between 1931 and 1950 (L/P&S/12).
- Official memoranda (Series A) prepared in the Government of India's Political Department, 1840–1947 (L/P&S/18).

Particularly at times of crisis, convenient collections of many of these papers were laid before the British Parliament, and are to be found in the Parliamentary Papers series, notably

- Vol. 40 (1839). India Papers Vols I-VII.
- Vol. 25 (1859).
- Vol. 75 (1873).
- Vol. 56 (1879).
- Vol. 53 (1880).
- Vol. 70 (1881).
- Vol. 77 (1885–6).
- Cmd. 324. No. 2 (1919).

Relevant private correspondence held in the British Library includes:

- Broughton Papers.
- Lytton Papers.
- Palmerston Papers.
- Peel Papers.
- Ripon Papers.
- Wellesley Papers.

The National Archives of India, New Delhi, holds the volumes of the Proceedings of the Foreign Department of the pre-Partition Government of India. Many of these are not replicated in the records held in the OIOC. Those referred to in the Notes are in the For. Sec. (Foreign Secretary) Group.

The Public Records Office, Kew, Surrey, UK, contains, in the FO series FO402 and the relevant papers in FO 371 and FO 408, the Records of the British Legation (later British Embassy), Kabul, after its creation in 1922. A number of Foreign Office records relating to Russia are also relevant, in particular, up to 1906, the sections of FO 65 and FO 106 entitled *Proceedings in Central Asia*, and, from 1906 onwards, the relevant papers from FO 371 and FO408.

Index

1/06 (4) 8/02
3/07 5 12/06
5/12 (16) 3/2